Minister's Shop-Talk

MINISTER'S SHOP-TALK

BY

James W. Kennedy

Harper & Row, *Publishers*

NEW YORK

FIRST EDITION

H-P

Library of Congress Catalog Card Number: 65-20454

TO

Roswell P. Barnes

MENTOR

FRIEND

MINISTER

WHO

STANDS

IN

A

LARGE

ROOM

CONTENTS

PREFACE

THIS BOOK is about the environment and life-role of the Christian minister. It is addressed to other Christian ministers out of the life and thoughts of one of them, as he pokes around in his past and explores subjects of mutual concern.

The aim of this book is to pursue the ideal of the "able minister" who "faints not,"[1] and to share a few common hopes, joys, fears, and experiences. The desire and hope of the author is that all ministers will be doing an ever enlarged and more effective job as *Christian* ministers during the cultural, social, and religious revolution the world is passing through.

"Unto every one of us is given grace, according to the measure of the gift of Christ."[2] Each Christian minister has his own particular endowment; but he is never a one-man show, for each is dependent on the other.

The world is changing with alarming speed, and so is the role of the minister. This means he must move with the times in order to make his ministry thoroughly up-to-date, that is, he must be in touch at any given moment with whatever changes are being made, whether radical or gradual, so that neither he nor the church will be separated from the world as it is in that moment. He must possess great mobility of mind and flexibility of spirit, using all the gifts of improvisation he possesses, as God directs. He must manage to survive and keep moving ahead, with the resources at his disposal well in hand.

There is a vast potential in all Christian ministers. Therefore, the earnest wish and best hope of one of these ministers is that some God-directed word in this book may strike home and release in the reader hidden powers of good sense and courage, compassion and exhilaration, and help to make him more grateful and ready for "the superb chance to minister to this age with its troubles and its triumphs."[3]

JAMES W. KENNEDY

The Minister

In whom there are signs of

"God let loose in the world."*

* John Masefield, *The Coming of Christ* (New York: The Macmillan Company, 1928).

I

His World

Facing Today's World

The plight of the minister viewing his world today reminds me of mine on a particular afternoon when I stood on the south shore of Nantucket Island as the fog rolled in and the great wind-driven surf of the wild Atlantic crashed and pounded against the shifting, roiling sands. Unable to see clearly in the heavy mist, feeling puny, small, and helpless before the whirling sea, I watched two young people foolishly venture too far out in the surf, until they were lost to sight as though swallowed up by the sea without a trace. One of them was my son. I watched and waited. Each passing moment I grew more panicky, not knowing their fate and fearing the worst.

When, after a frantic thirty minutes on my part, the two young people were able to return safely to land, I discovered I had been more frightened than they. They had been in the midst of the world of wind, wave, and fog, and had found it a less fearful place than it seemed to one who stood apart on the shore trembling.

Many of us feel this way in our less optimistic moments, as the weight, fearsomeness, and mystery of the world move in on us as if to crush us or swallow us up. For a long moment on that foggy, wave-lashed beach, I forgot that this is God's world, that He loves His world—every last flaw of it—and that from the beginning He has found it good. I should have recalled His words, "In the world ye shall have tribulation: but be of good cheer; I have overcome the world."[1] I should have remembered that "the gates of hell" shall not prevail against Him and His Church. Hell is on the defensive. The Church is not. That day I forgot.

Men are often thoughtless or foolish and expose themselves needlessly to danger, by choice or in ignorance, as those two young people did that day on the Nantucket beach; and yet my faithless fears led me to panic. This reaction to a loved one in danger, especially of a parent for a child, is quite natural and understandable, but the point I am making is that this is God's world and that He is "let loose" in it, and men must never forget this—even parents of children who fearlessly or foolishly advance into danger.

Disaster comes frequently to those who live in the world, and demands great courage of those who must endure it. Christ has promised to see His fellow-sufferers through the worst of such disastrous periods, provided they hold on in faith to Him who enables them to rise above the world while remaining in it. Valiant is the name for such Christians.

The Christian is always on the offensive, so what matter if the wind, waves, and fog come? Such challenge and danger should bring out the best in him, since he knows he is not alone in the midst of it. We live in an exciting, dangerous, and challenging age, when battles of the spirit are raging on many fronts. Therefore, it is good to recall Churchill's dictum, "Live dangerously. Take things as they are. Dread naught. All will be well."[2]

But suppose all had not been well. Suppose my son and his companion had been drowned? This tragedy, too, the Christian would not have to face alone. No matter who was at fault, the young people who dared the elements or the parents who failed to cry a warning, God would be there to help them take things as they are. Young people must learn to live dangerously but wisely, and parents at last must turn them loose, for they cannot ever be laid safely away on a shelf.

This darkening world of dimly seen shore line is a reality to be faced with courage by Christians. Too frequently those in the world believe that they, Christians, when danger threatens can quickly jump back into the protective circle of their own little "sacred" island world, totally apart from the mainland world other people live in. This is the image many people have of the Church, which too often fails to plunge into the dangerous surf, or even to stand on the shore line, but, instead, hides behind a sand dune. As historians continue to point out, the second half of the twentieth century is marked by superficiality and disillusionment. How can this fail to be, when those who live in it are face to face with a reality stripped of all idealism; and because of the annihilation of distance in a highly developed technological society, the plight of one is the plight of all. Regardless of what we may desire there is no escape for anyone from being involved in the world.[3] This means Christianity is being put to the test of discovering within the context of its long life and experience what can be done to cope with the sizzling pace of the contemporary world; and Christians rejoice that this is so. Again I recall a maxim of Winston Churchill, this time a mutual code of living between "Winnie" and his wife Clementine. "It is no use doing what you like. You have got to like what you do."[4]

No matter *where* or *what* or *how* things are in the world, we are mutually encouraged by each other's faith to make the best of what must be done. We are not afraid of struggle or mystery or suspense, for only when we struggle are we alive and human, facing the world with bulldog tenacity, matching our words with our deeds, our wits with our wisdom, and praying for signs of greatness in both. The one indelible mark of a Christian minister is his cheerful, unshakable, and undiscourageable faith, secure because it is faith in a Person, Jesus Christ.

Christian Answers in a "Post-Christian World"

Regardless of the world's dangers and difficulties, the minister lives no cloistered existence in some quiet sanctuary. His feet are firmly planted in the midst of reality while he sings an "alleluia." The world in all its complexity, beauty, fearsomeness, and ugliness confronts him daily as he goes about the business of the Kingdom of God on earth, which too often seems foreign to the world's business. How the minister faces the world often defines the limits of his ministry, for if he ignores the passing scene and attempts to live in the past, or in an unreal, nonexistent present, or in some imaginary future, he fails God, himself, his people, and his world. There are deeps to plumb, and he can dive in with no fear of hitting the bottom.

The setting for the minister's life, word, and works today is often described as "a post-Christian world," and he must know what such a world is like in its rapidly changing aspects, speak to it in a language it understands, and maintain an open-minded attitude in every realm and compartment of modern man's life. The minister must know what his people are up against and help them face it and "be of good cheer" even in the world's bad times. Every era is an age of revolution and change, and the minister must be adaptable, while at the same time he must maintain an unchanging core of conviction to anchor him as he evaluates situations, makes judgments, and guides choices.

Moods change. Spirit and viewpoint change. Before World War I, for example, men were, by and large, cheerful, well fed, and self-satisfied, contemplating with complacency the world as it appeared to be then—progressing smoothly and without interruption toward an ever enlarging and more perfect horizon. But World War I stripped nineteenth-century Western man of all illusion. After this war, the prevailing mood and spirit of the intelligentsia was uncertainty; the surrounding doubt, disorder, and anxiety left their minds profoundly disturbed. All seemed dark and hopeless. They were bitter over war's destruction of the flower of the world's youth. The future seemed to hold nothing but a question mark against a dim and cloudy background, which Christians did little to dispel. Such moods recur in cycles, not of centuries but of decades. Each postwar generation feels it is living in a depressingly dark and austere world of the question mark, and is as "profoundly disturbed" as I was standing on the beach that day on Nantucket Island.

But what of the Christian view of things? What of the challenge of commitment to the belief that this is God's world in spite of what men's choices have done to it—and certainly all sides bungled during the shocking stalemate and senseless slaughter in World War I. Have all men, even Christians, abandoned the Christian frame of reference within which the individual sees himself as a child of God, created for the purpose of enjoying Him forever, responsible to Him for his choices, and whose moral integrity is ultimately accountable to God, in and through Christ?

When we stop to think about it, we realize that ours has never been a truly Christian society. But there was a time when people lived under the illusion that it was, and at least gave lip service to the idea. It's all to the good to rid ourselves of any such lulling illusion, for the fact is that only as each person individually comes under the influence of the compelling truth of God's redeeming love in Christ, feels it keenly, and begins to live it out in his daily relationships, can any segment of the world actually *be* Christian. We have to choose as our preference among ways of life a Christian world in the making, act on that choice, and do what we can to make it a reality. The world and its problems must be at the forefront of the Church's concern and come under the judgment and redemption of God, or else how can His Kingdom ever be realized in any generation?

No image phrase like "post-Christian" tells the whole story of Christian influence, or lack of it, on society. Nevertheless it does set up a questioning in the minds of serious Christians as to the depth of their own commitment to Christ and His Church, and how firmly they believe He has "overcome the world." "Commitment" is the key word—commitment to a Person, Jesus Christ.

However, this intellectual approach can go too far, as it did tragically in one instance I know of, where a brilliant young clergyman lost the moorings of his faith through overintellectualizing, and was finally edged off into an abyss of nothingness, which left him in a moral as well as religious vacuum. What kind of redemption is possible for him? By the grace of God some miracle of comprehension may awaken him from his deadness and relate him once again to God's creation and man's redemption, lead him back to see and acknowledge the relation between Christ's Lordship over the world and His Lordship over the Church and over every individual, and bring him to another radical turnabout and another commitment to God's glory. I pray this will be so for him and others like him. It is our task to prevent this from happening to other young men.

Where is the glow and the banner for such young men—to inspire them and to win them to follow? One answer lies in the vision and dream of a young minister I know, who looked at the crumbling shell of a long disused girls' school in his community and saw, not the raccoons and squirrels running free in the building nor the cracks the winter frosts had widened in the foundation, but a flourishing institution, renewed and alive. He shared his vision with another young minister, who accepted the challenge enthusiastically and later became the first headmaster. Although the practical problems were immense, together they began the transforming process.

They continued the school's original symbolic name, Wykeham Rise. It was named, at its founding in 1902, in honor of William of Wykeham, fourteenth-century Bishop of Winchester, who was architect and founder of England's first great public school, in Winchester. The new school was built on a high piece of ground in a quiet Connecticut town—hence Wykeham Rise. The original high standards were kept and raised. To me the great contribution of this school, in addition to its remarkable contributions to secondary educational philosophy and its range of unusual activities, is its call to commitment. The school's able and creative headmaster put it this way: "A student at Wykeham commits herself not just to a school—to traditions, to buildings, to mottoes—and not just to excellence in education. She commits herself to people. A school is people, and, one would hope, loving people. François Mauriac has expressed what we know to be true: 'We are, all of us, molded and remolded by those who have loved us, and though that love may pass, we remain none the less their work—a work that very likely they do not recognize, and which is never exactly what they intended. No love, no friendship, can cross the path of our destiny without leaving some mark upon it forever.' We hope that those who choose Wykeham as part of their destiny will bear its mark with grace and gratitude forever. For of all things which they will come to know in this place, there is none more creative and redeeming than the love of those persons, students and staff, who make Wykeham what it is."[5]

Young men still dream dreams and have visions, and with God's help can overcome the difficulties and see their dreams and visions become realities.

What kind of a world confronts us today in this particular year or month or day of the twentieth century—the world we must live in, work in, and, above all, minister to? It may not be the kind of world we want, but it is the kind of a world we've got, and there are marks of God's presence in it which we must first recognize and then carry with us as we move into the lost and empty places where men cannot seem to find any evidence of Him—to awaken them, as we are awake, to the revolutionary changes going on all around us.

In such a world of surging speed, bewildering change, and perpetual dilemmas, the Christian gospel stands today in sharp contrast to both shallow optimism and black despair. The Christian doctrines of creation and redemption do not run away from any part of truth as revealed in the world. How could they, for they deal with all levels of truth. Those who think of God as a not very up-to-date old fellow, baffled by all the "new" developments—or maybe even dead by now—are way off base. We are at least smart enough to start from and come back to God as the center, the core, the anchoring point of all truth.

St. Paul reminds each of us to get back to our center, the God who revealed Himself to us in the person of Christ; get back to our center, the Word of God, spoken through Jesus Christ, and let it dwell richly in us by faith; get back to our center, maintaining contact with Him through prayer, worship, and communion; get back to Him and think according to our faith in Him as the Person, as Lord and Savior, and to do all things in His Name, as though in His presence. This is the minister's theme song in a strange new world which he must continuously adapt to and seek to change, never letting it fall below the limits of what is possible for it to be and to become with God's help. It is a time to speak, to act, and, if need be, to suffer joyously, with certainty that He is "the way, the truth, and the life."[6]

The minister needs to know how others view man's existence in this world, which can look so different depending upon whose eyes and mind we see it through, for, as Henry James said about the "house of fiction," man's existence has "the possibility of a million windows, any one of which can be fashioned to open on the spreading field of the human scene by the pressure of the individual will and vision." So, whatever the center, it is the individual, on his own, who decides on his viewing post, even though "the windows can be of any shape, 'either broad or balconied, or slit-like and low-browed.' Yet in themselves, Henry James says, the windows are as nothing without 'the posted presence of the watcher.' "7

In other words, what matters is what each "watcher" sees as he looks out of one or more of the windows, for this becomes his "post," and views and frames his existence. Today the countless windows vying with one another to offer "the finest view" or "the only view worth seeing" too often tend only to confuse and lead to no view at all. Philosophies and religions almost without number wave their flags, display their pageantry, and present their concepts with all the Madison Avenue tricks of persuasion they can muster. Each one is out "to win converts," "to save the world," "to fulfill life," "to bring happiness through identity and belonging," and each is a threat and a competing rival to every other.

The faithful adherents of Christ must man the battle stations where confrontation occurs and seek to overcome "the competition" by whatever means they can. The Christian minister has made his choice and is convinced his way is the best and only way. Also, he is of good cheer because he believes God in Christ has overcome the world and offers the only wide-open window for viewing it whole. He believes that "the task set to [the Christians of] every generation [every day], is to relate the abiding and the transitory in [their] experience, to bring together the truth which is not of an age but for all time, and the insights, derived from the actual situation in which [they] stand, . . . and not to shrink from the challenging but saving encounter with the living God today."8

The View from the Window

The Christian minister must use every "trick of the trade" to catch the attention of the potential viewers gathered around and lead them to the crystal-clear Christian window through which they can view existence and the meaning of life. No one is excluded from this window's view, which is there for every man, from the one with the most modest mental endowments to the brilliant scientist or philosopher, for him to behold, understand, and relate what he sees. The primary task of the minister is to communicate relevantly the Christian meaning of existence. Therefore, as spokesman for an age, he must seek life's full meaning and its best patterns of articulation, whereby words, spoken or written, become the language of power which overcomes the world. The minister must know and understand what such writers as

Sartre, Camus, Beckett, and Ionesco are trying to express, namely, man's endeavor to come to terms on a nonreligious basis with the world in which he lives, and to face up to the human condition as it really is, free from illusions and despair. He must look through their window, not at a painting on a solid wall.

On the other hand, he must be aware that there are others doing the same thing, but in religious terms, with the addition of faith, hope, and charity, and who love what they see. While thoroughly aware of the misery and shoddiness of mankind, he must acknowledge, too, man's grandeur, and that life's true meaning can be found from another point of view than the non-Christian existentialist—through a "balconied window." He, as should all Christians, understands that life and intelligence are divine gifts, not only the result of a biological process. He believes that the transformation and the true wholeness of a man's life comes not just through psychological and social adjustments, nor philosophical systems and points of view, but through knowing the Person, Jesus Christ.

Christians always discover at some critical point, that God acts, and has acted in history, in and through Christ, and that the "Christian gospel comes to all of us with a message which is very old, and yet new every time someone feels his own need deeply and turns to Him. For the gospel tells us that because God in Jesus Christ has taken upon Himself all our shortcomings, we can come into His presence not with fear, but in absolute trust."[9]

God knows the worst about us, but He also knows the best. He knows that there are the makings of a better person hidden away in all of us: the flickering impulses of genuine compassion; the decent motives which often become twisted in the web of our relationships; the inner core of sensitivity, humility, and hope which lies buried behind the protective shells of our personalities. The minister must speak to those who think that all these secret best things will die with them—locked up inside—and tell them that if they will learn how to come into the presence of God, even though this takes time, effort, and patience, they "will discover how to let the best that is in them come out into the light,"[10] and how truly to overcome the world.

In this besotted and crazy world, which is still God's world, whatever its correct descriptive label may be, the Christian holds to this certainty, namely, that he can ask and get from God, through Christ, guidance, steadfastness, something that will give meaning to his life, a true beacon which will lead him back to his proper spiritual center. He knows, too, that Christ brought the inner resources of a steadfast soul to the events which He encountered, and that He brought to life a sense of direction which finally led to a cross. He revealed the secret of His power and the source of His strength as God-given, and He made the same spiritual power and strength available to all who have the courage to look at material possessions and at human society as they are, and to examine the innermost secrets of their own souls in the same clear light that God in Christ sheds upon them as they come into His presence.

God thus enables Christians to see this too familiar cockeyed world with clear eyes, learning to love it as He does. To anyone who penitently asks God for direction, strength, and forgiveness through Jesus Christ, He gives the power to awaken to the same familiar earth, the same people, the same self, but to find everything in wonderfully different perspective, because with God's help he stands up as a free man. The great fact to remember is that we grow tall and knowing in His presence, and this is the view of life the minister sees and points out through his balconied window—an unobscured panorama of the world's life.

The minister must pay particular attention to the young people at his window, whose temptations to succumb to flight, opportunism, and despair must be stayed. This can be done only by giving convincing and solid answers, hammered out of reality, to show them that absurdity and nothingness are not answers; that there *is* hope and purpose; that present facts must be faced with the courage and dignity of manhood instead of with the railing and complaining of an unnaturally prolonged, sophisticated childishness; and that all life must be evaluated from the perspective and meaning of the Christian viewpoint to make any sense at all. The Word of God must be brought to bear on each situation as the determining influence on choice and action, with love uppermost. Living in the world as forgiven sinners, as loved sons of a Father who suffers in the midst of His free and erring children, we, together with them, when they are willing, achieve wholeness and purpose.

World War II is over and the next world war has not yet begun, but the warrings within and around every life go on without ceasing. The demand is for something strong to bind and hold life together so that it will not come apart when faced with the new theology, the new variations on the existentialist theme, the new morality, the new revolution, the new concept of "Church," and the new ecumenical climate. The minister opens the Christian window on the world and is responsible for the comprehensiveness and validity of the view his people get and hold to. However, it is useless to apply such phrases as "post-Christian" or even "pre-Christian" to modern thought, for they only confuse and frighten the faithful. The minister needs to view calmly from his window the shattering changes going on everywhere in the world, and begin seriously and with urgency to make the timeless Christian gospel timely and relevant to each moment, within the context of that special moment in history. The minister is not shocked or disturbed or discouraged by what he sees, although profoundly sad and sorry, for it is God's world, over which He shall reign eventually, in His own good time. Nor is he confused or surprised at what he sees, because he knows the doctrine of original sin, that men will cater to their self-centered worst until won to seek their God-given best. He is concerned with a sense of urgency—always on the offensive, never the defensive. Meaning and relevance must be to the fore in the minister's exposition of the Christian faith, and he must be continually "concerned to bring out what Kierkegaard taught us to call its 'existential' significance for the active conduct of our lives and the solution of the problems we have every day to face,"[11] such as "the new morality."

Moral Law versus Chaos

No one would question that many things are wrong with the world, from whatever window it is viewed. For instance, no one would question that there is moral deterioration in society evident on every side to all who are not absolutely blind. We read about it in newspapers, magazines, and books. We see it delineated in movies, on television, and in ads and cover pictures on every newsstand. It is the so-called "new morality" which confronts us. What this really means is that we must take another look at our hard-and-fast opinions on morals and ethics and be sure they jibe with the morality of the New Testament, which is the control center of our existence.

There is moral laxity, civil disobedience, and naked violence everywhere, which "strike heaven in the face," and too few ministers even deplore, publicly or privately, what is going on. But just closing one's eyes and ignoring it—pretending it doesn't exist—will not banish it. When such moral sickness is so prevalent and contagious, and the beginnings of a nationwide and even worldwide epidemic are so clearly discerned, certain questions must be raised and answered. For example, are right and wrong important matters, or should we ignore the conditions around us and close our eyes, letting things rack along just as they are? "After all, what can *we* do?" When moral restraint is loosened, when the inner law of conscience is disobeyed without a flicker of regret, when the devious minded convince themselves black is white and any wrong is right as long as no one is caught, when men think kindness is softness and cruelty strength, the seeds of decay are already sown and another civilization is on its way to decline and fall.

Youth is our main concern here. To them society and culture are on the defensive. They need to see that this defensive attitude does not include the Church, which ever marches into the world prepared to give battle. Also, they need perspective on moral problems. The young are uncertain about many things, especially the future. They need to live dangerously—not for kicks, but for their soul's salvation. Youth has no clear challenge so to live today—to live for others, to live for a future— and thus this need to live dangerously and purposefully is perverted, and they often get into trouble. They need to hoist banners, to fall in behind strong leaders, to be committed to something. There are too few banners. The Church must find a substitute for the pageantry of war, and must offer more than an anemic youth-group meeting on a Sunday night: something large enough as a challenge to win a response. This problem demands the vision and the indefatigable energy and ingenuity of every parish minister.

Take one specific instance. In New York City there are innumerable manifestations of this full-blown moral sickness, as every minister who works there will testify. There is a shocking need for Christians to wake up and look long and soberly into the consequences of disobedience and moral lawlessness, and into the condition of their own souls which makes this possible. We can begin in a hundred places to pile up the evidence. We can catalogue the headlines: sexual promiscuity, and a wide assortment of sex crimes; dishonesty, embezzlement, racial hatred, and murder. We can look at the titles and themes of books, movies, and plays, many of which are outcries *against* the moral degradation they depict so vividly. We can glance at the pictures in magazines for sale on every newsstand—often tasteless, vulgar, suggestive, or downright obscene. We can note the come-on blurbs and story titles of so-called "comics," the pulps, and the degenerate "art" magazines. The very fact that so many are sold and gloated over in private is one of the symptoms of this moral sickness. About all we do is wonder and cluck our tongues, especially over the dreadful doings of young people, sometimes from the finest homes, who get into serious difficulty without their parents seeking to understand the direct relationship between the atmosphere and materials of corruption and lawlessness and the unrestrained, unashamed conduct of impressionable youth.

Those who do not uphold the moral law and do not teach it ceaselessly are partially to blame. The minister must pound home the age-old lesson to every succeeding generation, that those who deliberately flaunt the moral law must suffer the consequences. My quarrel is with those who ignore the moral law and those who, without remonstrance, let the flaunters get away with it. It is quite true that right and wrong are not always clearly discernible to everybody and are often distorted according to one's point of view, leading to quarrels over conduct; but at least we are on safe ground in assuming that we agree there is a difference between right and wrong, and that most of us can understand enough to make our choices for one or the other.

What gospel is there for today's youth? What certainties? What absolutes? These questions must plague and nag until elementary answers are found. Search the Scriptures daily and show how to apply the Christian frame of meaning to a young person's life today; reach out and get a hold on him before dope does, or crime, or alcohol, or before he sinks into depression and discouragement beyond our saving, even though he may never be beyond God's redeeming help. Youth needs a gospel for tomorrow, today.

The major trouble is that many people really don't believe in the moral law, that it is a part of the very stuff of the universe, which is God's universe, and that disobedience to it really *will* bring dire consequences. They think that our alarm is just "Mrs. Grundy" sounding off, and believe that it is nobody's business what they do. But those who think they can choose to live life just as they please, without reference to the laws of God, are dead wrong, for "the inescapable element of choice infects everything in life. . . . There is no way to secede from humanity and its problems and live our own life in isolation. We have the choice only of being either ineffective members of the human race, failing to carry our end of the load, or positive and loyal members, doing our best to take our part in the life of the body. . . . All of reality comes to us in terms of what we want to do about it. . . . What we are is what we choose to be—with God's help."[12]

The supreme asset of man is an inner respect for moral law, living in conformity to the dictates of a well-nurtured conscience, in other words, possessing the saving humanity and wisdom called by the Hebrew seers "The fear of the Lord." That is why the window he looks through is so important. The ages of history pointed to with pride are those when civilizations flourished at high points of moral consciousness and moral living. Gibbon's historical insight, borne out by Toynbee and others, was right. Rome's decline and fall was due mainly to moral causes. In order to treat the moral malady with which so many are afflicted, we need some form of deep therapy that we have not yet discovered, which will be effective and relevant, and will penetrate to the very heart of our contemporary situation.

The Minister's Stand

With his clear-eyed view, the minister can apply the corrective to so much of the distortion found in men's thoughts today. In modern literature, for example, where often "the curdled disillusionment of the worship of the creature instead of the Creator"[13] is portrayed with such ugliness, he will call attention to those writers who are "continuing or reviewing the great tradition of man as a rational, free, responsible, purposeful—even though fallible and imperfect—creature of God."[14] He can never hope that evil, in all its range, will completely disappear from the pages of books and magazines, for man is inextricably compounded of good and evil. But the minister can see to it that his people "will no longer be given the illusion that the seamy aspect of man is the sum total of man."[15]

There is need today for a great "Thou shalt not," a mighty and certain sound from the trumpet of God's righteousness, and the lips on the mouthpiece are the minister's. He must trumpet the existence of God's love in God's world, the basic goodness of men and society, and believe that the doors of hell shall not be proof against the forces of God's spirit. Man needs at all times the commanding authority of the gospel, firmly and unhesitatingly presented as calling for his allegiance. For the Christian developing in the world, living and conduct are increasingly governed by cooperation with God's laws as revealed in the Gospels, the beatitudes, the decalogue in its Christian reinterpretation, the laws which God has "put in men's inward parts" and "written in their hearts,"[16] which prepare and fit them to receive the power of the Holy Spirit. Inward moral law is the rule of decent behavior which governs conduct and is of God, the freedom under obligation which we call conscience.

Man alone is responsible for his choices and his sinful acts. He cannot whine forever and lay all the blame on inheritance, an inherent weakness, environment, or a bad break, although these may make his choices more difficult.

The principles which should guide a conscientious Christian in cases of grave perplexity are those which the Apostle Paul sums up in his Epistle to the Romans. He cries, "Who shall deliver me from the body [bondage] of this death?"[17] that is, "Who shall take me beyond this desperate point where choice ends and I am left to struggle alone in the moral conflicts which beset me?" Then he gives his answer in one word, "Christ," who strengthens him.

Jesus Christ was St. Paul's answer as to how to overcome the world, and He is ours likewise, for He is God's help for all men, who in His life gave direction for all of life and taught men how to walk by the spirit, to accept God's love and their own sonship—to walk and not faint. We need Christ, and the principles He left for us in the New Testament, by which to test and regulate the chaos of impulses that surrounds every intended action in the world. And we need the grace of God for the strength and ability to choose the good and to hold steady on course where it leads us.

Our struggle to satisfy the moral demands of His law, and to go beyond the letter to the spirit, means developing humility of the creative sort. God's grace alone is sufficient. He will enable us, but not automatically; we must pray for insight and understanding, and for a growing sense of our own worth to Him, to be able to accept wholeheartedly His love toward us. The minister is confronted daily with God's world, and seeks to address it with persuasive power and love that can both charm and change the individual, and through him, perhaps, influence a tiny fragment of the world's life.

Man without God

The Christian minister today is being forced to take a long look at the Church as an institution, to see whether it is still finding, opening, and articulating "a way in which [men] can, with dignity, confront a universe deprived of what was once its center and its living purpose, a world deprived of a generally accepted integrating principle, which has become disjointed, purposeless, absurd."[18]

The minister can offer but one major premise for all he says, namely, that man without God cannot successfully face life and find happiness in any age. In any resumé of man's cultural, political, social, or spiritual history, it is quite apparent that man has not been able to go it alone and build society and set the world aright. The doctrine of inevitable progress has had a staggering setback in the twentieth century. Man's scientific competence has increased a thousandfold, yet wars rage, dictators rise and fall, the cruelty of man to man has reached a new high and in the United States undisciplined family life has brought the teen-age generation, in large cities particularly, to the brink of anarchy and disaster.

Life can do strange things to educated people who try to live by intellect alone, who go their own perverse ways, dashing their heads against the stone wall of God's law in a moral universe. Reason alone is not sufficient to orient a person in this mysterious universe. For a balanced concept of the meaning of existence, there must also be faith in a God who cares. In every age and every place faith and reason can and must join hands. Neither competence nor conscience, neither reason nor faith, is taken straight. It is the mixture that counts; and the mixture is perfect and thoroughly realistic in Christianity.

The minister's twentieth-century world is full of sham, pretense, lust, and ugliness, and the face of his parish reflects all of it, but he knows that Christianity has no illusions about man and his world, and therefore he does not sink into cynicism or despair over what he sees and hears. He knows that God is in his world; this is a major premise of fact. The Christian Church holds an answer to the dilemma man is in and offers him a faith which it believes comes straight from God. This faith is not an ideal to be striven for until frustration leads to despair, but a Savior in and through whom all men can know blessed peace and healing forgiveness, and in whom men can go from strength to strength, possessed of a new reality, no longer estranged from God or wandering lost in the world.

The minister forever confronts man and his world with the right perspective, not with that of some small insect on the vast expanse of a patterned Persian rug, seeing only a fragment of the color and design, but as a mature man gazing from the heights above the blinding and blurring sensory perceptions of self, viewing life whole, not allowing glimpses of unrelenting ugliness here and there, or lack of order and purpose all about, or moments of disillusionment, to down him or discourage him. God lifts us up to a point above self where things are seen in proper perspective and life makes sense, as seen through the balconied window of the Christian religion.

The Church is in the world and part of it, as it has been from the beginning. The Christian fellowship struggled to make an impression on its world; its progress was slow but sure, until, in effect, the Western World was Christian. Note how the Church grew in the world and became an accepted part of its life. In the first few centuries, the center of things was wherever the fellowship met, which in the early Church was mostly in homes. In the centuries following Christianity's adoption by the empire under Constantine, church buildings were erected as centers for Christian meetings and worship at the crossroads of life, in key places like market towns. In the middle ages the Church was the center of every community around which people lived and worked with stability and continuity from one generation to another. In modern times the Christian fellowship is demonstrating its original mobile, flexible nature, for it is once again on the move and, as so often in other centuries, is being forced to adapt itself to changing times, seeking the form that will best function today, when people often live and work in two different communities.

Now that the minister's task is more complex than ever before his temptation is to let things ride. Procrastination is the curse of our age. We haven't time to wait for an eventual change. There is an urgency forced upon us by science and speed in communication; and contact with the people of his often heterogeneous world is of the essence of the minister's life.

This pressure was described in a lecture I heard, "The Face of Science Today," given by a Harvard physics professor. He told how the explosive speed of scientific knowledge was such that even the scientists couldn't keep up with themselves. Even before books on scientific progress can be written they are already out of date, he said, and articles in scientific journals are often obsolete before the subscribers can read them. This may have been a slight exaggeration, but I gathered from what he said that a frantic prepublication interchange of the latest discoveries and bursts of new knowledge is necessary in order to correlate the pattern of progress in this jet-propelled age of scientific knowledge. The scientist, however, is in search of facts rather than truth, with a passion for re-examining his hypotheses. And there are so many different kinds of scientists—those dealing with human behavior (sociologists, anthropologists, psychologists, psychiatrists), and those dealing with physical things (mathematicians, chemists, physicists, doctors). While, on the other hand, the "nonscientific" philosophers and theologians are seeking the discernment and grasp of moral truth, and are engaged in a search for meaning beyond the facts. No matter how far the scientist's research takes him—and it is already opening the unknown universe in outer space to his ever closer personal scrutiny—in order to keep life balanced and in proper perspective, he must find an ultimate meaning for life in the midst of all this, or else what is the point of it?

One example of this search comes out of a fictional surgeon's experience, but is based on a true incident. In his novel, *The Surgeon,* W. C. Heinz has his main character reach this conclusion in his gradual change through long experience from a brash and doubting young medical student to a serious and believing man of science. "You can't be a surgeon," he said, "and not believe in some kind of supreme law. You can't witness the whole series of dynamic, immutable changes that is life from beginning to end without believing. I have seen death hundreds of times. I have seen brave men die and men you would call cowards die, and at the end there is no difference between them. There comes over all of them that same blessed euphoria and only their survivors suffer. You may not want to call it God's numbing, as I have heard it called, but you can't deny it. . . . So there must be a God." In another passage, while witnessing a complete autopsy, "he watched the emptying and then the careful, skilled, hidden, and disguised closure, [and] it came to him that what they had removed would tell them why this manikin-man died, but it would not tell them why he had hoped and feared and lived."[19]

The minister who is in tune with his times will discover he is as much at home in the field of science as he is in the realm of Christian faith, and that the concepts and language of one fit easily into those of the other. Also, the shouts of non-Christians are never ignored by the Christian minister who is on the job, for he knows no one is beyond God's influence. He becomes God's instrument of good cheer in overcoming the wrong and frustrated thought-ways of the world. By proclaiming God's love for His world, he can furnish an answer for those who believe the world is "post-Christian," or that the Christian Church as an institution, and what it stands for, is obsolete and unnecessary.

In Tune with the Times

The minister lives in a world of blinding speed, a world which won't wait for calm deliberation—with its population exploding, with pigmy nations rising overnight to be counted on a par with giants at the level of statesmanship, with political left and right fighting for control, with men's hearts failing them for fear—and he is not afraid. Indeed, he is thankful to be alive in the midst of so much excitement and danger. This is his world, this is God's world, and he is God's voice and God's servant in His Church in the midst of it, not looking backward or forward in fear, but around in awareness and ahead in hope. He knows the battle of good and evil goes on, but no Christian minister is ever in doubt about the final outcome and so he works and fights and prays.

I I

His Church

An Analogy

While attending a meeting of the World Council of Churches one
summer in Nyborg Strand, Denmark, I gazed daily at a tiny island
directly in front of my bedroom window, some two or three miles out in
the Great Belt of the Kattegat. It rose like some miniature Mont St.
Michel out of an arm of the North Sea, against the barely discernible
shoreline of the larger island of Zealand far in the distance. It was
always a beautiful sight, looming as a patch of green slope revealed in a
sudden burst of sunlight, or when its lighthouse flashed out intermittent
brightness in the dark, or as a silhouette visible in the mist and rain. All
the while the white ferryboats plied back and forth between nearby
Nyborg and faraway Korsor, never once stopping at the island.

I often think of this little island, so alluring yet so often passed by
and so seldom visited—always admired for its distant beauty. We often
see such islands but pass them by as something unattainable or perhaps
not even desirable—we wonder if we really want to explore them. This
is an analogy to the Christian Church to guide our thinking as we
ponder the meaning of its existence and its relationships.

The Definition

For a long time theologians have been trying to define the phrase
"Christian Church" to the satisfaction of all who call themselves Christians. I am thinking of the Christian use of the word "Church" in two
ways in this chapter: first, as a Trinitarian fellowship; and, second, as
an ecumenical fellowship. I am thinking of the Church "not as an
institution, or a place for the conservation or the defense of moral and

spiritual values, but as a group of witnessing people, charged with the responsibility for making the good news of the Kingdom of God heard in the world. Everything else must be subordinated to this proclamation, everything else must revolve around this message, for that is the Church's very *raison d'être*. . . . The task of [the minister], then, is constantly to recall and restore to the Church its *raison d'être*, which is the content of its message."[1]

The Christian Church is much more than this, of course, and the theologians must continue to seek for its most accurate and widely expanded definition; but as a working definition for this chapter the concept of the Church as a witnessing and ecumenical fellowship will do nicely, with the addition of these words from St. John's great prologue to his gospel. "As many as received him, to them gave he power to become the sons of God, even to them that believe on his name."[2] Those who accept Jesus Christ as the Son of God become one with Him as sons of the same Father and are led by His Spirit. But "power to become" implies a choice made and a promise given, both depending upon our accepting and growing more and more until we are one with Him. "That ye may be blameless . . ., without rebuke in the midst of a crooked and perverse nation, among whom ye shine as lights in the world."[3] Christians are those who belong to the fellowship of Christ's followers, who bear witness to God's life and words revealed in and through Him, which witness shines as a light in the midst of the world's darkness, and offers a purpose and a goal for every man's life. Therefore, "the Christian view of history must involve both judgment and hope, held in constant and almost paradoxical relationship."[4] And over the centuries Christians have been highly successful in keeping this balanced view.

The Church's Basis

The Christian Church has depended upon memory for the very ground of her being. In fact, the emphasis from the beginning of human life has been on remembering. It was what men remembered as important—ancient stories, laws, customs—and passed on, first orally, then in writing, that became their religious code. The whole history of religion is a cycle of remembering and forgetting, with special emphasis on the consequences of forgetting God's laws. The original purity of the Christian faith as contained in the New Testament was in essence the record of what the disciples remembered of Christ. The importance the disciples attached to Christ's words and deeds[5] determined the content of their message, the versions of the gospel they held precious and passed on.

The most wonderful thing they remembered was Christ's birth into the world as the Son of God. This became the doctrine of the Incarnation, which is celebrated around the world each year with joy and solemnity at Christmas. The most awesome thing they remember was His death—that it was for them He hung and suffered on a cross—and because this one man died, many were reconciled and lived. This became the doctrine of the Atonement, and is widely and intensely commemorated on Good Friday everywhere men believe in Him. The most mysterious thing they remember about Him was His Resurrection and reappearance to them as a living Person. This became the Easter doctrine of eternal life, and is held to tenaciously by all Christians everywhere. The most potent and life-changing memory, however, was of Pentecost, the descent of the Holy Spirit. This experience, which rounded out their basic knowledge of God, gave them a core of faith which grew into the doctrine of the Trinity, the tenet that held the Church together through the centuries of discord and disunity as the minimum statement of the Christian faith. In spite of endless differences and most un-Christian quarrels, the Trinitarian belief has been a firm bond of unity between Christians, no matter how far apart they have been in other beliefs and traditions. Out of it grew the historic creeds of the Christian Church. Against it, heresies have been measured and rejected, and without acknowledgment of it no group is accepted as fully Christian in either the New Testament sense or according to Apostolic tradition.

This concise doctrine really says all the essential things for Christians to believe and remember; and each Christian makes his commitment to it at his baptism, for he must believe, accept and hold to this formulation of the nature and being of God: "the Father, who . . . made [him], and all the world"; "the Son, who . . . redeemed [him], and all mankind"; "the Holy Ghost [Spirit], who sanctifieth [him], and all the people of God."[6]

It is this Holy Trinity, One God, whom he will praise and magnify throughout his Christian life, "founded upon the fact of the presence of the Word of God already in the common life of the world. All of which is remembered, recorded, and passed on, that is, projected, as the practice of the Christian life founded on the very same Trinitarian formula. This formula consists of the discernment of, that is, both seeing and hearing; and the reliance upon, that is, the reckless and uncalculating dependence upon; and the celebration of, that is, the ready and spontanous enjoyment of; the presence of the Word of God in the common life of the world—the world we touch, smell, hear, and see. It is *this* world just as it is, into which God comes, for which God cares, in which God is with us, [and] in which the word of God resides."[7] This is what the early Christians remembered and handed down to us.

We talk about the authority of Scripture and the authority of tradition, and of continuing in the Apostles' teaching and fellowship. What we really need is a neat summary of the basic Christian beliefs which will provide a solid foundation for all men to stand on in order to get a steady, whole, and undistorted Christian view of life, which we believe is virtually the same today as it was in the beginning and will be from now on.

Such a set of basic Christian beliefs is important, for they determine what Christians think about the world they live in, about other persons, and about their own duties and responsibilities in this life. They also determine what Christians think about the life to come—that is, man's nature and man's destiny in relation to his belief in One God as revealed in Jesus Christ and ever present as Holy Spirit in the Church. There is no tighter summary of essential Christian belief than the Trinitarian formulation of the Christian faith as condensed from the Apostles' Creed, which we have just reviewed.

The Church's Authority

But acceptable creedal formulas for one century may not apply with equal force in another century. For hundreds of years the traditional language and statements of the orthodox Christian doctrines were quite sufficient. However, the battle for the minds of men, which has never ceased, has grown more furious and more devastating in the quick-changing and explosive world of the twentieth century. In this century, whether man emerges as monarch of all he surveys, including himself, or whether God reascends His throne as ruler of the kingdoms of this world and the dwellers in them—or whether there still is a kingdom to rule and dwell in—depends largely on which of the first-century Christian answers to existence he remembers, selects, and holds to, and how he uses them to relate his life to a fully satisfying way of thinking and living within a basic frame of meaning and reference for today. What the Church becomes in him who reveals its nature and position in the world is the only evidence of the Church some people will ever see.

Nietzsche's words condemn us all. "I will not believe in the Redeemer of these Christians till they have shown me they are redeemed."[8] But how long will it take for this evidence to be shown in every time and every place? The words that John Baillie addressed to the First Assembly of the World Council of Churches in Amsterdam in 1948 tie together Christians of the twentieth century and the first century on this point. "The defective Christianity of His followers has indeed in every age been the most difficult hurdle Christ has had to overcome in reaching the souls of men; yet there have been ages and places in which faith and charity walked hand in hand, in which profession was so matched with practice that men said not only 'Hear what these Christians believe,' but also 'See how these Christians love one another!' "[9] From the first century to the twentieth, Christians have tried to reformulate Christian truth for each age of its developing life.

But before any further attempt is made to capsule the Christian faith or to expound the essential minimum of the New Testament "credo," whether in first- or twentieth-century form, let us look for a moment at this process of remembering and its climax at Pentecost, when the Christian faith both fused and exploded at the same time—fused as a oneness, exploded as a dynamic—and the Church was fired into being as the focal point of God's life in Christ among men.

The first searching of the disciples began on a dark night of uncertainty before the tragic moment when the three silent crosses were etched against the lightning-ripped sky—a moment never to be erased from the minds of men. It was late that night on which He was betrayed—after the meal with His followers, the falling asleep in the garden, the kiss of Judas, the arrest and the cowardly scattering of those who had sworn never to betray or desert Him.

"The same night in which he was betrayed"[10] He broke bread with the faithful twelve in an upper room in the house of a disciple, and afterward departed for a nearby hillside with His friends, all the disciples save Judas, by His side. In this dramatic prelude to His passion, almost like the first morality play, we find the essential meaning of this night made vivid.

The darkness and the night air brought freshness after the warmth of the upper room, and the silence of the garden retreat brought peace and close comradeship. Danger seemed far away—or was it that His presence made all living things deaf to the sounds of fear? So much had happened in the upper room that night; the eleven faithful friends were weary from trying to remember—and fearful of forgetting too soon— all the words He had uttered beyond their comprehension. He had poured out His life in words to His beloved disciples that night on which He was to be betrayed, but He knew time must pass before the focussed meaning of what his disciples remembered would be projected beyond the upper room and the olive garden. They slept. He prayed.

But sleep and prayer were shattered by the tramping feet of soldiers.

As Christ was led away in the night, the voice of Judas crying "Master, Master" lingered in the disciples' ears.

But shortly after midnight, along the sleep-stilled streets figures crept stealthily, turning up the outer stairs into an upper room, a room with the lingering scent of poured-out wine and broken bread, there to hide until the danger was well past. They drew close together, starting with fear each time another one entered. After they were all there, save one, they dared to light a single lamp; and in the wisp of light they whispered puzzling questions back and forth, trying to make some sense out of the swift-moving events of the night.

They began to sort out and share their memories, not only of that night but of their whole time with Him, and the things that held them to Him. Their shared memories were punctuated by the bitter jabs of words like failure, betrayal, fear, desertion, shame, denial, all piercing their agonizingly sensitive consciences. But other words, too, were remembered to balance the hurt and despair—comforting words like forgiveness, love, faith, trust, joy, humility, oneness, hope, promise, power, prayer, memory, life. Each one contributed his dearest memory of the Master's words and moments of close relationship with Him, putting together each "one thing needful" with each "one thing I know," and made ready to move out and live as if He were still with them. Did they not know He was still with them? Had He not promised?

But there was still a crucifixion to witness, another dreadful period of doubt, fear, sorrow, and despair to pass through, as the body of their Lord was taken down from the cross and sealed in a tomb. But then came Easter and a confirmation of their memories and their conclusions, and the Ascension, and at last, Pentecost. It was at Pentecost, again in that sacred upper room, as they were attempting to marshal their forces and agree on what He wanted them to do, that He came among them with power, and they knew what they must say and what they must do.

This time, when they left the upper room, guided and strengthened by the Holy Spirit, they were restored, fearless, and with a single mind, eager to proclaim what they remembered. No return now to the old tasks, now become strangely unalluring, or to the old life to face the mocking voices of those who had never caught and followed the vision. This vision was for them now a promise given, stored in memory—a way and a truth clear and strong. They had now a Life and a Presence to sustain them on their way as they spoke the truth, and to keep them to their course, come what may. They were His emissaries now, sent to proclaim His Kingdom of love on earth. They remembered and held to

His words for life, so different were they now from those faithful few
who gathered in that darkened upper room while our Lord's passion
grew in intensity, just before the bitter death on the cross. They remembered from that night for life the events that came clear as God let them
identify with Christ's sufferings and His whole life.

Each disciple contributed at least one memory.

"I remember Gethsemane:

I remember how Judas betrayed Him:

I remember how Peter denied Him:

I remember how they all forsook [Him] and fled:

I remember the scourging:

I remember the crown of thorns:

I remember how they spat upon Him:

I remember how they smote Him on the head with a reed:

I remember His pierced hands and feet:

I remember His agony on the Cross:

I remember His thirst:

I remember how He cried, My God, my God, why hast thou forsaken
me?"[11]

And out of their collective memory came a church and a creed. The
long line of remembered things stretches as far forward and as far back
as men will allow, for commitment is not out of style, and we, His
followers, receive and project His life and His light. That light came
from God; the light of God became incarnate and was made coherent in
Jesus Christ through the Holy Spirit. Christ was the emission point of
the light that God released, and those who received Him became the
"excited atoms" that enabled the "coherent" light of His Word to be
beamed to the world and into the future through the Christian Church.
The voices of history have been preserved and carried as a cloud of clear
witnesses to the light projected to the point of visibility in every age.

The coherent light took shape that night as Jesus was tortured, tried,
and condemned, but it was untested until the meeting of Jesus with two
of His followers on the way to Emmaus and until Pentecost. These two
stories and the indelible experience they portray bring to full circle the
oneness of the "Last Supper" and the "Holy Communion." In this
sacrament of His continuing life, this perpetual memory of His precious
death and sacrifice, He left the re-formed group of disciples the
dynamics for the projection of the "coherent" light of His earthly
presence into the darkness of the future; "they continued steadfastly in
the apostles' doctrine and fellowship, and in breaking of bread, and in
prayers."[12]

We who live in this world need to remember Pentecost. On that day the power of the Holy Spirit, which changed the disciples so miraculously, was as bright and clear and powerful as a beam of light, and as difficult to explain. The doors of the age were shut until by the operation of the Holy Spirit they were opened.

The analogy of coherent light seems to make the event of Pentecost—that bursting beginning of the Church, when history first discerned it—more concrete and understandable within the context of today's life. In the Christian religion, God's coherent light concentrated in Christ is like a single note from a violin. In contrast, the world's incoherent light is like the raucous noise of Times Square. Ordinary light spreads out, disperses, loses power in transmission; God's light in and through Christ, however, can travel thousands of miles or years without losing any of its power or spreading significantly. Light waves vibrate tens of millions of times faster than ordinary sound waves. God takes these light waves, which move like an unruly mob, and transforms them into "coherent" light—makes them move like disciplined soldiers.

A diagram helped make clear to me the tremendous possibilities of this "coherent" light, which is Christ. Two atoms were shown: the first, an unexcited atom that absorbs the light wave and ends its transmission; the second, an excited atom that takes whatever light waves strike it at the same frequency and is stimulated to transmit them, increasing in power, in the direction of their propagation. By itself, an excited atom contributes little to the science of communications, but many such atoms vibrating together become a powerful source of high-frequency energy. Henry Drummond anticipated this analogy when he said, "Every atom in the universe can act on every other atom, but only through the atom next it. And if a man would act upon every other man, he can do so best by acting, one at a time, upon those beside him."[13]

Pentecost made the difference between unexcited atoms and excited atoms, for on that day God produced the powerful coherent light of His presence, reorganizing and reorienting life around a different center, the living Christ, and focusing it on a different goal, His Kingdom on earth. I believe that this analogy brings new understanding to the event known as Pentecost, when God's spiritual power, wisdom, and direction descended as the Holy Spirit upon the disciples gathered in the upper room, ready, waiting, expectant, already believing because they had seen and known God incarnate in Jesus Christ.

The pre-eminent result of Pentecost was not the speaking in tongues but the triumphant progress of the gospel over all barriers of language and distance, from a place in Galilee in 33 A.D. to Main Street, U.S.A. in A.D. 1965. Paul, as one of the excited atoms, picked up and carried on the Pentecost theme when he admonished the Philippians to "be blameless and harmless," as "sons of God, without rebuke, in the midst of a crooked and perverse nation, among whom ye are to shine as lights in the world; holding forth the word of life."[14]

After Pentecost, these new Christians were to keep their eyes fixed on the light that is in Christ, which is disciplined, coherent, excited, always moving on, not permitting them to concentrate only on the darkness of the world or the crooked age. Because of this, the light began to shine in them and from them, and to penetrate the darkest parts of the world.

In spite of our vastly different twentieth-century world, we are called upon to do no less than the first Christians. We are to help hold the world together through our knowledge that in Christ we see what God is like. In responding to His love and by serving His purpose we find our own fulfillment and freedom, which we share with all men.

The Ecumenical Past and Future

Can we, therefore, pull into one coherent whole the essence of Christianity, the basic content, the corpus of His teaching, the absolute core of Christian truth to be projected and never lost? Is there a spectrum to faith which coheres as white light for projection but which breaks down into its component colors for bearing witness—for example, in our own age in a specific situation? We recognize that the white light of Christ's eternal presence is a combination of rays of all known colors, which cohere and project as excited atoms, ceaselessly bombarding the atoms next to them as links in the chain of history from the day of Pentecost until now.

The coherent light of memory spans the centuries, and all of it is focused in and on a Person. Christians rode this beam of light, which is Christ, through history, and, although sometimes "off the beam," they sought with courage and hope to see that this coherent light was projected without diminution or dissipation or interruption or deviation or distortion from Christ the source, straight into the infinite future.

But remember also that the light was made coherent only in His person; that God was incarnate in Jesus Christ; that the Holy Spirit gathered the light of His presence and projected it through time and space to now—to us—through Him.

This ideal of the disciplined and focused concentration of God's light in Christ, as projected by the Christian fellowship, has suffered in transmission from age to age, country to country, person to person, and has lost some of its coherence, unity, and power. As an agnostic once said to Reinhold Niebuhr, "I oppose the Church, not primarily because of its dogmas but because of its triviality." Dr. Niebuhr observed, in response, that "The Church sinks into triviality when it fails to deal with 'the weightier matters of the law.' "[15] The coherent beam of Christ's light has often been interrupted and diffused by trivialities. This is what makes the minister angry, the willingness of people to deal only in trifles when a life and death struggle is going on all around.

The outward signs of the Church change but Christianity does not. Styles change in church architecture, liturgy, vestments, theology, even morals, but the inner life and its needs remain unchanged, just as the human body remains basically the same though clothed in different styles.

If the Christian Church is not to be a clothes dummy to exhibit current styles or a waxworks display of an array of period pieces, it must face that moment of unveiling when the outward and visible coverings are removed and the naked truth is beheld. Whether we have worn the "fine linens" of a liturgical tradition in our fragmented segment of the whole Body of Christ, or the "filthy rags" of a shouting sect on the fringe of orthodoxy, God will see us, as we shall also see ourselves, as we really are, men made up of erring flesh and blood, all equal in His sight, in need of His love, care, forgiveness, insight, direction, mercy, and grace. The ecclesiastical clothes of hypocrisy are among the greatest blocks to the reunion of Christendom.

Far more than doctrine divides the churches, as those negotiating for the organic union of two or more bodies of Christians have learned. C. H. Dodd's famous letter provided a revealing moment of truth which has been hard to swallow, but what he wrote is obvious when we are honest with ourselves.[16] Is it not true that there are many "unavowed motives" in ecumenical conversations, such as denominational or confessional loyalties, separate religious traditions, implications of social and political factors, which, when unity and agreement seem within sight, shunt the discussion to a siding or bring it to a complete impasse?

Doctrines do need the serious attention they are getting on all sides in all parts of Christendom, but the early general councils of the Church discovered that most of their time was needed for going over the practical, nontheological factors, which in some ways were more difficult and touchy than the deeper theological issues. The list is long and could be further lengthened without difficulty, but the following factors are common knowledge: national antagonisms, habit, sentiment, vested interests, institutional pride, prejudices, love of status quo, personal ambition, political pressures, distrust of the unfamiliar, sociology, race, misrepresentations, and doctored history.[17]

The slowdown in approaches to unity within and among Christian churches, where reform and renewal are so urgently needed, is the unwillingness of unity negotiators to go beyond the point of no return. Fortunately, there are significant exceptions. One example is the Church of South India, which has succeeded mainly because of the willingness of the churches involved to be guided by the Holy Spirit—the presence of God with them here and now—and to trust Him to lead them into whatever future He wills for them. It is lack of faith that has prevented more such organic unions.

The Place of History

Almost from the beginning of the Church's life there were quarrels and internecine warfare over one thing or another—as far back as the severe disagreement between Peter and Paul over whether to admit Gentiles into the Christian fellowship or not, which the Council of Jerusalem settled in favor of Paul's inclusive catholic view of Christ's followers.

During a thousand years of turmoil and darkness, men grappled with ignorance and superstition, and the spread of Christianity was largely dependent on both, in addition to the conquering force of arms. But in the ferment and discontent of the fourteenth and fifteenth centuries, when the rumblings of rebellion stirred in almost every country, men's minds as well as their consciences were aroused. There was a gradual emergence from the darkness of the middle ages through new learning, the invention of the printing press—which made possible the wide distribution of this new knowledge—a rising sense of nationalism, and a reappraisal of the Church and its life through new vision and insight, which beheld and articulated the visible truth so long unseen before men's eyes. The tempo of reaction was stepped up. The Scriptures were translated into the vernacular. This firsthand knowledge of the word of God caused men to think, to compare, and to question.

But, instead of cleansing, reforming, and renewing the Church from within as all the reformers intended, it became a sweeping flood tide of change which got out of control and led at last to Christianity gone berserk, with the variations and fragmentations multiplying so fast it was hard to keep track of what was going on. Paul had his problems of changing loyalties when ambitious and misguided leaders, like Apollos and others, tried to take over for Christ as head of the Church. Christianity could not possibly have been all the things that emerged during the Reformation as "Christian" and as "Church" in the roaring confusion of the claims put forth by those who thought they were doing the Lord's work. As men sought to find the light which was Christ, it became so diffused there was no way to focus it for continuity. Was it shining in and from the Pope in Rome, or from the Patriarch in Constantinople, or from Calvin in Geneva, or from Luther in Germany, or from Knox in Edinburgh, or from Cranmer in London? Some of the light was shining in each person in each place, but there were many confusions and problems.

Whenever any man makes an unalterable stand and wins followers, there is usually strife and bloodshed. It is hard to stop the overzealous conduct of those won to a new idea, and there are always the iconoclastic concomitants of every revolutionary movement; the original purity and intent of "new truth" is always twisted, distorted, and carried to extremes in some followers. This was true in Germany and Switzerland, and later in England. Making a stand for a conviction is a costly and often disorderly business in any age, but to those who make it there is no alternative. While the forces of the time played on the thinking, writing, and speaking of Luther, Zwingli, Calvin, Knox, and Cranmer, the essential significance of what they did was religious, a return to the Bible to find out what it had to say on every disputed point—the authority of the Bible to back up the authority of the Church.

The Protestant tradition needs to be redefined for us today in the light of the modern ecumenical movement and the things we hold in common. But first, what do we mean by "Protestant," *the* word of the Reformation?

"Protestant" is not a word to be eliminated or forgotten but a word to be understood. It means essentially an appeal to God in Christ as found in Holy Scripture and in the Early Church; it is the good news of God's grace. It means also a protest against all degeneration, apostasy, grievous distortions, and abuses found in the Church. "Protest" was used in a positive sense, as Shakespeare used it when the wrote "I do protest [insist] I love thee." The word was first used to describe the protest against Roman Catholic intolerance as evidenced at the Imperial Diet of Speyer, Bavaria, in 1529, which decreed that Roman Catholic ministers were not to be disturbed in territories predominantly Lutheran, but that Lutheran minorities were not to be tolerated in Roman Catholic countries. The same is true today in Italy, Spain, and Colombia, and we still protest such measures. Christians were first given their name at Antioch, Protestants at Speyer.

The reformers arrived at purification and reformation, not abolition and overthrow; they expounded the implications of the ancient creeds which they felt had long been unnoticed or obscured. As early as 1529 two great fundamental convictions of Protestantism were set forth: the awareness that there could be another kind of churchmanship than was possible under the Papacy; and the setting up of the First Century Rule of Faith as the standard of all Christian life and Christian belief—that man's final appeal is to the Word of God, and that man's primary allegiance is to our Lord Jesus Christ.

Within the varied ranks of Protestantism today, men still argue over such doctrines as Luther's "justification by faith alone," but all will grant the need for emphasizing faith as well as works and man's dependence on the grace of God. "Did we in our own strength confide our striving would be losing."[18] Among Protestants there are also varying degrees of acceptance of the doctrine of "the priesthood of all believers," but all are grateful for the new emphasis on the role of the laity and the recognition of their ministry in the Church, which has become an important part of the ecumenical movement.

The reformers were not so intent on developing new doctrines as they were on exploring and exploding old doctrines, or giving them a different orientation. They did not throw out the sacramental system, for example, but claimed that every man also had direct access to God, which led to a break with ecclesiastical legalism and to greater simplicity in organization and worship. But again, it was hard not to go to extremes as far removed as possible from what was deplored.

Whenever a reformer, who must be a judge of others whom he holds in error, forgets that he, too, is under judgment—for no man is perfectly good or has hold of perfect truth perfectly—he may do more harm than good. It was good to get rid of the rigid and infallible aristocracy of the Church, but bad to put man on the throne and then lose sight of the profound truth that he is not God but an imperfect, erring creature, and to forget that sometimes every man stands in need of a Savior. It was good to be emancipated intellectually, but bad to accept without question the general secular humanism of the age which accompanied it.

Just a word about Anglicanism, which is unique among Reformed Evangelical Protestant Churches, for with its principle of continuity is preserved its Catholic heritage, even as it rediscovered the evangelical witness of the gospel. The insistence upon continuity of succession has produced continuing tension within the Anglican Communion and caused much misunderstanding outside. We know that no communion can lay claim to possess alone the wholeness of the gospel. While we all believe in the continuity of faith and the historic ministry, most of us count the truth of the gospel, and Christian life in accord with the gospel, at least as important as episcopal succession. Some Anglicans do not. However, for all parts of the Christian Church the ultimate concern is that every man should know the forgiving love of God in Christ. We stand on common ground in the emphasis on the Word and the inner witness, and this emphasis has endured for over 1,900 years.

There are undoubtedly some who think it would have been better not to have had a Reformation, since the fragmentation of the Church was one result. Such regret is futile. The unity of Christendom claims our earnest attention today and progress is being made, but there must always be new and corrective insights within the Church, and under God a constant process of reformation. We can never stand again with Ephraim as Hosea describes him, "a wild ass alone by himself."[19] We must stand together and witness to the truth of God in and for the world, as each man sees this truth, based on the Word of God and the experience of history, and within the framework of the Trinitarian formula.

A New Reformation

What is wrong with the Church today that needs to be made right, as we seek to remove some of those distortions of "sins and wickedness" by which we are handicapped in running "the race that is set before us"?[20] Let us concentrate, not on the superficial and usual things we "ought to do" or have left undone, but on deeper, vastly more important matters—what we must *be* and *become*. As learners, worshipers, teachers, and witnesses, we must breathe out a healthy sense of wonder and serenity over the things of this world, as well as manifesting a sense of certainty and expectation over the things "not of this world," and always seek God's light for every darkness.

What about the abuses today? Where do we find the aberrations which demand our protest? Again, the answer is within the churches, made manifest by our divisions, our lack of understanding, and our failure to speak the truth in love. We need much plain speaking—but within the fellowship; there should be no open letters, no panning of Protestantism, and no snubbing of Christian brothers at the local level.

We can make our stand today on a common understanding of our Protestant Christian heritage from the very beginning of the Christian Church, not ignoring the long life of the Church before the Reformation, nor minimizing the Reformation and post-Reformation changes in the Church's life, but holding firmly to Paul's words: "But speaking the truth in love, [we] may grow up into him in all things, which is the head, even Christ: from whom the whole body fitly joined together and compacted by that which every joint supplieth, according to the effectual working in the measure of every part, maketh increase of the body unto the edifying of itself in love."²¹

Any kind of reformation means putting right what is wrong. It is amazing how easy the reformation process is, once we get the basic facts straight as to what we believe. All else then begins to fall into place, as it did when Luther was convinced good works alone were not sufficient for saving one's soul. Men are made valuable only by the grace of God, which is freely given to those who see that they need it and will accept it. When the individual Christian and the parish both come alive by manifesting such a God, others will be drawn to worship Him also. Insofar as our basic Christian beliefs are related to the facts of everyday life, the Christian influence permeates the life of the world, proving that you and I are the Church wherever we are.

There were other reforming theses flying in the winds of sixteenth-century change—those of Calvin, Knox, Zwingli, Cranmer, and others. Why were these questions so violently taken up by the people and as violently refused answers by the hierarchy of the Roman Church? Because both sides failed to discern the signs of the times. As a result, along with reformation, the sixteenth century produced fragmentation. The Church is not according to Rome, Constantinople, Worms, Geneva, or Anglia, but according to Scripture. The new or second reformation today is a reunification of the Body of Christ as a living reality in the life of the world, not a dummy for displaying changing styles of religion according to one man's whim or caprice.

Agreed that many things are wrong with the Church in the world today and many changes need to be made. Agreed that all is not wrong, that there is much that is good and right, and true to that coherent light projected in a straight, uncluttered line from the day of Pentecost in the first century. Agreed that God is not dead or on vacation or outmoded. Agreed that the Christian Church, with all its need for reform, is no anachronism in the midst of a scientific age but, now more than ever, has an essential role to play in the lives of men. However, when the outward evidences of a Christian civilization begin to disappear, it means something is organically wrong within—a neglected Church loses its *raison d'être*.

"Jesus Christ [is] the same yesterday, and today, and for ever."²² This is a true statement, but He is differently perceived and made evident in every age. He is the same. It is we who are different—each year of our lives. Therefore, we heed the admonition, "Be not carried about with divers and strange doctrines. For it is a good thing that the heart be established with grace."[23]

The coherent light which is Christ is constant and powerful, undiminished after almost two thousand years. And it projects its beam into the next era of Christian influence, when the Church must move into the areas of life where there are spiritual vacuums, pockets of darkness, or unknowns still to explore and conquer, and into the wide-open universe to keep up with a space age. This is only the beginning. The minister and his people—they are the Church, each bearing his own witness in his own way wherever he is. And while they are not always "without rebuke, in the midst of a crooked and perverse nation," they are always aware that they must "shine as lights in the world"[24] for His sake.

III

His Parish

Here's the People

Georges Bernanos wrote of a country priest to whom the Church and
the world were all concentrated in the small parish and the few people
he served in a French provincial village. In his diary the priest reveals
the consuming passion he had for this localized ministry in a parish that
was "being eaten up by boredom." He said, "we can't do anything
about it. . . . If only the good God would open my eyes and unseal my
ears, so that I might behold the face of my parish."[1] This French
country priest speaks for all ministers in all parishes, for to him parish
and people are synonymous. We, too, want to see "the face of our
parish, the look in its eyes." We, too, want to tend "the flock of God
which is among" us,[2] leading, feeding, and heeding them willingly,
with a ready mind and hand. We want to teach them all things a
Christian ought to know and believe, and to guide them into all truth.[3]
We want to "do good unto all men" while there is time, "and especially
unto them that are of the household of faith."[4] The minister's task as
shepherd is unlimited, but it begins with his own small segment of the
fellowship placed in his immediate care—a local and personal task, yet
unlimited in scope and consequences.

There is more to that childish hand game than one thinks. You have
probably played it. You interlock your fingers and say, "Here's the
church." You put next the two first finger tips together and say, "Here's
the steeple." Then you say, as you open your hands to show the interlocking fingers, "Open the door, and here's the people." The Church is
the people. It seems so simple to define what we mean by "Church"
until we try to weave into a single statement all the loose strands of
meaning. "Here's the church" can mean anything from a first-century

fellowship, as described in the Acts of the Apostles, to a twentieth-century hierarchy, as evidenced in the Second Vatican Council.

In this chapter I am more concerned with the local manifestations and variations of the concept and image of the word "Church" than I am with the larger aspects discussed in the last chapter. I want to explore just how the small or large band of Christ's followers penetrates the nightmares of ugliness, pollution, and noise, and accepts the challenge, of the places where people live and work—how Christ is made known there to each person in each parish by getting under the skin and into the hearts of the people.[5]

Reformers

There is a score or more of restless young thinkers today who have settled on a new image of "church" for Christians, going so far as to dispense with church buildings entirely, leaving them to remain what so many of them are—museums. In Russia many of the churches have been turned into museums, and the government is tearing others down one by one, with but a single aim in view, the complete effacing of the evidences of Christianity from the Soviet Union. It is not yet quite like that in the United States, but our impatient young Christian *avant garde* has begun to develop a new theology for "correcting the prevalent paralysis" of Christianity; they want a non-gospel for a non-you in a non-world, sans buildings, sans organization, sans the institution labeled "church."

In order to keep in touch with this group and not dismiss them with a shrug because we have "lost" them, we must take a new look at what we mean by the word "church." One way is to check the excited atoms and declare what we mean by individual Christians being the Church, each standing in his own place. How can we reconcile the core meaning of "church" to the Russian Orthodox conception as opposed to the Pentecostal view, since both churches are now members of the World Council of Churches? The problem is best solved by defining the outward and visible signs of the Church at the parish level, since all of the "marks" of the Church are seen at last locally in persons and in parishes, whether or not they are those found in the Acts, the Nicene Creed, or in classical Reformation documents. The New Testament marks of the Church are given simply in Acts 2:42: "They continued in the Apostles' doctrine [the word of God] and fellowship, and in breaking of bread [sacrament], and in prayers." The marks in the Nicene Creed declare boldly and succinctly that the Church is "one, holy,

catholic, [and] apostolic." The marks of the Church at the time of the
Reformation are summarized generally as follows: "The true Church is
a visible fellowship of believers in which the pure word of God is
preached, and the sacraments are administered according to the or-
dinances of Christ."[6] For the Christian today the earliest marks of the
Church are the most essential, namely, those found in the Acts of the
Apostles: making the word of God central, breaking bread together at
the Lord's Table regularly, and praying without ceasing. The effective
witness of Christians in whom the marks of the Church are found is of
paramount importance to the Christian mission in the world.

Jacques Ellul, a French lawyer and lay theologian, put his finger on
the sore point for churchmen when he said, "the dilemma for Christians
in France nowadays is this, that, on the one hand, the churches there are
so debilitated and apostate that a Christian can hardly bear to remain in
a church, and yet, on the other hand, no Christian can leave a church
lest he fail to confess his own part of the responsibility for the very
conditions in a church which provoke protest."[7] This is true in the
United States, too.

So, our dilemma is: To what door of what church in what land shall
we nail our theses of protest—and how shall we list all those factors
which enter into the debilitated condition of the churches so as to bring
about a change?

The basic question is this: How are the people in churches to change
in order to meet the "exigency of times and occasions?" What will
enable these members of parishes to effect the needed changes in their
own community? The Parish and People Movement in Britain is
marshaling some of the answers. They are seeking ways of deploying the
clergy more fairly and effectively, to move them from the static situations to where the people are. They are trying to release the parochial
system from its bonds and its bounds. They are moving swiftly to
capture a neglected area of the Church's ministry among the working
class. When the workers left the villages for the industrial centers they
were uprooted culturally and spiritually, and were largely lost to the
Church, which has shown hardly a ripple of concern until now. The so-
called house church is one attempt to reach them in small groups where
they will feel valuable and effective as individuals.

In this country we need the same concern and approach, and the
asking of pointed questions which demand answers. Locally we might
ask such questions as "Is the church building essential?" or "What is
impeding the progress of the Church in this neighborhood or community?" or we might try to answer at a simple level such weighty
theological questions as "What is the priesthood?" or "What is the

Church?" or "What is the ministry?" or "What is the liturgy?" The
face of my parish changes.

Luther used a set of theses as his catalyst for change. Today a tool or
weapon is being forged in God's workshop as the instrument of change
within the Church.

An Answer

That single word "Coventry" conjures up a host of mental pictures.
For all who went through World War II it has become a symbol to the
civilized world of senseless, total destruction. For those who have
been on pilgrimage to this sacred spot, the word holds many vivid
memories. Here is evidence of resurrection: a church outwardly destroyed by enemy action rises from its ashes to fit a new day and
generation—now ready and eager for dialogue with the world.

Here the reforms have been built into the very fabric. The Cathedral
Church of St. Michael in Coventry, with Epstein's sculptured *St.
Michael and the Devil* on guard, is concentrating on communicating the
gospel through dialogue. In every area of life there must be this kind of
dialogue, the Christian gospel confronting the various non-Christian
ideologies with the full force and vigor of the Christian message,
enunciating its doctrine of love in the face of such isms as communism,
scientific humanism, and whatever distorts and stultifies life's meaning.
This new cathedral, resurrected from the sacrifice, suffering, and destruction of war, would project the Christian Church into the future, not
have it retreat into the past. It was built on the ruins of the medieval
church started in 1043 by Lady Godiva and the Earl Leofric, which was
dissolved by Henry VIII and pulled down in about 1539, and subse-
quently used as a quarry. Adjacent are the ruins of the parish church,
completed in 1433 but not raised to cathedral status until 1918. This
was the structure destroyed by Hitler's fire bombs. The new cathedral
stands not only as a magnificent replacement, but as a tool and a weapon
forged for immediate use in the twentieth century. "Here is the church."

Coventry has brought the Christian religion and the life of the
Church to bear upon the modern industrial society which surrounds
it—preaching, teaching, and practicing the gospel for tomorrow, today,
seeking to make men desire to board the ship of the Christian Church
rather than the "Ship of Fools," for their journey on the sea of life.
Paul Tillich sharpens this thought in these words: "We must receive the
ever contemporary Christ in our own contemporary way employing
whatever artistic forms, liturgical patterns, theological concepts and

social diagnosis that can best enable us, here and now, to re-encounter the God of history and to reapprehend and actually receive His eternal time-oriented word."[8] In other words, we need to recognize and find a gospel for the age incarnate in the gospel for the ages. Coventry has done just this. Her cathedral rose from the ashes of war's destruction, "as a triumphant reassertion of the vitality of Christian civilization" and "the permanence of Christian truth," as a symbol of the "determination of Christians to capture and direct the revolutionary forces which are shaping the post-war world," and as a way to relate prayer and praise to every phase of a man's life. The face of this "parish" is discernible to all who visit Coventry.

St. Michael's Cathedral Church was specifically rededicated on May 25, 1962, to be "the spiritual dynamo behind a city" and for a special purpose—"to proclaim and to foster reconciliation, to build bridges of understanding between nation and nation, class and class, between men of divergent religious outlook and, not least, between the Church and the Arts." The image of this new cathedral is to be as "a living House of God, a great laboratory of experiment to establish the relevance of Christianity to contemporary society." In this "workshop for the Kingdom of God," the goals will be to close the gaps between the Church and the world, using every form of communication to speak the language of the people and society, always seeking for a greater participation by the people and oneness with every phase of their lives. It is quite true that Church "structures are heretical if they belittle God's mission or action" in the world, and if they "prevent the gospel from reaching its intended goal,"[9] all men in each place.

So when we say "Here's the Church," we mean "Here are the visible, tangible marks of the life of the Christian fellowship, as described in the New Testament, made concrete in parish and community life." By this we really mean "Here's the people," for they are the "face" of the parish, they are the Church. So the minister deals with his people who, with him, are the Church in that place. "Take heed therefore unto yourselves, and to all the flock, over which the Holy Ghost hath made you overseers, to feed the church of God."[10]

The Shepherd's Flock

His people are the minister's bane and his blessing, but always *his* people. He is committed at ordination to maintain "quietness, peace, and love, among all Christian people, and especially among them that are or shall be committed" to his charge, "as much as lieth in" him. He is the shepherd of his flock. He knows his sheep, even the black ones, by name, and cares for each of them, even the most unlovable among them—especially these. They are his people, even those who do not support him or who criticize him—often with great intensity. In fact, this positive reaction is better than to have them neither hot nor cold, that is, indifferent.

From some thirty years of dealing with "my" people in six different parishes—widely scattered geographically from Texas to New York—I find I can divide them into fairly clearly defined groups found in every parish, in spite of the difference in individuals. "My" people fall into one or more of the categories described below, and the "face of my parish" must be fashioned into a Christian fellowship out of this assortment of human beings who have only one thing in common, belief in Jesus Christ as their Lord and Savior.

I am reluctant to label each member of my parish according to his or her present category, for people do change. Also, a first impression is often a lasting one, even for the minister, who must watch for signs of change in each one of his flock as he seeks to discover marks of God's presence among them, and to develop these marks whenever they are not found. In a real sense, whatever is found in this chapter must be related to all the rest of the book, for the question "Who are they?" is directly connected with "Who or what am I?"

As a background for considering all types of people who make up parishes, Dr. Kraemer gives us this analysis: "The urban dweller's everyday life is not concentrated upon one point, geographical or social, but revolves around a series of different points, spread over a broad range of relationships and territories. Without actually, or even supposedly, being a disintegrated personality . . . he leads several part lives, synthesized within himself. . . . Many a faithful member of the congregation is often acutely conscious of the fact that his membership is in reality purely a sparetime occupation."[11]

St. Paul wisely declared, "Every man's work shall be made manifest: for the day shall declare it,"[12] be it bricklayer, plasterer, plumber, doctor, weaver, lawyer, seamstress, student, or minister. So when we open the door and see the people we single them out as persons and sort them out as individuals according to their several relationships. The following "sortings" deal specifically with persons in relation to their ministers. However, these are not intended to be hard and fast compartments to limit the description of any parishioner's existence.

The true friends and followers. Some of the parish hit it off with the new minister from the beginning, and support him wholeheartedly in all he undertakes to do. These are the loyal ones who make life a joy for the minister and give him the courage to go on. There is always someone in every parish who saves the day, someone who can be trusted when the minister needs to blow off steam. These he cherishes and gives thanks for daily. He makes sure, however, that he does not let them possess him totally, to the exclusion of others in the parish.

The friends and followers of a former minister. A few parishioners' lives are linked so closely with a previous minister in some way that they resent his successor and withhold their loyalty and support. They are often sharply critical of the new man because he is not like the old one, and does things so differently—in an inferior way, of course!

One thing to remember when taking on a new parish is to assess the previous minister's work, retaining and building on what is good and being very slow to plunge into something drastically new and different. Win over the parish first and, whatever changes are make, make them gradually, with a clear explanation of why they are needed and what you hope to accomplish by them in the enlarged and more effective outreach of the parish.

This category of parishioners lives in the past. They are not willing to change, and often cause divisions and give the new minister a rough time. He must bear with this attitude patiently and do all in his power to overcome it and to win them over. He must never, by even so much as a small hint, denigrate what any former minister has done.

One of the best descriptions of this situation is given by Henry Knox Sherrill. He tells about Dr. E. Winchester Donald, Phillips Brooks' successor, who was one of my predecessors at the Church of the Ascension in New York City. Donald "was an able man and preacher, but he felt the burden of his predecessor. In my observation there are two ways of meeting such a situation, to ride the wave or to buck it. Apparently Dr. Donald, with all his good qualities, attempted the latter. It was a heart-breaking, if not impossible task."[13]

The minister must build on the past and be ready and generous in giving all due credit to past ministers for what exists in the present. A bit of good, sound advice is this: Never belittle a predecessor.

The chronic complainers. The epithet is description enough for these persons, who are forever doomsday bent and critical of any change. The question of votive candles is a case in point for me. When I came to the Church of the Ascension there were candles at the side altar for worshipers to light. The original intent, during the war, had been to have something tangible for the worshiper to do in addition to saying a prayer. When I became rector I removed them, for they had outlasted their original purpose as part of a wartime ministry and gave many people the wrong impression. The most vociferous and persistent complainer was not a member of the parish at all. I learned a lot about candles in this brief encounter.

Of course, no minister can please everyone all the time. There will always be complainers. It is, therefore, best to let them speak their piece so that their complaints can be known and dealt with whenever possible. Otherwise they can cause a seeping infection in the life of the parish.

The neurotics and the queer. The latter are easier to deal with than the former. The minister must be trained to recognize those in both categories and to differentiate them from those who are headed for a true psychosis and mental breakdown. I shall never cease to be grateful for my summer at Worcester State Hospital learning about the outward and visible signs to watch for in an onset of mental illness. The various clinical training programs for the theological student are splendid additions to the tools of his "trade."

In a large city like New York the minister can spend all of his time just listening to neurotics without really aiding a single one, except through the therapy of listening. These pitiful people must be dealt with, whether they are parishioners or not, and in every city and diocese there is, or should be, some proper agency or person to whom they can be referred, which the minister must know about. In New York City both Trinity Church, downtown, and the Cathedral Church of St. John the Divine, uptown, provide an expert couseling service.

The troublemakers. There seems to be at least one in every parish who is not happy unless trouble is brewing for the minister in some area of the parish life. These persons are pesky, and usually sick in some sense of that word. They start rumors and in general raise a ruckus, or else ask disturbing questions, as in our Sunday School fire-escape issue. One parent—not a member of the parish—made quite a to-do over the lack of what he considered adequate fire escapes from the building where the Sunday School classes were held, especially for the younger children. He made a nuisance of himself, conducted weekly inspections, talked to many parents at the coffee hour, demanded regular fire drills, and so on. We had what the fire department considered adequate exits, but several improvements did come out of his campaign. We widened the fire escape at considerable expense, installed a fire bell, and instituted routine fire drills. By the following fall the family had moved away. There were no more complaints about fire hazards. All is well in the parish until another troublemaker emerges. The minister must and can handle all such situations with patience. He must refuse to lose his temper, which is not so easy, since these troublemakers do tend to get one's goat. But he must remember that he or any person is only as big as the thing that infuriates him, and that everyone has a right to his own opinion. He must try not to air publicly how he feels about any person, except on the rare occasions when a stand must be made on some critical issue.

Gossips are also troublemakers and a great deal of time must be spent in correcting impressions and allaying rumors set in motion by hasty and wicked tongues. But the minister himself must be watchful, for he, too, can be a gossip about gossips and other troublemakers and do great harm. Silence is golden unless something good about another is suppressed. In judging others with what Roger Lloyd calls "the burning charity," the "only thing to be done is for the people concerned to apply as honestly as they possibly can the standards of charity [as found in I Corinthians 13, for example] to the particular situation in which they have been placed and to *all* the other people involved in it."[14]

The hard workers. Fortunately there are some who never say "no" to any task assigned and who take pleasure and pride in serving in even the "meanest" or smallest capacity; and these are jewels in the minister's crown. Every parish must have an effective volunteer service program, and the minister with a little persistence can always come up with the right person for every volunteer job in or out of the parish. I have always campaigned to make my parishioners willing volunteers under the slogan "No nos!" But this has not always worked. Motivation must be inspired by representing the job to be done as something important, urgently needed, and which fits the capacities of the particular person chosen. If not, that "no" is likely to come, since in every community the competition for people's time is on the increase. The minister gives much care to making these choices.

The leaners. These demand the minister's time and strength. They expect him to be close behind them, ready to prop them up lest they fall, always at their beck and call. This is a hard task, but I've found no escape from it. The only solution is to transfer the burden by teaching the leaners about God's strength within them and get them to stand on their own two feet with God's help, which is often a long and demanding task. But wean them we must, for their sakes and ours.

The learners. These make up the minister's team of growing Christians. They attend lectures, read books, organize study groups, and are insatiable for more knowledge. These form the hard core of a new spiritual dimension to the parish and are the nucleus of a team for winning others. Here we must deal with "evangelism," and how it is done locally by members of the parish, as the cutting edge of the Church's approach to the world, "for in Him we live, and move, and have our being."[15] Religion deals with man's "ultimate concern" (Paul Tillich's favorite phrase), and this ultimate concern and commitment depend on how we approach the basic and persistent questions of existence, how we who are the Church present Christianity to others through our understanding and living, as the enlightened and strengthening answer to the great question, "What is the chief end of man?" We need always to recover the gospel's authentic freshness and power and have it instantly available, for this content is the Church's *raison d'être*.

Christian answers to the meaning of a man's life for today are emerging, for example, in the writings of such younger men as William Stringfellow, "The reconciliation of God and the world in Jesus Christ means that in Christ there is a radical and integral relationship of all men and of all things. In Him all things are held together."[16] To communicate this is evangelism. As disciples, that is, willing learners who know that Christianity is not a non-gospel for a non-self, a nothing in a non-world, we are all evangelists. Christianity to us is the faith of a man in God, in God's universe, in Jesus Christ who is God's Son, and in himself as a child of God, become so through God's mercy, love and grace. With him we are everything. Without Him we are nothing. Without God's grace we are nothing. Without God's love we are nothing. Without God's revelation of Himself to us in His world we are nothing. I am a nothing without God. I am a something only with God's help. As a nothing "I can't go on." As a child of God "I can." The *primary* task of Christians is to *be* the Church. In Him we have found that indestructible core of self-indentity without which we could not be what we are—persons, for whom God cares. And this must be passed on by us to others as part of a lay-minister team ministry. Therefore, we cherish these learners and know that in them true discipleship is to be found, for every disciple is a willing learner and an eager sharer.

But how are we to reach the vast army of the unchurched? How are we to win the laborers and technicians in factories, farms, and laboratories? The answer lies in some form of small-group ministry, for small groups make people feel more at ease. This is one reason the house church movement has played an important role in the new outreach of the Church in the twentieth century. The "Parish and People" movement in England, already referred to, in an attempt to release the people from their long paralysis in vicarages, large churches, and parochial systems, concentrates on study groups, Bible-reading groups, and prayer groups, seeking a renewal of spirituality, of theology, and of ethics for our time.[17]

The devoted Christians. These form a major part of any minister's parish membership, at least most of the parishioners think of themselves as devoted Christians. How hard it is to make men see themselves as they really are—to change them from pseudo-Christians to real, devoted Christians. This is the primary task of the minister. But how? The answer is: from the pulpit, in the weekly message in the parish bulletin, in face-to-face challenge, in holding up constantly before his people the ideal Christian life. What we really mean by the word "devoted" is the layman who employs his time and talents in developing a Christian "style of life."[18] He incarnates what it means to *be* a Christian in the world, fully aware of and sensitive to the world's profane and secular life, and he uses this knowledge as a genuine point of contact for communicating the gospel.

The nominal Christians. There are far too many fakers and hypocrites who make a great show of church attendance and church work but who are really what Jesus called "whited sepulchers." Both the outside and inside of the cup of faith must be clean. There must be no evidence of "holy masquerade" of "the deadly charade of merely nominal Christianity," or of the hypocritical facade of righteousness, for all this will be unmasked and known at last. These people are hard to reach and change, but it is possible through their receiving new insight. *The Southwell Litany* furnishes a perfect guide and mirror[19] for both the minister and his people.

On the other hand, one factor that keeps many people from coming to church at all is that they cannot believe everything as presented and do not want to be hypocrites. The minister is often hard put to deal with these people, but he must keep after them and give them a toehold sufficient for them to hang on until a firmer and more complete understanding and acceptance can be won. He must try to keep them at least interested and exposed.

The doubters. The known and unknown doubters should be given sympathetic attention; there is a streak of honest doubt in us all. This is an area of major concern for all ages, especially when the teenager and the college youth begin to ask questions, and this is only part of the ferment in the Church everywhere. The really intellectual and scientifically minded are specially hard to reach, but every effort must be made to do so. Many college faculty groups are seeking answers for correcting the disillusionment of those who come to college and "lose" their faith as their minds are turned on full steam for the first time. Men like Henry Drummond in his day, and C. S. Lewis in our day, find reason the best approach to religion. There are also men like C. E. M. Joad, and many others, who have reasoned their way back into a Christian faith.

The minister can be of great help to doubters by sharing his own doubts and how they have been resolved, like D. R. Davies in his two books, *Down Peacock Feathers* and *In Search of Myself*. Talking things through with the doubter gives him a chance to air his doubts. This often clears the air sufficiently for a person to rethink his position—especially one who has been estranged or put off by what he thinks the Church means by words, phrases, and doctrines. The minister is often able to draw him back into the worship and work life of the parish by such understanding and clarifying dialogue.

Henry Drummond furnishes a good example of the pioneer debate between science and religion.[20] In the last century he helped Christians bridge the disturbing gap between Darwin's theory of an evolutionary creation and the Christian's story of creation by fiat. His attitude is as soundly constructive today as it was then. Henry Drummond is not just a "period piece" of the nineteenth century; he avoided with amazing success most of the scientific and religious cant of his time, and much of his writing is still good intellectual nourishment.

The zealots. The objectionable ones are those who work themselves to death for the wrong reasons, those who push a pointless cause or one that is unwise at that moment. These are the extremists, the wild-haired and harried ones, who fasten like a bull-dog to an idea and refuse to be deterred or to give an inch. Among these are also the demagogues and hatemongers who make a mockery of freedom by using it irresponsibly. The minister must be alert to spot and combat such zealots. But what about those others in the Old and New Testaments—the prophets, Jesus Himself, and the disciples? Were they not all zealots, too? True, they were. We need to separate out the possible good which comes from such zeal as found in the Bible, when it is God-inspired, and be guided by that kind of zeal.

Zeal can be a good thing and often injects the needle necessary to shock awake a dormant or hesitant Church, as illustrated by the famous Barmen Confession in which the Church in Germany expressed its opposition to Hitler. This document categorically proclaimed allegiance to God alone in Christ, and repudiated any other "events and powers" which claimed to supersede this primary allegiance. Only God is our *Führer,* they declared, boldly and unequivocally, and paid the price. Another instance of courageous zeal in this same period was the founding of a theological journal in Germany, launched by Karl Barth and his friend Edward Thuneysen in July, 1933—a trumpet blast as a manifesto to German Christians, which many listened to and heeded.[21]

Zealots are often a nuisance and a problem to the ordinary, placid, run-of-the-mill church member. They are so disturbing and upsetting. Why can't they be content with things as they are? However, when we try to lump all zealots under one label we run into difficulties. One thing they do have in common—things as they are have become intolerable and must go. But all zealots are not extremists who would use any means to obtain their ends. We cannot react to all zealots in the same way, that is, damn them and banish them. We need them in our midst to keep us from complacency, and we should be thankful to have a few of them around to stir us up, for they very often awaken us to needs unseen and unmet, or to roadblocks of the faith which must be removed.

It often takes a few prophetic extremists to keep us moving forward, willing to look at what's wrong and reforming what is amiss. The hymns "Rise up, O men of God, have done with lesser things," and "Awake my soul, stretch every nerve," give us our cue in recognizing the place of zealots, although their zeal sometimes gets out of hand and must be tempered by the fellowship when the final changes are made. But we need more tolerance and understanding for those who advocate radical change—they may have a valid point we have missed which has slowed or stopped the influence of the Church in our time.

Thank God there are zealots among us, who believe they are doing God's business, and who are willing to speak and face the consequences. They needle us and pain us, but they make us get a move on.

The aged and the lonely. Old people are on the increase in most parishes. They are becoming a problem, and the minister is squarely in the middle of the whole complex "science" of geriatrics. Every minister seeks the best way to handle the problem in his own parish—perhaps by forming social clubs, visiting the lonely, helping to make life worth living up to a hundred and old age a "golden" age in reality; but also he must make it clear that no one can live forever in this life, and that holy dying, joyfully, in hope, must be in the background of the mind of every older citizen. Getting older sick people into hospitals and nursing homes and homes for the aged takes time and patience, and, whenever possible, the minister should have someone who is especially gifted or trained to assist him in dealing with this problem.

The Sick. The minister always gives priority to the sick in parceling out his time. By the word "sick" is meant not only those who are ill with bodily sickness, but every other form of abnormality called sickness; when all is not well within, the whole person is affected. The sick are always with us, as are the poor, and must be given every possible attention and aid by the minister. The subject of healing comes up again and again, especially healing services, which have been dealt with in another section of this book. Also the subject of social case work will arise frequently and how far the Church can go in cooperation with welfare agencies to meet the calls which come. This is a local problem which must be dealt with by the minister in that particular situation.

The meddlers. There are always a few of these, who might have been included under "troublemakers." They go out of their way to put in their oar when they have no place in the boat. They give advice without being asked. Each minister can draw on his own experience for examples. I am thinking of several who did not mean to meddle but were "just trying to be helpful," and of how I have tried to deal with them. One thing which is dangerous, and so easy to misunderstand, is to write letters. Don't! Both the words and the spirit are so often taken the wrong way. Whatever is done or said, do it or say it face to face. How can the minister say, "Mind your own business," or "This is none of your affair," or "When your advice is wanted I'll ask for it?" He can't. He must always keep himself under control in dealing with the meddlers. Meddlers are a trial every minister wishes he could avoid.

Gross and perpetual sinners. There are the most obviously sinful, like sex offenders and alcoholics, who come under this label, but the not-so-obvious sinners in this category are the hardest to reach. The Oxford Group taught me how to deal with alcoholics, sex offenders, and other gross sinners, teaching me never to forget that if the sin is cured so is the sickness, and, therefore, to seek out the sin *first*. While in Richmond, Virginia, I learned a lot from my weekly meeting with a small group of such people in the process of being changed. Jesus first demanded that the sinner sin no more before he could be healed.

Parishes differ as to the numbers in this category. It requires some sharp probing to get anyone to admit his guilt, for no one wants anyone else to know—as if sinfulness could be kept secret. This is sticky and unpleasant business, but no greater blessing can come into a minister's life than to see the confusion which results from sinning cleaned up and the person straightened out and restored to family, society, and Church. The story of every "Bowery bum" contains the inability to shake off some dreadfully tenacious gross sin. These sinners are difficult, but often rewarding. They, too, are "his people."

The no-shows. This group completely baffles me. They belong to the parish, their names are on the books, but they never show up, except for baptisms, weddings, and funerals—a few may drop in for an Easter service. Nevertheless, it is better that they come once a year or on state occasions than not at all, and an Easter-day service is no time for sarcasm on the subject. No matter how often the minister reminds his flock that one of their bounden duties is to "worship God every Sunday in His Church," it does no good unless there is some inner motivation like that found by Liz Burns as she at last sought for something in a church service and really heard for the first time the words, "Almighty God, unto whom all hearts are open, all desires known, and from whom no secrets are hid."[22] She told what they meant to her. "The ageless words rolled down from the altar and poured over me, their beauty the beauty of the centuries, time-tested. Some call them soporific and for some they are, but for me they were and have remained electrifyingly vivid, these simple words of common prayer."[23] But the words did not speak to her until Liz realized she needed to go back to a church and went, seeking and ready to find.

No minister can admonish, reason, or browbeat people into coming to church. How do we succeed, then? By making the worship so attractive and valuable, the sermons so compelling and revealing, when people do come, that they will never want to miss again. For His sake, every service must be the very best a minister is capable of conducting.

The Shepherd's Duty

However discouraging the array of people with whom the minister must work and live, he must attempt to mold them into a portion of God's Kingdom on earth and to make each individual into a portrait of Christ. The face of his parish is enough to discourage the most dedicated among us, and yet marks of God's presence are there. So what do we do? Remember that no person is really what he seems to be, as Henry Drummond points out in his famous essay "Spiritual Diagnosis."

"The study of the soul is difficult because it far transcends the mind in complexity and in variety as the mind does the body. The minister is the one to whom men should turn if spiritual darkness spreads across their souls. But how few have penetration enough to diagnose such cases? Men in need too often think, because of their limited contact and knowledge, that there are few ministers to observe our least apparent symptoms, to get out of us what we [resolve] not to tell them, to see through and through us the evil and the good. Plenty there are to preach to us, but who will interview us, and anatomize us, and lay us bare to God's eye and our own? . . . To take [a person] by himself; to feel his pulse alone, and give him one particular earnest word—the only word that would do—all to himself—this is the simple feat which [we] look in vain for men to perform. . . . [God] hath appointed us to be our brother's keeper nor will He do for my brother what could be done by me. We cannot expect the Spirit's help to teach us what only laziness and personal indifference hinder us from learning; and to despise a power which He gave us capacities to possess is not the way to show that we trust Him who gave it. . . ."[24]

The minister must care about all people, even the most despised and unlovable, to learn what makes them tick and to introduce them to themselves and to God. People are the minister's business, all kinds of people, and the whole purpose of his parish ministry is to change people's lives from what they are to what God wants them to be. This is what attracted me to the Oxford Group back in the 30's; they had a life-changing emphasis and technique I had found nowhere else. I really thought this movement was what it appeared to be, the answer to my ineffective ministry. It did give a new bent to my life and contributed to my hour of awakening, but the solution was not as simple and easy as it seemed in the first rosy blush of finding "all the answers" pat, everything black or white. The Christian ministry begins and ends with the emphasis on winning men for Christ and His Church, substituting Christ for self as the focal point of their lives.

I recall vividly an Oxford Group meeting in Aiken, South Carolina, and the bishop who said he'd give anything to have known their technique at the beginning of his ministry. So I felt, and I tried it with zeal. Why didn't it always work for me? The answer is not yet fully clear. However, in this period I came to know of Dwight L. Moody and Henry Drummond, and found that the latter's essay "Spiritual Diagnosis," just quoted, revealed many clues to the kind of personal evangelism which worked life-changing miracles in his day and gave new meaning to "preaching for decision," used today by Billy Graham, along with personal confrontation. All ministers long to recover the converting power of the old revival preachers and to make the old inquiry-room technique work, as Dwight L. Moody did in the last century and Billy Graham does in the twentieth. I made many attempts over the years to work out a modern version of the inquiry room and after-sessions, by sermon quizzes and coffee-hour huddles, but I was haunted by the Oxford Group insistence on "scalps" won and displayed and pointed to with pride by the scalper—with embarrassment for the scalped—until I finally lost contact with the group and gave up many of its techniques.

I concluded that "The mission of the Church is not removing fish from a dirty river called the world and placing them in a clean pool called the Church. . . . The mission of the Church, which can never be separated from the Church itself, is to work by God's grace for the life of the world to come, in every circumstance and in every event of our lives, here and now."[25]

As a minister looks at his parish list he visualizes each name as a person living under a particular set of circumstances and sees what could be said or done or prayed about to change that person's life so that it may more nearly fulfil the dimensions of discipleship which will mark him as a Christian for all to see. To be converted, a man needs the courage to change what can be changed and the patience to put up with what cannot be changed—at least not yet. He must be twice-born. As related in the next chapter, my own experience of conversion has given me the ability to understand, in part, what another is going through, but it has given me no miraculous entry into the lives of others, only a better understanding of their needs and a deepening desire to help.

The old sawdust-trail technique worked better in the past than in the present, and "mass" evangelism is almost passé as a universal panacea to sin. There are many new and creative approaches to "saving souls" today that are working effectively in many different parts of the world. The World Council's Department of Evangelism has catalogued many of them in an effort to communicate ways of winning men to Christ, from the worker-priest approach in France to the house church movement among the workers in Sheffield, England, and the ways and means that are being developed in each country to fit its own peculiar situation. One of the best adaptations of the Church for reaching men of all conditions is the Cathedral of St. Michael in Coventry which has already been referred to. Here, the major goal is to close the gaps between the Church and the world, using every means of communication to speak the language of people and society.

Just how does the minister bring a man to that moment of decision to follow Christ and surrender his life into God's hands? Not many ministers will find success in a person-to-person approach on an "Are you saved?" basis. Is there any difference, really, between today's method of life-changing and the technique used by Philip the Evangelist with the Ethiopian eunuch? Look to that story for guidance in evangelism.

Read carefully Acts 8:26–40. Note the order and technique of approach and follow-through by the zealous Philip, who was alert and ready to strike when the opportunity came to bear witness. He was an excited atom, ready and anxious to share his Christian life with another. He was on fire with the gospel message. He seized quickly, without hesitation, his opportunity to instruct and to win another seeking person who was in a receptive frame of mind. Philip lived as a Christian and spoke as a Christian. He was full of his faith in Christ and his new way of life and always ready to talk about it, and as he talked men listened. Philip was a light to the Ethiopian, illuminating his darkness, guiding him into the truth about Christ, leading him to decisive and immediate action. When Philip finished this job he went on to the next opportunity to which God led him.

Since most of our stirrings-up and confrontations of choice leading to change occur in round-about ways, we need to be as concrete and helpful as possible at all times, and concentrate on making Christian people aware that they are "being the church" as they live and talk, wherever they are. The minister will be insistent upon an evaluation of spiritual growth each year as essential, reminding again and again of the need for daily increase.

I suggest reading J. D. Salinger's unusual story, *Franny and Zooey,* as an excellent illustration of how talk can lead to understanding when all facets of an idea are explored until the truth shines like a pearl of great price.[26]

I feel very close to Father Dillard, the French priest-workman who wrote about his people, painfully asking the following questions of himself: "What was I to do? What was I to say to them? I felt that I was a stranger to them. My liturgy, my prayers, my priestly dress—all cut me off from them and made me a being apart. Can Christ have lost his power of attracting or the strength that he is able to communicate to others? Am I an isolated being—one who has found the pearl of great price, and has to keep the secret to himself?"[27] Father Dillard was seeking to find the way to reach the hearts and minds of his own people, those committed to his charge. This is difficult, as he says and as we have seen. But there are more people outside than there are inside parishes. Those people who are outside the fold, who are technically not the minister's responsibility, what of them? The new Testament has an answer. We learn they are often more responsive than those inside the church.

My sidewalk preaching and the open-door ministry at the Church of the Ascension in New York City are but two examples of the Church's outreach into the world to minister to and win all men. For example, every Sunday afternoon in late spring and early summer, strollers along lower Fifth Avenue or visitors to the famous Washington Square Outdoor Art Show had a chance to witness a preaching mission which is rare in the cosmopolitan atmosphere of such a sophisticated avenue. I conducted for six years a "short-story hour" from the lawn of the church, standing on a low platform behind the old wrought-iron railing, for all who were willing to stop and to listen. I used a musical prelude to attract all within reach of my voice and praised God first on some musical instrument, ranging from Scottish bagpipes to the Salvation Army brass band. When CBS television picked up one of the sidewalk services they called it appropriately "A Word in Passing." I was always fully vested, and preceded by the parish sexton, who was also vested and carried a mace.

It was a bit unusual to find such a thing going on in front of a dignified Episcopal Church. But for a number of years I had failed to attract into the church many of the hundreds of people who flowed down toward Washington Square on a Sunday afternoon in the spring-time. I tried special musical services and good preachers, but few responded. There were always some who came in for a moment to see the famous John La Farge mural of the Ascension or for a quiet prayer, but most of them flowed right on past.

It finally occurred to me that if I was ever to reach these people I'd have to talk to them out there on the sidewalk. I was used to having a protective pulpit in front of me; it was quite different standing unprotected in front of those who stopped, first out of curiosity, but who stayed if I caught and held their attention. It was frightening at first to be out there face to face with people whose attention I had to seize in spite of all the noises and competition of the avenue.

My format was simple. After the music I told them a story, usually in parable form, striving to get across at least one point about the Christian religion relevant to the people and the moment, attempting to plant a seed of thought in their minds for later growing. At the close I always invited them into the church for a few "going-home prayers." I also invited them to drop into the Church of the Open Door at any hour day or night. I then closed with uplifted hand in benediction, saying "God go with you." The musician of the day played as I preceded the people into the church. Anywhere from one hundred to two hundred people stopped for the service, and about one-fourth of them came into the church for the prayers. While most of the value of these services is unknown, there were sufficient tangible responses from those seeking to discuss religion, who have since renewed their contact with the Christian Church because of them, to make the effort worth while.

If by one word a single person has been touched and the direction of his life changed for the better, and the Church's outreach has been increased by even a fraction, it was worth doing. It has been a challenge to my ministry, a chance for me to test my vocation as one called to speak a good word for the Lord Jesus, and to use God's instrument of the voice to catch and hold people's attention long enough for the Word of God to be heard.

God's Way

The minister's care and concern is for all of God's people, whoever they are, wherever they are, never content until everything possible is known about their background, education, family, training, and relationships, for only thus can he understand their current attitudes and conduct, and minister to their needs. The ancient words of hope in Jeremiah, "I will . . . be their God, and they shall be my people,"[28] give him a clue as to his responsibilities, as do the psalmist's words, "We are the people of his pasture, and the sheep of his hand."[29]

His people are sometimes blind and stupid, squabbling often, failing constantly, and they are vulnerable and helpless. But they are Christians, one of God's channels for holding the world together, and they are His people, and He seems to have made them a part of His plan for winning His world to His way. People banded together as a fellowship, forming the visible Body of Christ on earth, can act for Him and help to keep Him central in the world's life. Therefore, no matter how frail the instrument or imperfect the tools, Christians wage the battle against evil, which they believe is still worth waging; and they also believe that these efforts are "something less futile than carpenters mending the deck of a sinking ship."[30]

But God may have other ways and plans for saving His world. It would be presumptive arrogance to claim that the Christian Church is the only means He is using. We must trust, obey, and believe that Christians, in the fellowship of the Church, are the best means we know of for God's purpose in the world to be fulfilled; and we must pursue this as if it were the only way. But we can never know all the things God is up to in shaping the world for His ultimate plan.

IV

His Life

Understanding Himself

When I wrote the story of my airplane crash I chose this title, "Not Appointed to Die." When the story appeared in print I found the title had been changed to "The Day I Learned to Live." That twist in meaning from negative to positive played an important part in my life. Later I'll tell more about that airplane crash on a hot August day in Texas, but so much that happened as prelude to that critical incident must be told first.

Mark Twain prefaces his story, *Pudd'nhead Wilson,* with these words: "What a man sees in the world is only himself in the deep and honest privacy of his own heart." This is exactly the point I want to probe in this chapter, the inner life of the minister, the treasure he has in the earthen vessel of self, in his aloneness and in his relatedness.

"Every individual," so Herbert Stroup says, "in some degree belongs to a community which is appealed to by symbols and concepts [images] that define its distinctive life."[1] And this is where the minister shines as he holds high the Cross of Christ as the true banner of his existence.

Practically all the material in this book could come under the title of this chapter, but I want to delve into the minister's private life a bit first, using my own life as a laboratory specimen. However, each chapter that follows will unfold a part of the minister's life as he lives it in his parish, community, and home, as part of his Church and his world. In this review of a minister's life, words, works, and ways, I single out the minister I know best and present him for microscopic scrutiny as one thankful and glad to be alive. I believe, with William Golding, that "what men believe is a function of what they are; and what they are is in part what has happened to them."[2]

There are two texts for this chapter. The first one is from St. John
1:4—"In him was life; and the life was the light of men." All that has
been gathered up in the life of Jesus Christ reveals what God is like.
God's Word has come to life in a knowable, describable person and
moment, bringing God and man into a new relationship. God's light of
understanding broke upon men's minds as He appeared to them in Jesus
Christ. The second text is from Romans 14:7–8—"For none of us liveth
to himself. . . . we are the Lord's." No matter what comes, "we are
the Lord's," and are bound together in mutual dependence because we
are related to Him on a one-for-all, all-for-one, basis. Being a Christian
involves mutual responsibility and interdependence in the fellowship
where we are "mutually encouraged by each other's faith."[3]

I am what might be described as an average ordained minister, who
has served parishes in Texas, Georgia, Virginia, Kentucky, and New
York over a period of some thirty-three years; I am not especially
talented or well-known. Each one of my parishioners has beheld, perhaps, a special and different aspect of me as a minister, depending on
how I have affected him or ministered to him. How would he describe
me? How would I describe myself? What is a minister? Certainly he is
of the species *homo sapiens,* the knowing one, the contriver, the
manipulator. One of the greatest miracles of the universe is that man is
able to comprehend it, but a still greater miracle is when he learns to
comprehend himself. That is the aspect of the minister which concerns
me most in this chapter, the miracle of the minister who, in Einstein's
words, "learns to comprehend himself,"[4] and who looks within "the
deep and honest privacy of his own heart," to quote Mark Twain's
phrase.

Can a man ever learn to comprehend himself? The enemy a man still
has to conquer, the last and worst enemy, is himself. But he must never
give up trying. Winston Churchill, when the people of Britain rejected
his leadership after World War II, heeded some of his own advice.
"Never give in! Never give in! Never, Never, Never, Never!—in
nothing great or small, large or petty—never give in except to convictions of honor and good sense."[5]

Perhaps the minister may be able to understand himself, in part, but
there'll always be a lot of mystery left. Even St. Paul scarcely understood himself, and St. Peter never fathomed his own inner contradic-
tions. This makes it all the more interesting as we continue to discover
new facets to our nature and new depths to our being. Husband and
wife often appear to be strangers to each other. Minister and congregation often live in isolation from each other, covering the parish fellow-

ship with a cloud of unknowing. But what I am trying to do is to get each minister to understand himself more completely and to discover what makes him tick.

The Image

What image do most people have of the ideal minister and his life— one ordained of God to be His minister? The answer to this question is not easy. I was brought up on the shining ideal of the ministry as the highest calling of man. Ministers were "stewards of His grace," a special breed, chosen and set apart. I was a bit vague about the minister's task, although I clung to my long-held image of his preaching the word of God with clarity and power to large congregations, and his pastoral function of ministering with miraculous effectiveness to all of troubled and suffering humanity, as portrayed in certain romantic novels. Beyond this I did not usually go in my thinking about ministers, although I knew vaguely that they must be able to run a parish, raise money, teach, organize, and be socially acceptable as well as conduct services of all kinds, in addition to being preachers and pastors.

Basically, the image I had when I entered the seminary was twofold: a minister was ordained with authority, after long and thorough preparation, first, to truly preach the Word of God, and, second, to duly administer the sacraments as "expressions of Christ's relationship to the real world where the Church is called to witness."[6] In the minister's proclamation and interpretation of the Word of God, I mixed my image a bit with touches of a knight in shining armor riding to someone's rescue. I believed firmly that the minister should always be ready "to take seriously the questions and assaults of the world and the congregation and not to withdraw into the comparative safety of the pulpit, the lecture platform, or the parsonage."[7] But, as a young man growing up in a Southern Baptist environment in Fort Worth, Texas, I had no minister hero. Our family moved frequently and there was no one minister for me to hold up for long as an ideal example to follow. I had to make up a semifictional minister as my hero, whom I wanted to be like.

Before World War II, and even earlier, in the aftermath of World War I, especially during the roaring twenties and through the depressing and disillusioning thirties, all this ideal seemed possible of attainment within the still stable confines of the Church, against which neither the forces of evil, both within and without, nor change of orientation could ever prevail, in spite of a few bitter scoffers heard from occasionally. I was certainly not then prepared to face the searching challenge thrown down by numerous Christian thinkers and writers today, who would bring the minister out into a "post-Christian" world to make sense out of "religionless Christianity" and to "relate God to where men are." And yet, this is where all ministers are called upon to stand today and bear their witness.

The story of finding one's true life as a minister of God and striving toward whatever image one has of this ministry, requires a long journey back into time—an exploration of childhood and youth, interpreting the strange twists and intense struggles of heart and mind as well as one's education at home, school, church, college, and in the seminary. But even this will not be sufficient, for the process is never ended. We are what we are because of a million choices made and consequences suffered, covering miles of misunderstandings, mistakes, and just plain perversity of fate. What I here uncover and share will be only a small part of my own life's journey, some of it hidden far back in the past, as a clue to understanding my present life and ministry. What I am now, is determined by, and can be traced back to, what I was then.

The Neophyte

By nature, and neglect of the habit, I have had a lifelong reluctance to share my thoughts. I have always been hesitant to put down in black and white what I believe or to attempt to articulate it verbally. The few times I have done so meant sticking my neck out and furnishing a target for questions I was afraid I might not be able to answer. It also meant giving up that secret knowledge which, kept to myself, made me feel more secure. Any "discussion" of my beliefs was limited to neat statements and conclusions. I made no attempt to account for how I arrived at them, and they were not always firmly believed nor clearly formulated. I fled from bull sessions. I suppose this feeling stemmed from a childhood full of nameless fears, when every phase of religion seemed unreal.

Those who know me now will find it hard to recognize me from this description, but I was once a shy lad, and there are traces of this shyness still visible. I have always been reticent about my true feelings, which were disclosed mostly only in private, and then hesitantly. As a boy I wanted above all else to be thought brave and blasé, a man of the world; and what a heroic figure I made of myself in my daydreams. I was a true romantic, but earthly minded. I tested daily the strength of my own personal powers to control my life; I was a lonely-island ego. As I look back and see myself so ruthlessly selfish and seeking my own ends, it fills my heart with thankfulness that God opened my eyes and let me see my true self at last. This experience was like a delayed parachute jump, with the rip cord pulled dangerously late, making a very rough landing. Yet even then, before my bump of awakening, there were moments of choking aspiration pulling me out of myself, when the very heavens opened and beckoned me to be free from self-limitations. I felt deeply such moments, but failed to respond to them. I did not know how.

All of my religious life as a church member, up to that point of self-discovery, first as a Southern Baptist and later as an Episcopalian, had served only to feed my own sense of self-importance, whether as a youth leader, a Sunday School teacher, a lay minister, or a singer in the choir. Naturally upon this diet of pithy fruit, produced on the barren vine of self, I failed to grow in wisdom, in understanding, or in favor with God and man, and life was frustrated at every point. I sought to wash away a much too vague sense of guilt and frustration by good deeds and pious dreams, and by the outward observance of what never really possessed my heart and mind. Almost the only encouraging sign was that in spite of all this self-centeredness, I was sincerely stirred to great pity by the plight of the underprivileged, and sought to help everyone in need, especially children. My late teen-age years and early twenties were tied up with many amateurish excursions into the fields of social service, institutional work, and child welfare.

Another sign that all was not lost was my instant response to beauty through both sight and sound, and my desire to possess as much of it as I could. With this love of beauty went a positive and opposite response to ugliness and pain and a passionate desire to rid the world of as much of it as possible. I believe God first began to speak to me through art, music, and beautiful sights and sounds, all parts of His creation. There was buried deep within me, too, the consuming desire to create something. As a child I wanted to invent something; later I wanted to compose music and write novels. Perhaps this was God's way of tugging at my heart and mind to tie them in with the processes of His creation, especially as revealed in and through people. Work and ambition pushed churchgoing aside for part of a long formative period of my life, during which I took many wrong turns down uncharted roads leading nowhere. No one had ever told me to "expect the best, prepare for the worst, and take what comes."[8] I had a penchant for wrong roads, and was often lost on them.

Selfish, ambitious sociological tendencies guided my actions and were revealed in my unstable choices. God was not real, even though I believed in His existence and spent hours in times of upset and crisis in an emotionally sentimental appeal for aid, which seldom came. God and I seemed to live in two different realms, and we met only upon the rare occasions, in situations of crisis, when I forgot to shove myself out on the center of the stage. But out of this more or less unconscious seeking for certainty came the decision to serve mankind; and here again, God had very little to do with it, or so it seemed. It was a purely humanistic desire to help the poor and needy, with nothing very tangible in mind as to what they needed, except the obvious food, clothing, and shelter. Even in the years of actual preparation for the ministry, I achieved very little understanding of religion and what it could do for me and others, and was content with superficialities. There was one exception, a "rainbow" survey course on the Old Testament, which was a living and vital presentation of what religion meant during those long, hard, primitive years of man's growing up. But for me there was very little carry-over to my life.

If someone had asked me what I believed in those days, *and no one ever did,* I would have had to quote the words of another's belief or say that to do good unto all men is the highest task and therefore my first concern. In order to make up for the lack of religious reality, I attempted to formulate a personal creed by taking much time on the side for the study of psychology and social casework methods—so much more exciting to me than theology or, say, the synoptic problem. I even sought to prepare myself as a great "physician of souls"—a phrase which came from something I read—by spending time in such institutions as the State Mental Hospital in Worcester, Massachusetts, Cook County General Hospital in Chicago, homes for underprivileged and crippled children, and houses of detention for old and young. Indeed, I spent some time in almost every kind of institution, both penal and remedial, to discover ways and means of becoming expert in the techniques of helping people. But myself, the helper-to-be, went unaided, and the store of specialized knowledge did not cure my blindness.

I was too quickly launched on a ministry based upon such preparation, a ministry which was enthusiastic but never really vital. With so many tremendous handicaps it was not surprising that my ministry, though zealous, was without marked success. For several years I did my best to cope with its demands, finding heavy moments of disillusionment, making many mistakes, and seeking greener pastures always where I was not. But I was involved at all times in helping to meet human need, for the service motive never slacked off, even though there was no satisfying certainty concerning my religious life. I steered clear of preaching or speaking too specifically and personally of such matters as prayer, God, death, atonement, and the other great themes which are the daily sum and substance of the Christian's faith.

And yet I had the Church year to guide me. The round of the Christian Year makes a good frame of reference for anyone who wants to see the phrase "a post-Christian world" changed to "a more Christian world," and who is willing to follow John Keble's advice, "Live ye by the calendar," by which he meant keeping the round of days that are marked in color as key checking points for life. Especially the days and seasons which unfold the events of Jesus' life and His disciples' furnish a reminder and an opportunity for checking and relating the meaning of each event to that day and that moment of one's life. We might add to our personal calendar other important red-letter days, such as birthdays, anniversaries, baptisms, confirmations, conversions, and other days fraught with deep personal meaning.

My early sermons were largely quotations from books, without impact, persuasion, or conviction, and my people slowly starved spiritually. I would have done better to have used one of those old volumes of homiletics containing an approved sermon for each Sunday of the Church Year, with special sermons for Christmas and Easter.

God does move in mysterious ways beyond our understanding, and He must have sought me night and day as I figuratively crossed mountains and deserts, wild seas and much wilderness in order to elude Him, like the "Hound of Heaven" in Francis Thompson's vivid poem. God saved me from near failure several times, and I ploughed doggedly on, for it never once occurred to me to give up. I tried hard to be one of the ones who give the lie to the phrase "god is no more," and to be a mature man who has acquired the ability to take criticism, evaluate it and, when it is valid, apply it. It took me a long time to come by such knowledge and to arrive at a point where this made sense.

Twice-born

When it seemed as if my life and ministry were both doomed to failure, two things happened. I crashed in an airplane, which took about a year out of my normal life, and immediately after my recovery, I got married. St. Paul said that for some marriage is necessary. It was a necessity for me; I needed a wife. These two significant and timely events prepared the soil for the change in my life which followed about a year after my marriage to a dark-eyed Texas girl, who balanced and restored my life. My return from a far country was soon to begin. I thank God daily it came in time to save me from disaster. Every Christian's life story will take a different turn here and there, but at the end we find more or less agreement on what in our Christian faith has really mattered and has had a part in the new dimensions of character developed over the years of failure and near success. A person may find it hard to pinpoint that moment when he came to himself, and even after deciding when and how it came about, find it hard to capture authentically for others to read about.

As with so many moments when one's life is completely changed, there was nothing spectacular in my case, just a wonderful feeling of giving up a struggle and gaining the sense of a victorious sustaining Presence never more to be separated from my day-to-day existence, a Presence both to be reckoned with and counted on. It happened over a long period, really, but the actual moment is hard to express as vividly as I would like. Here are the several stages of the experience as I remember them, beginning with the first understanding of my own deep needs which came when trial and failure had repeatedly pointed out to poor, blind, stubborn me that something was very wrong inside me. My mind began its long search for the root cause of my difficulties and mistakes. A lot of resolutions were made and new leaves turned over and forgotten before there was sufficient courage and faith to carry through what I knew must be done before I was in the clear in my relationships with God and with others.

For two years in a small mission in Texas, the search went on. It came to a flashing point of certainty during the reading of a book sent to me as a follow-up of a conference held in Washington, D.C., which was, strangely enough, on preaching. In the book, *Twice-Born Ministers* by Samuel M. Shoemaker,[9] I found myself, with all of my weaknesses, presented in the stories of the ministers who had finally come to themselves and were now apostles of reality, with every channel open for God to speak *to* them and *through* them. There was no mistaking what had to be done by me, which I did to the best of my ability, with God's help. I gave up my long-accustomed right to my own way, and decided, without question, from that moment on, to abide more completely by God's law and way for me, as revealed in Christ's life and way—always with His help, never alone. This meant some drastic changes in my thinking and living, as a person, a husband, and an ordained minister. It required a long time to dig out the refuse, face the past, and make up for all I could. It involved some costly sharing and, worst of all for me, admitting what a fool I had been in so many ways. I had come to myself and could never again flee from the truth of what I saw.

That was the turning point, the beginning of my daily quiet times of

intense devotion, no longer performed perfunctorily as something expected of me, but genuinely seeking what God wanted me to do—really
wanting to know. My ministry began to assert itself and I began to
grow. In the first rush of happiness I felt all was settled and that now
nothing could ever be wrong again. But not so, for I soon found so
many things still wrong, so many incidents and thoughts which I felt it
my right to withhold and conceal from view. It took two years more to
break down the last barrier, the most costly one of all. When that was
shared and put into the past I was free, suddenly and completely, even
in the midst of the very sorrow I had caused. I was no longer shackled
by anything. The last great blocking burden had been laid at God's feet,
and every area of my life was turned over to Him as fast as I possibly
could. This last costly step was an intensely personal and private thing,
and really does not matter to anyone but those who shared in it. The
miracle was that beyond all my shallow understanding and inadequate
motives, God kept me aware that I had not yet reached the ultimate
goal, that there was something more, something firmer to base my life
and ministry on, and He kept moving me toward what He had in store
for me.

From that time on—many unfading years ago now—there has been
more or less continuous growth, although with considerable back-sliding
and occasional stretches of aridity in between the good times. The Bible
has opened like a flower never before seen, and rarely does it seem dry or
senseless or obsolete. God seems to place His finger upon the right
words when I call on Him for guidance. Of course, the struggle has
never ceased between the jealous man-self pushed out of the center of
things and the God-self which now takes charge of more and more
moments of my life, but there is rarely ever any doubt as to what God
expects of me and wants me to do when I really want to know and do
His will. The prodigal-son experience made all things new and fresh,
and while perfection is still a long way ahead, the light of His presence
has never dimmed from that moment to this.

One thing I've learned is the constant need for personal reformation
and renewal, the importance of response in every phase of one's life, and
the necessity to keep awake and aware in the midst of each current
revolution. I often think of reformation as it applies to my own life and
how it is like recovering and restoring the lost beauty and radiance of a
stained glass window through the meticulous removal of layers of many
years' accumulation of dirt, making visible the original design and
color—not like the restoration of a window out of bits and pieces of
broken glass put together carelessly, with little resemblance to the
original.

I think of my reformation also in another way: that it is like taking a service of worship, written in sixteenth-century English and falling on the deaf ears of the twentieth century, and revising and rewriting it in a modern idiom for men who are repelled by the use of ancient terms that have lost their bite and vividness. Perhaps, in response to worship, my life has become a kind of interlinear interpretation of the archaic words and phrases. Is not this also the minister's task?

Who am I? What am I?

Most of us spend a long time in our search for identity; each one of us has an ideal image of what "my life" is to be. Life sometimes appears to be a complicated maze as we wander in it, hoping at each turning we will find our way through. The worst plague of man today is his sense of lostness and hollowness, his aimless moving from day to day, from event to event, from person to person, without purpose or goal. Any minister who has gone through this experience can be of tremendous help to others in the same condition.

D. R. Davies, in his autobiography *In Search of Myself,* shares with us his progress through every conceivable phase of mental, social, and spiritual change—like a human chameleon—until at last he found himself and knew where he was and what he was. The story of his life was a continuing drama "of great vicissitudes, of alternating success and failure, of frustration and despair, which sank to the abyss; but [it was also] a story of renewal, of re-birth into hope and faith, the story of a new man."[10] Here, in microcosm, is the story of a generation, in which one soul experienced "the bitter death of the illusions" of that generation, but in so doing, found his own identity as a "child of God," and in the chaos and disillusion into which he had fallen, he found God in the Person of Christ with whom he could be identified and in whom he became a new man. Davies began with only a tiny pinpoint of belief that there is a God who lives and cares and saves, a Being whom to know even slightly and to be with even for one brief moment, changes everything. In his deepest despair he came face to face with God, the ultimate truth, and His grace was sufficient to enable him to walk back into life, denying his own pride and the world's power.

The minister, through his personal pilgrimage, is able to give substance to such fundamental questions as What is man? and Who am I? and to make good use of St. Paul's wrestling with the same question in his Epistle to the Romans. Through his own grasp of the meaning of compassion, he can face and come to grips with others' lostness and sickness—the prevailing "sickness of modern man" revealed in current fiction. Edmund Fuller says modern fiction debases man, strips him of moral responsibility, gives him a state of mind from which arises an "irresponsible and degraded sexuality, a cult of violence and brutality." We are often asked to believe that prostitutes are the only truly compassionate ones. However, a pseudo-compassion that doesn't really redeem, but which leaves the needy one in a worse state than before, is a nostrum of the cruelest sort.

In some such way the minister learns to see himself, and in so doing learns how to look into the depths of another's soul with discernment and compassion.

Henry Drummond points out that every man is in reality a *threefold* man. That is why soul analysis is so difficult. When two people are in conversation, he says, there are really *six* persons in conversation. Suppose that John and Tom are in conversation, there are three Johns and three Toms. There are three Johns—the real John, known only to his Maker; John's ideal John, John as he thinks of himself, never the real John and often very unlike him; Tom's ideal of John, or John as Tom thinks of him, never the real John nor John's John. There are also three Toms—the real Tom, Tom's Tom, John's ideal Tom.[11] How are we to speak to all these persons? How can the gospel reach them?

In all I have written about a "search for identity," there is but one point to make and remember: how to find life and how to live it based on His words. To be quite honest, I am still pursuing my full "moment of truth." But as each glimpse of truth comes more and more alive, in concrete and creative responses in worship and mission, the truth separates out into living acts of witness and service. All the good things I've recalled in sharing portions of my life, have had many times of eclipse, but the memory of them, with many variations, has held and kept me inspired over the years. There have been deserts to be crossed, questions to be answered, the overlong "absences" of God to be accounted for, the failures to communicate which need correcting, and a "post-Christian" world to be overcome and lived in. That sense of God's presence "never more" leaving me is still there, but now that I know He is ever near, I am content to be patient when He does not manifest Himself every second of every day's life.

Every minister *pursues* the ideal of perfection. Every one of his people *expects* perfection in him. Neither he nor they are completely satisfied. "Be ye perfect" is an admonition to keep one's eye on the goal; it is not a state ever to be attained, but stage after stage in the growing process on the way up the steep ascent. There is potential greatness in us all. It takes only the right stimulus and motivation to release it and move us a little closer to the goal He has set for us, within our reach if not yet within our grasp.

Conclusions

We have examined who and what a minister is, as partially revealed by fragments from one minister's life. What have we found? What must we conclude? He is a man, like all other human beings, erring often, weak in the face of strong temptations, never self-sufficient (too often he forgets he needn't try to be), strong only in the Lord and in the power of *His* might. He is stubborn, like all the rest of humanity, desiring his own way, finding humility an awkward guise to wear even for a moment. But he is a man with a label; he belongs to God, and everyone knows it. He can never hide his commitments and his loyalties. He can never forget the ideal, that the minister is first of all a Christian—as St. Paul would say, a "saint"—and a member of the fellowship, the *laos*, the people of God, on special assignment. He is a minister in the Church of God before he is tagged with a denominational label. He holds to this order: first Christ, then His Church; first Christians, then churchmen. That is still a good image to have of the minister and his priorities.

It is quite true that "we are afraid of slander, of losing our reputations, of losing face. As individuals, nation, party, Church, we are eager to make an image of ourselves and to make it appear spotless in the sight of men."[12] That moment when I came down from my pedestal was when my ministry really started to make sense, and I began to reach my people. "Life is justified by the imponderable, the unexpected, the impossible. It is justified—if at all—in the living, and in our work, only when it is part of our living and when we are not anxious as to what men will say about us."[13]

But Who am I and What am I? These questions still nag my mind, pushing me forever deeper and demanding fuller answers than the ones already found and to be recorded later. I know that at the heart of every answer is a Person, Jesus Christ, so there should never be an end to the quest or the questioning. I am exactly what I am at every given moment of my existence, striving continuously for consistency, fulfillment, responsiveness, and a dependable responsibleness, as one who belongs now to the twice-born, never forgetting that "each of us has been given his gift, his due portion of Christ's bounty,"[14] to keep and to *use*, and that "In him [is] life, and [His] life [is] the light of men."[15]

V

His Words

Brevity, Grace, and Salt

It may be setting too high an ideal for public utterances, but Strunk's "Rule Thirteen," when followed, can save a minister's public-speaking life from failure and help him win men by his sharpness and precision instead of repelling them by his dullness. "Rule Thirteen. Omit needless words! Omit needless words! Omit needless words!"[1]

The minister has a passion for truth and is unwilling to leave anything obscure. Whatever theology he has involves him in the world and helps to make God's design clear and understandable in the midst of man's disorder. While he recognizes that there is a new man of a new age emerging who needs a new theology and a newly reformed church, in presenting the gospel he must remember those who still find its power flowing through traditional words and ways. He keeps close to the needs of both.

The minister is ever conscious of the fact that both the Word and the sacraments exist for the world. "The Word is not truly preached unless it is a dialogue with the world's need" and "the sacraments are not duly administered unless they take on their true character as living signs of God's gracious salvation coming into being in His world."[2]

The minister must articulate his convictions and commitments with persuasive power to the "pious" and to the "emancipated" alike, if his life is to count vitally in Christian witness, especially in man's new creation known as "Metropolis."[3] The proclamation of the gospel, the *Kerygma,* has played such a central role in the life of the Christian Church "that it is inconceivable that its place should become secondary. . . . The work of preaching is to maintain the relationship to the present identity of the Church with the saving events of its foundation; it mediates the true being of the present moment as *trust.* The recounting of the saving events, their interpretation in terms of the contemporary situation and the illumination of the new mankind in the light of these events: this proclamation testifies to the grounding of the present in the source of all being."[4] There may never be a moratorium on preaching, as someone—Dean Inge, I think—once seriously suggested, but many, I am sure, have thought at times, without expressing it, that the minister as preacher needs to reevaluate his task and how well he is doing it. I agree.

St. Paul's words make the point of this chapter clear. "Let your speech be alway with grace, seasoned with salt, that ye may know how ye ought to answer every man."[5] Let your speech always be pleasant, attractive, full of meaning, zest, and good humor, spoken to fit each man individually. There are no stock answers to the attitudes and questions of men, only a framework, a basic core of belief on which to draw, as we have already attempted to show in Chapter 2.

To Christians all over the land, both clergy and laity, the Sunday morning sermon is the minister's most influential moment, in which the largest group of people can be made aware of the gospel message as it relates to their day and to their lives. Certainly, in the non-Roman churches great emphasis is placed on "the preaching of the word," without, of course, neglecting the sacraments. But homiletics is not always every minister's forte, and the Sunday-morning sermon hour is for him often an anxiety and a trial. One proof of this is the steady sale of books of sermons and sermon helps, and of magazines containing sermons and articles on how to write and deliver them. No minister is exempt at times from sitting on the edge of the anxious bench, angling in whatever pool is handy for a fresh idea which will see him through the next sermon, the next address, the next speaking or writing stint, using whatever he can devise to "hook 'em and hold 'em."

It is almost impossible to separate a minister's preaching from the rest of his life, for each sermon is a reflection of his own thinking, experiencing, reacting, and viewing applied to each subject he deals with—based on his knowledge of the Word of God and his conviction concerning God's message for the age and for the given moment. His faith, or lack of it, inevitably shines through as he inspires, convinces, and convicts, or misses fire and fails to communicate the word given him to proclaim.

It is no easy religion he proclaims. There is no instant salvation, no discount redemption, no guaranteed spiritual health, nor joy without suffering.

Since pen and ink, type and carbon, voice and manner, along with heart and mind, are the minister's kit of communication, how he uses

them to express his ideas and convictions is most important. His whole
life-purpose is to make the word of God clear and compelling enough to
change the lives of men. God expects of His ministers their utmost in
preparation—often this means agonizing over what to say and the
clearest way to say it. If they do their best, God will give to that best an
added insight, power, and blessing, but only if it *is* their best. The
minister as preacher is charged with overcoming the human gospel of
despair by the Christian gospel of hope, and he is constantly being
forced to stretch his limited talents to their utmost in order to face, and
help others to confront, the world and its ideas as they are today.

The Invariables

Whatever one's profession or trade, it is governed by a set of invariables to be learned and followed in meeting the many variables and
unknowns which confront him. A mathematician depends upon his
axioms, theorems, equations, and laws; a chemist upon his formulas,
structures, reactions, measures, and weights; a philosopher, upon his
"system"; a minister, upon his doctrines, and the authority of Scripture
and tradition. The scientist, however, although he works under certain
well-known laws, specializes in testing his own hypotheses. For him
there are no invariables. Indeed, in this scientifically oriented age, men
are a bit suspicious of invariables, absolutes, and dogmas—in philosophy and religion especially—as if they spelled out a static condition with
no possibility of change.

But every man must have a few elements in his life which are stable
and can be counted on not to disappear at the slightest signs of change
in conditions. This is what I mean by "invariables." For the Christian
minister, his basic core of belief gives substance, meaning, and purpose
to his existence, a reason for being what he is and where he is, something secure to stand on in the midst of continual change all around
him. However, he is not fearful of change which leads to human
betterment and to a better understanding of himself and his world.

The great question for all men, always, is that of meaning, making
sense out of what is to be done, being able to read the directions of one's
particular do-it-yourself kit so as to produce results. Whether it is the
assembling of a model airplane from bits of plastic and smears of glue
by an enthralled lad of eight, or intricate assembling, by an amazingly
complicated series of mechanisms and data, of a space-ship for landing
on the moon, the process is similar, leading to the completed "object"
ready at last to prove itself.

It is easy to be one-sided and follow either the scientific or the artistic bent; but the minister's approach to life must have a good balance of both emotion and intellect. What a man does with his life is directly relevant to the substance of all preaching. He wants that life to make sense, to have some semblance of worth and meaning, asking only that one thing lead, logically or otherwise, to something else, with the end result reasonably satisfying and secure—something tangible to show for all the sweat, tears, and suffering life demands.

The search for meaning is never new, but always present, and is especially acute and desperate after periods of senseless conflict in war, or senseless suffering in depressions, or senseless destruction by disaster of earthquake, flood, fire, and epidemics. That is why it is so imperative for Christians to have a frame of meaning for their lives—a frame strongly made and possible to defend, with more answers in it than questions. Enough hope and conviction must be evidenced by those who believe it is the only way of life to persuade and win those who have found no purpose nor meaning nor sense in the life they have lived thus far without it.

The minister always tries to keep the Christian frame of meaning and reference before his people, showing them how to relate the substance of their faith to the current scene. Sermons, therefore, must constantly enunciate this basic core of truth and certainty held by Christians, and seek to clarify the statements of faith often made unnecessarily puzzling and difficult by theologians or by the archaisms of the Authorized Version of the Bible, particularly some passages in St. Paul's epistles, which need special illumination.

Christians live in the present-day world with eyes wide open to the mercies of God, "taking life in [their] stride, with all its duties and its problems, its successes and its failures, its experience and helplessness."[6] Christians live in the world, not apart from it, but they are supported by the knowledge of the true nature of man, the true nature of God, and the reconciling love of God in Christ, and sermons must remind them continuously of this fact. That is how they, as Christians, can "overcome" the world.

It is in the setting of the world *as it is* that Christians manifest an understanding of life different from the world's understanding, because theirs is rooted and grounded in God's kind of love, a love growing, or which ought to grow, ever more mature in the oneness with Christ's way, to which all Christians are committed by choice, even if they follow only from afar.

"The sermon brings to focus the many difficulties all Christians face in our day as we try to make the faith relevant and reasonable to others

and as we try to live in the modern world ourselves. To be able to preach
effectively demands not only a knowledge of the *faith* but also of the
world and of the minds of lay people—their hopes and fears, their
problems, their language."[7] Religion never comes vacuum-packed,
untouched by the breath of life.

Since the pulpit is "one of the most important places in the world,"
no minister should ever dare enter it "content to mouth pious irrele-
vancies and sanctimonious trivialities."[8]

In Thomas Hardy's novel, *The Mayor of Casterbridge,* there is a
penetrating observation by Mr. Fall, the local seer, who prophesied
concerning weather and crops, and who "was sometimes astonished that
men could profess so little and believe so much at his house, when at
Church they professed so much and believed so little."[9] The test of a
Christian's faith today, as Reinhold Niebuhr points out, is not "the
number of beliefs or the order with which they are held, but simply the
quality of the Christian's life."[10]

The law of love and the Christian gospel *are* relevant when we look at
the facts with an open mind and realize that such an injunction as "love
your enemies," which sounds so impossible, is simply, to quote Niebuhr,
"a symbolic way of describing a disposition of heart which will bridge
the chasms that nature and history create in the human community."
Take the Christian doctrine of grace. While this "is more directly relevant to individuals in their shortcomings and sorrows, their hopes and
frustrations, than it is to nations and civilizations in the throes of earthshaking revolutions," it is still "of vital importance to all of us. . . .
But Christian insights [contained in such laws and doctrines] may serve
modern men in coming to terms with their common fate, their common
frustrations, and their common dangers, provided these insights are
presented not as a single panacea for all collective ills but as the frame
of meaning for the tragic facts and awful responsibilities of the day."[11]
Niebuhr contends that all this holds true for both social and historical
situations.

The Christian Frame of Meaning

Whenever I think about a structure of faith I recall the time of my
spiritual awakening that showed up my weakness at this crucial point. I
discovered the storehouse of my religion contained almost nothing upon
which I could really depend with certainty. The cleansing of my heart
and mind had left a great emptiness, as well as a great joy and peace.

My first concern, as the days unfolded and the immediate tasks of making amends, and the like, were more or less well on their way, was to think through, under the divine impetus of a new motive power for every thought and feeling, what I really believed about the fundamental truths of the Christian religion. I knew this must be what *I* actually believed, whether apart from or in conformity with any creed or statement by my Church or another. But even this was not sufficient. I needed certain basic, minimum essentials for a creed of my own, not in opposition to the creeds of my Church, but simply to interpret and translate their ancient and often archaic-sounding words and phrases, which would guide my thinking consistently every day. This meant a few easily mastered and remembered things. One of them I already possessed—the absolute faith in a God who could make all things new to those who turned to Him and who was made forever undeniable because of a man named Jesus. From this point on, other beliefs began to assert themselves as paramount.

From the first, God had been more or less a hazy conception, an inspirer of good works, but because of Jesus Christ and His life and words, God now began to emerge, at first not so much as a form or a being, but as life and light and love reflected in a Being. I had heard all this many times before, but now I realized that believing this, and living as if it were so, made everything contrary to it a denial of that belief.

Since I believed in God as Life-giver, as Life itself, I believed my life, that which was really me—my personality, my soul—was a part of God flowing through me; and, therefore, I must, so believing, live that life as God designed it or as God had planned.

Since I believed in God as Light-giver, as Light itself, I believed that my mind, which is one of my life-controlling centers, was a part of God and was meant to help me conform to His laws and to keep me under His control, moving always according to my understanding of His will. I could thus be lifted out of my own self-will and stubborn resistance to know His plan for me; therefore, I must keep all my thoughts, and this also meant every act, under this belief, and let God use my mind for controlling and directing me according to His purpose.

Since I believed God was Love, Love incarnate, I believed my own love, which gave me the capacity to feel toward others as God had planned, to be but the minute expression of His love; therefore, any act of mine contrary to this belief was a denial of God as I thought of Him then. Martin Luther King, Jr., described this powerful Christian love in action in these marvelous words: "We'll match your capacity to inflict suffering by our capacity to endure suffering. You can throw us in jail,

you can bomb our homes and our children, you can drag us out in the
middle of the night and beat us but, as difficult as it is, we'll still love
you."[12] God as Life, Light, and Love—these three central beliefs about
the manifestations of the nature and being of God have furnished me
the basic help around which all other beliefs have been built and seem to
have in them the core answer to almost every perplexity which has come
to me. When one believes in them as descriptive of God's nature and
man's response, and tries never to forget them, he must live constantly
under their truth. As anyone grows in understanding of His words of
"life" and "light," he falls ever more intensely "in love" with His
"glory."[13] Jesus Christ made these and other things so clear to me that
I have never needed to adjust them since then, but simply adjust to them.

That was a long time ago. Where do I stand now? Has my theology
changed, deepened, broadened, and become more ecumenical? I would
say that the core is still there but many enlargements and variations have
taken place; the theological battle and search for identity and truth must
never end, for me or anyone else.

The frame of meaning for our fellowship in the gospel can be elabo-
rated almost endlessly. But the very heart of the gospel message is Jesus
Christ, who is the revelation of what God is, "the Word . . . made
flesh, [who] dwelt among us,"[14] and what man through Him may by
choice become. God's life, love, and light come to us in the visible,
down-to-earth form of a man like ourselves, in a Person, Jesus Christ,
who is God's self-expression to us. Our world is created and ruled by a
Christlike God. Christ makes God the Father known to us, perfect and
infinite in love and righteousness. Christ is God's love at work in the
world, a love which constrains us and strengthens us to obey His commands.

The variations on this theological frame of meaning are often confus-
ing—even the leading theologians disagree, as they always have, as ex-
ponents of this "queen of the sciences." For the minister, who must
guide his people to the "correct" frame of meaning to live by, this poses
a whole flock of questions. Even Paul had his problems when he sought
to present Christ's Person and what He really was like, as opposed to
the many competing interpretations of Him in every community of believers. All men seriously concerned with truth must follow where it
leads them, but most of us proceed gradually, and solidify each advance
by resting on the sure ground of what we know is consistent with Jesus'
teaching.

It is just here that we who live in obedience to our faith are part of
God's action toward His goal. The decisions of God's action are made

in our life with Christ. Therefore, according to how we live with Christ or do not live with Christ, we are part of God's mission, or we stand in its way. Therefore, the Christian life cannot be lived without the wide horizon, the view of the world which God has in mind, the world which God loves—man's disorder seen from the perspective of God's design.

Trivia versus Matters of Moment

Since I am dealing with the minister's words, I must insert a comment about the modern phenomenon of "glossolalia," which has had a remarkable revival in recent years in those churches which were always thought of as too enlightened for such primitive manifestations as "speaking with tongues."

Since I have never been so possessed, nor witnessed such expressions of the outpouring of the Spirit, I find it extremely hard to evaluate what I have read. I do not for a moment discount the gifts of the Spirit which some have found in the miracle of tongues, but I have not yet been able to fit this phenomenon into my own frame of meaning, within which I view the world and live in it and relate the gospel to it; I try to see that some aspect of that meaning is clearly articulated in every sermon I preach. I find St. Paul's words fit my frame of meaning more perfectly. "Except ye utter by the tongue words easy to be understood, how shall it be known what is spoken? For ye shall speak into the air."[15] And also these words, "I had rather speak five words with my understanding . . . than ten thousand words in an unknown tongue."[16] The whole purpose of words is to communicate ideas and feeling, and if these words are in an unknown tongue, not even understood by the one who utters them, how can God's purpose be furthered?

The testing of the Christian faith today is constant and manifold, and all Christians face the responsible task of making men aware of that faith and relating that faith to each and every situation. This means that side issues and trivia must go, that all Christians in each place must somehow be brought to an awareness that they are all Christ's, and that Christ is the one great truth to be applied.

In our industrial society, for example, the minister is involved in all issues of injustice. No one can forget the dreadful days of child labor, the exploitation of men for gain, the struggle of the working man for a decent living wage. The battle for a decent wage has been won, although pockets of poverty and periodic unemployment still exist. A new battleground of power is emerging between capital and labor today, and the minister must play his role, as he sees it, in maintaining justice and fairness in relationships for the common good.

Christian doctrines and insights based on the gospel and the experience of the Church over the centuries can help modern man come to terms with the fate, frustrations, and dangers which all men must face; and they must be applied daily wherever he works and lives. Against the bewildering procession of critical events today, we cling to the basic Christian understanding of life which we are able to speak about, and relate to, without reserve or embarrassment or hesitation, both in and out of a pulpit.

Credo

The Christian must apply a Christian frame of meaning to five crucial areas. He must look at the *time* in which he has been born as God's time—only a small fraction of historical time, but every minute of it precious and to be lived to the full, with the sure hope of God's eternal time beyond history. He must look at the *world* as God's world, in which he must live and work out his own salvation, and as much of the salvation of the world as possible, with God's help, and in which are the signs of His coming Kingdom. He must look at all *humanity* as part of God's creation, each part related to every other part, all men his brothers under a common Father, *"Our* Father." Just think of these two words in connection with civil rights, for example. He must look on the living *God* as the Creator, Redeemer, and Sanctifier of his life, to whom he must give his commitment and allegiance, and whose laws he must obey. He must look on the Christian *Church* and community as the fellowship which is God's instrument for carrying out His plans and purposes for man and His world. His primary concern must be to accept and share in it, with more emphasis on the fellowship than the institution.

I am indebted to some forgotten source for these five areas of Christian concern—time, world, humanity, God, Church—which are related points where each must apply his own Christian frame of meaning. Is this not the whole point of the Christian faith, to see that in spite of the devious maneuvers of a man to escape facing his true self in God's presence, he is rescued and landed at last on the solid foundation of faith and insight? Once again balanced and restored, he finds the new life of consciousness of being a child of God worth all the repenting, confessing, renewing, and atonement demanded, since the sense of moral responsibility has been rediscovered and reaccepted. As for me, there must be a "hitching post" in my universe, regardless of Einstein's observation to the contrary,* and that hitching post is the Person of Christ.

Christians stake their all on the truth that "when men turn to God through Jesus Christ in faith, and are incorporated through baptism and the Lord's Supper into the Body of Christ, the Holy Spirit is able to furnish them with the gifts that they need for their growth in grace and for their witness and service in the world."[17] These gifts Christians rely upon. His presence and leadership Christians depend on. We all believe God is with us and in us and among us.

The basic Christian beliefs provide the foundation of the whole Christian view of life and determine what Christians think about the world they live in, about other persons, about their own duties and responsibilities in this life, and about the life to come. In short, these beliefs determine what Christians think about man's nature and man's destiny. That is why it is essential for all Christians to know what the really basic beliefs are.

Let us summarize them.

I believe in God, the God who created life and sustains it, and in whom all creation is incorporated.

I believe in God as He revealed Himself in Jesus Christ, who demonstrated God's love for each human being by giving Himself completely in love to save man from his worst self-centered self and to close the gap between God and man through forgiveness and reconciliation.

I believe in God as He constantly provides His grace and mercy through the Holy Spirit in His Church, through worship, prayer, and sacrament, to men as they live this life, and promises fulfillment for men in oneness with Him in the life to come.

These are basic beliefs. Once we have them straight and in proper relationship and perspective, we have a workable frame of reference and meaning for handling all the secondary beliefs and variations of belief which confront us daily as we seek constantly to apply what we believe to what we do. "For the life [of God] was manifested [in Christ], and we have seen it, and bear witness, and show [it] unto you."[18]

Logic

The *first* point, then, is to build upon a solid foundation of Christian faith. The *second* point, which follows logically, is to feed that life inwardly on thanksgiving, and the joy of having found what God is really like through Jesus Christ. We must keep feeding that faith on

---

* "There is no hitching post in the universe."

prayer and thanksgiving, forever learning, deepening, relating, and enlarging the fundamentals, until our Christianity becomes the all in all of our life. This leads to the joy of living each day in the light of His saving grace, and the knowledge of His love at work in and through us.

In possessing such a frame of meaning, the Christian is able to reverse the balance of the forces of light and dark, placing the greater emphasis on light and survival, in a world already too heavily weighted on the side of darkness and death. The Christian meaning for life is to look for the light in every human situation, the light which is Christ. By the phrase "look for the light which is Christ" I mean what St. Paul meant when he said, "For the invisible things of him from the creation of the world are clearly seen."[19] That is, God has shown to all men His power and goodness in the world He made, but men have refused to look at Him and have turned away from Him. St. Paul indicts men for worshiping the things which God has created, such as possessions, pleasures, and, above all, self, instead of worshiping the Creator. The light is in Him, our Lord Jesus Christ, who came and comes into our world to restore us to the worship of the Creator rather than any of His creatures. Such a frame of meaning can help us to understand both the tragedies of the world and the life, purpose, and message of Jesus Christ.

This light which is Christ is desperately needed, as we know from the trend of the day, which is creeping laxity in moral convictions and in respect and reverence for other human beings. The minister can never keep silent about these issues. His tongue and his pulpit can be powerful forces for change in the right direction, and help bring men back from some far continent to a safe landfall.

Arthur Miller, the distinguished dramatist, in his search for light, claims that "there are no longer any philosophies and programs to give one any external support," which leads him to conclude, "I am on my own."[20] I long for Miller and others like him to listen to a really good teacher of Christian theology. I believe he would be surprised and heartened to find that Christianity has been announcing all these years that God is even more concerned about the condition of His free and erring children than Miller currently is, and has acted in history in Christ so that we might understand the truth about ourselves and about God Himself. Miller looks in the darkness for the light, when all the time the lamp of truth is nearby, all lit, trimmed, and burning, ready to light his way. When man tries to be God he remains in darkness and trouble. That is why we look for the light which is Christ.

The minister must never be fearful of crises which test his faith, for a crisis is worth all it costs if a man learns through it how to remove the clutter he has created which has walled off his ego from the Spirit of

God. It often takes a crisis situation to smash the wall made up of the bricks of bitter resentments, cherished grudges, selfish indulgences, self-pity, and the comfort and ease that make cowards of us all. Stoicism, existentialism, romanticism, humanism, ancient or modern, none of them is sufficient as a frame of meaning for facing life in unexpected crises or for carrying through the long haul of a chronic condition. In order to resist the pressures which daily increase in the world and not break under them, St. Paul's words must become ours, because we believe they are true: "I can do all things through Christ."[21] We cannot repeat them too often.

One never ceases to add to, strengthen, and eagerly apply his own Christian frame of meaning and reference, not in isolation from the Christian fellowship, nor as an individual's own created formula of faith, but in accordance with the classic gospel delineation of that faith, which all Christians have, in essence, in common. The coherent beam of God's light is continued in and through us. There is as yet no agreed-upon "ecumenical theology," but the basis of membership in the World Council of Churches is a core of belief sufficient to hold us together and to give us something solid to stand on. "The World Council of Churches is a fellowship of churches which confess the Lord Jesus Christ as God and Savior according to the Scriptures and therefore seek to fulfill together their common calling to the glory of the one God, Father, Son, and Holy Spirit."[22]

Regardless of his theology, the minister is called upon to see that his people "shall behold the land that is very far off."[23] He must keep them moving toward it with their sails of hope billowing in the strong winds of the Spirit, guided by the rudder of faith, and with a frame of meaning to life, present and future. He must teach them to interpret the chart God has placed in their hands for keeping on course in the journey from where they are—too often lost souls in the midst of a lost world—to where and when He shall reign within and among them. This chart of our basic Christian beliefs can be summarized in many ways, but in all the variations we find in common at least this outline of an ecumenical synthesis:

God made us and every other thing in the whole universe; life and time are His gifts and they are in His hands.

God revealed Himself to us in a man, Jesus Christ, who taught us what God is like and demonstrated His love for us, and at last died to show us the end result of our rebellion and self-will as opposed to obedience to Him and His way of life.

God stayed with us and is ever present with us in Spirit, to guide, strengthen, and bring us to the knowledge of all the truth we can know—of life and death, of man's nature and God's, of the way to walk in, of the faith to live by, of the kind of God we can trust and depend on.

And the Christian faith insists on a life commitment to this God revealed in Jesus Christ, as Christians banded together by this choice in a fellowship which exists to live the kind of love-life God planned, in relationship with Him and with one another.

Upon this rock of faith Christ has built His Church, and we are all members.

The Challenge of Today

And yet traditional words and imagery need constant scrutiny and revision lest they cease to communicate their meaning to a generation that speaks a different language and holds to a new set of images and meanings. There is often need for radical reinterpretation to the modern mind and its widespread questioning of ancient formularies and doctrines, as attempted by such books as *Soundings*[24] and *Honest to God*.[25] Men still search for the meaning of existence and life's ultimate purpose, but the traditional words often fail to reach them. That is why the minister must keep abreast of the times and search constantly for new ways and new words to bring the gospel message alive for modern ears to hear and accept.

Living Words

We started this chapter by calling attention to the importance of the minister's words in sermons. The age-old question which should haunt the preacher, and which he can never escape answering, is Ezekiel's question in his famous allegory of the valley of dry bones, "Can these bones live?"[26] In seminary, embryo preachers learn about the bones of sermon construction, but it is only as they live, and learn to relate the frame of meaning of their Christian faith, to their lives, that flesh and blood content brings the "bones" to life. This is the Word men need as their stalwart companion on the way each man must walk through his days of life on earth; this is the story of the Incarnate God every man yearns to hear, "the journey of the Son of God into the far country"[27] of man's life.

Elizabeth Goudge holds up an example of what the minister as preacher can never stoop to be. She speaks of Parson Ash who "never really preached a sermon at all, he read it out of a useful little book containing a couple of short homilies for each Sunday in the year, with Christmas thrown in extra, and read it so fast that no one could hear a word. Not that anyone wanted to. The sermon gave them a chance of a nap after the musical exertions that had preceded it. Parson Ash had no objection to his congregation going to sleep—he'd have done the same in their place—in fact, he always obligingly woke up the clerk, Job Stanberry, himself, leaning over the edge of the pulpit and slapping him on his bald nodding head with the book of sermons."28

There is less value than danger in preaching another's sermons: value in having a good pattern, outline, and content possibly beyond one's own capacity to produce; but there is the danger that one will cease to be creative and lean too heavily on another's mind, and so pass on God's word secondhand. Best avoid using the sermons of others except to prime the imagination for one's own sermon.

The Word of God is found in a Book all know about and some still read, but few understand and apply its contents. The preacher's task is to expound the Word of God, as Philip did to the Ethiopian eunuch that day on the road to Jericho, to relate it to life, to bring it alive in the hearts and minds of the hearers so they will catch and hold its meaning, and act upon it. He must proclaim the Eternal Word, the mighty acts of God, as contemporary to his world. He must make clear Karl Barth's point, "Man is unworthy, *nevertheless* God elects him,"29 communicating the good news that this is why man can hope, believe, and trust in God.

All the great preachers who have made any lasting impact on their generation have been witnesses to a truth they strongly believed. They have also spoken with forthrightness about the great issues of the day. But just how forthright and honest can a preacher be and survive? Many laymen want to have him "stick to his last," that is, to confine his remarks to what they call "religion," by which they usually mean faith, and never digress far enough to relate that religion to the issues of the day. But how can a preacher worthy of such a great heritage fail to apply the frame of meaing of his faith to the events of his day? He will most certainly attempt to give guidance to the thinking and conduct of his people, "fearlessly to contend against evil, and to make no peace with oppression."30 The preacher's task is exceedingly difficult, but whatever the cost he must express the Christian view sharply and clearly, without equivocation. The nature of God and man, also God's will and purpose for man, must never be silenced in the pulpit. That is why Martin Niemoeller's stand against Hitler in those critical years leading up to World War II looms so large in history. It is not a comfortable gospel we must preach but the Word of God as it relates to the problems of our time even though we often disagree as to the application of the gospel and the right moment for action.

His job is much more difficult today than it was even a hundred years ago. The many voices seeking men's attention, the many ideas and ideologies competing for their allegiance, make the task tougher; all the old obvious techniques no longer work as well as they did when the preacher could cry, "Come and be saved or go to hell." Modern man no longer believes that "the fear of the Lord is the beginning of wisdom." He can no longer be moved, except to laughter or pity, by the attempts to scare him into religion by angry ministers mouthing angry words about an angry God. While there are few of these ranters left, there must still be passion in preaching; but it must be backed up by sound biblical scholarship and rigorous theology, and a conviction born of a personal experience of the saving grace of God in Jesus Christ. And yet there must be a holy and healthy fear of consequences instilled, to accompany St. Augustine's "love God and do what you please" theme, if modern men, especially the young, are to learn to regard law and order with respect and have a wholesome fear of disobedience. Absence of fear leads to a don't-care attitude, and this, in turn, leads to a life with no purpose, too often just frittered away in amorality. The minister should instill fear, awe, and wonder when he inspires holy faith.

The Spiritual Kingdom

The minister as preacher must always set the feet of his listeners "in a large room."[31] The keynotes of our age are anxiety, fear, and absurdity. On the surface, this fear in our age is sometimes a cringing fear of bodily harm from atomic cindering, and sometimes a haunting fear of nothingness as a person or as a member of the human race and citizen of the world. A man is a fool if he is not afraid at times, but he is not a Christian if this fear has a paralyzing effect which congeals his thoughts and freezes his limbs. "The fear [awe, reverence] of the Lord" is to the spirit like the sharp increase of adrenalin to the body when fear strikes, marshaling forces within to meet the fear with all senses alert. Only the dull of mind and spirit are not afraid at times. The cynical keynotes of our age are just what the preacher needs to challenge him.

We hear of a God grown silent and man become an automaton. We are being squeezed to the wall, and phobias without number crowd in upon us to smother us, carrying us in a kind of subway-rush-hour tide away from our large place of dignity, fulfillment, and respect for values;

sweeping us into a packed subway car, locking us in, and jolting us off to nowhere. We live in a free land, but that freedom is endangered by men who have no vision, who narrow the limits of their sights to racial and social exclusiveness; men who further national arrogance and international irresponsibility. The minister must be alert to see and fight against these threats, but he should be even more troubled over the gullibility, naïveté, and ignorance of those who listen to such men and believe them, and are disturbed by what they say.

The minister-preacher proclaims the good news that from the beginning of creation God has placed our feet in a large room, a vast spiritual kingdom of His love, big enough to include all men, wide enough for every man to expand in, to the limits of the potential of his body, mind, and spirit. This is where the world's struggle lies today, just here in the realm of man's dimensions, and that is where the minister stands, trusting in the Lord and ready to abide by His laws. His preaching point is always sharp and clear: a man must exercise his freedom of choice by choosing to say "yes" to God and His way. Only thus does he find his feet placed in the large room of God's presence; for when he chooses to say "no" to God he finds the only space left to stand on is as narrow and coffinlike as a single "I." And the hearer, whether he appears bright with enthusiasm, intensely concentrated and serious, or dubious, is never merely bored or critical—just sitting back and accepting or rejecting what is said—but is working *with* the man in the pulpit, giving him support, yearning for the truth he would communicate.[32]

The Sermon

There are many kinds of sermons heard every Sunday in the United States. There is the theological and often technical preaching aimed at the intellectuals. There is the highly popular, all too often superficial preaching to a congregation rated on the same level as the average television audience, with a median age of twelve. All can recall many kinds of preachers they have heard over a lifetime of sermon tasting—"the shouters, the between-you-and-me-ers, the drama merchants who vary their tones and drop their voices like amateur reciters, the hearties, the mincing aesthetes, the unemphatic voices providing their congregations with a weekly ration of the abstract."[33] The standards for preachers should be the same as for actors and writers. All are professionals, and from them should be demanded the same skills in the art of communication.

Sometimes novels of suspense are more widely read than any book of sermons, and I have found in some of them gold nuggets ready for gathering and sharing. For example, I like Josephine Tey's description of the preaching of the vicar of Clare in her fine mystery novel, *Brat Farrar*. "He sounded as if he were arguing the matter out for himself; so that, if you shut your eyes, you could be in a chair at the other side of the rectory fireplace listening to him talk."[34] This is the ultimate in sermonic communication—to make each listener believe that the sermon is for him alone; each point is being argued out in his presence for his special benefit.

Since this is not a lecture on homiletics given to a class of seminarians, I shall not speak of the techniques for curing that prevalent clerical disease of speaking "in unknown tongues"—and I'm not referring to the spate of "glossalalia" breaking out in odd spots here and there; I am speaking of ministers who preach over the heads of their congregation. On the other hand, I would suggest that another reason more people are not affected by preaching today is that they never give the preacher a chance to be heard. One cannot be affected by a sermon unless he hears it or reads it. Teachers and preachers both have a captive audience for a service or a term, but unless each one hits the mark and arouses a response, next Sunday or next term the listeners are fewer.

It is hard and essential work for the dedicated preacher to see to it that he leaves no stone unturned, no "gimmick" unused, no "hook" untried, no technique untested—always provided it is in good taste—to win attention and to influence those whom he addresses. Whatever it takes he must do: endless study and reading; ceaseless drafting and editing; keeping in constant touch with the people preached to and with the world in which they must live and work; and whatever else is essential to those who would persuade men from the pulpit.

I once noted in my diary the conviction that I must never miss such an opportunity again, as I had done that Sunday by preaching a very poor sermon. I wrote that there is no excuse for a poor sermon, since someone's lifelong impression of the Christian religion may come from that sermon; that, no matter what the expenditure of time, I must prepare it well—keep at it until God begins to shine through the words. My life is lived for God, I added, and when I do not serve Him or speak for Him I let Him down. I have always, since then, used the small hours of Sunday morning for testing my sermon and making it as worthy and effective as I can.

George Herbert writes feelingly about the minister as he conducts a service of worship and preaches a sermon, and his advice is still a helpful guide to the weekly approach to "the heavenly throne" on Sundays in church, from chancel, pulpit, and sanctuary.

"The Countrey Parson, when he is to read divine services, composeth himselfe to all possible reverence; lifting up his heart and hands, and eyes, and using all other gestures which may expresse a hearty and unfeigned devotion. This he doth, first as being truly touched and amazed with the Majesty of God, before whom he then presents himself; yet not as himself alone, but as presenting with himself the whole congregation, whose sins he then beares, and brings with his own to the heavenly altar to be [cleansed]. . . . Secondly, as this is the true reason of his inward feare, so he is content to expresse this outwardly to the utmost of his power; that being first affected himself, he may affect also his people, knowing that no Sermon moves them so much as a reverence, which they forget againe, when they come to pray, as a devout behaviour in the very act of praying. Accordingly his voyce is humble, his words treatable,* and slow, yet not so slow neither, as to let the fervency of the supplication hang and dy between speaking, but with a grave liveliness, between fear and zeal, pausing yet pressing, he performs his duty."[35]

All preachers worth their stipend are on the anxious bench, weighed down by the burden of their responsibility to proclaim God's Word to their people with power and understanding Sunday after Sunday. They are often discouraged because the earthshaking, life-changing words they would utter are seldom spoken. In their desires they are lions, or even mice, that would roar, but instead the sound they make is too often a squeak. And yet, who knows what happens when the preacher does his best, using to the utmost whatever talents God has given him, for he seldom knows what the effect really is on those who hear; his lot is mostly to reap unseen and unknown harvests, and not to be fooled by the kindly meant, sweet words of flattery at the church door after service.

Preachers are, to use a rather crude expression, "brazen persuaders"; or ideally they ought to be. How can they be subtle or ashamed of the message they proclaim if they are to win listeners? Those to whom they preach have a right to expect bones with living flesh on them offered them on Sundays, not lifeless piffle. They have a right to expect of preachers a clear aim, and a purpose not lost sight of from beginning to end, carrying them along, step by step, to a definite conclusion and summary, packaged for remembering and taking away. They also have the right to expect preachers to follow the minimum rules for good speech-making, namely, that they overcome the listener's "ho-hum" by

* That is, tractable, gentle; conciliatory, moderate.

delivering a hook, avoid "Why bring that up?" by making the subject important and relevant, open a window in answer to the plea "Give us an example," and accept the challenge "So what?" with telling effectiveness.

The job of the minister as preacher is to communicate as well as to proclaim the gospel, and to present some portion of the Christian message intelligibly each time he enters the pulpit. He is, therefore, vitally concerned over the intensity of interest in those who are listening. He sometimes wonders if anybody is listening at all. There seems to be so little impression made on those who come. No one wants to waste his breath speaking to a bunch of robots. This unimpressionable attitude sometimes arises from hostility—those listeners who ask themselves, "Does he really believe what he says?" or "Is he trying to manipulate me in some way?"—which he will have to work out how best to overcome.

The minister expects most of those who take the time to come to church on Sunday morning to be attentive and give him a chance to speak to them. Every time a minister conducts a service of worship—as he reads from the Bible, preaches from the pulpit, prays, and announces the hymns—he wonders how many are really listening. And he should never cease to ask, for it will force him to check and seek to correct his own faults in blocking off communication between the pulpit and the chancel, or the sanctuary and the pew. No meaningless reading of Scripture in a droning voice, for one thing. No routine praying, but making prayers ring with real sincerity, for another. No careless giving of announcements, but carefully preparing each one and committing it to memory, for still another. Above all, no casual delivery of a few words from the pulpit, but the proclamation of a vital portion of God's truth to a congregation waiting to be fed solid spiritual food.

Some listeners will inevitably be preoccupied with other things during sermon time, but the minister must assume that most of his congregation are listening, obviously and eagerly, and give his all in preparation for them, speaking to their needs, relating them to their world, keeping God's word specific and timely. The minister's job is to make them hear, or, rather, to win a hearing from them by the persuasive and electrifying powers of the Holy Spirit, and to spend long hours of labor to make His word penetratingly clear. What a moment of joy came to me when one of my leading parishioners, who had admitted cutting me off the moment the sermon began, came to me and commented on the value of a particular sermon. To win listeners is the preacher's task.

Those who make up a Sunday morning congregation come to worship, which is an offering, a speaking, and a listening, especially a listening. Worship is the central expression of the Christian religion, and the heart of worship is the awareness of God which it cultivates and the consequences of that awareness. But alert listening is necessary to awaken and sharpen this awareness. The minister's major task in worship is to help men adore God, to lead them to repentance and thanksgiving, to bring about inner change in the presence of God. Worship is not an instrument, nor is the minister an instrumentalist, to *make* people do or be things. The person at worship is renewed because he is in the presence of God. The minister who conveys the sense of being in God's presence inspires worship. Those present catch his spirit; hypocrisy and phonyness in him here are hard to hide. St. John said it perfectly. "The hour cometh, and now is, when the true worshippers shall worship the Father in spirit and in truth: for the Father seeketh such to worship him."[36]

It is true that the minister hopes God will capture and hold for listening all who come, and send them forth renewed by some new impact or insight of His word, with an increased dimension to their faith, beyond the usual superficial perception. Worship should give a new depth and commitment to one's faith.

If anybody *is* listening, two questions follow at once: one, what will they hear; and, two, what should they do or be because of it? In other words, worship stirs to action and sends the worshipers forth inspired and strengthened to do whatever God has given, or shown, or directed them to do. When a man listens, really wanting to know, God communicates His will to him. When he listens and hears, be begins to find the answers for each week's living from the portion of the Bible read at the lectern or from the altar; or from portions of the Prayer Book used—such as a psalm, a canticle, a prayer, the Creed; or from the special music sung by the choir; or from the sermon preached with power from the pulpit.

The living words of our Christian worship keep after us until we are caught and held by them, and are obedient to them, and they bear fruit through a new dimension to our Christian living. The vital meaning of God's word for us is always tied up with the Person of Christ, with the Holy Spirit, and with God as Savior and Comforter. Only by seeking and finding Him in the pages of the Book, in the feast of His life at the altar, on one's knees daily in His presence, and by living with Him and with others who have accepted Him, can anyone know and do His will. Each time men listen and hear God speak through some word of worship, a new dimension of Christian life will follow. They will discover, at least in part, one or more facets of truth, opening one time as new life, again, perhaps, as release from sin, another time as a truer evaluation of man or a new understanding of God—and always with implications for their lives.

Jesus Christ is the one who makes the difference in our listening, hearing, knowing, and heeding, for He is really our Lord and Savior, whom we accept and under whose commands we begin to live, unquestioningly, according to His demands. We come to worship the reconciling Christ, to be better equipped by Him for life. We come ready to surrender, to give up love of self alone, to respond to Him, to wait upon His guidance, His directions, and then to follow obediently as He sends us out upon the way of creative adventure. We come to ask for His grace so that we may love and live, not hate and perish. The test of the faith we declare in worship is the living of it. Because we believe in Him, we are able to love one another and keep His commandments, not perfectly, but increasingly. All ministers strive to win listeners. This is their business.

Their special business as preachers is to present week after week Christian specifics, pinpointed and relevant to the current scene with its ever-present worries, fears, and troubles, as well as to engage in the age-old battle between the flesh and the conscience, obedience and disobedience. Ministers are indeed persuaders.

If ministers are to give their utmost to win men's minds and hearts by the spoken word, they must not let the curse of gobbledygook—that is, nonsense that catches no man's ear—possess them. St. Paul gave a tidy summary of what I have been trying to say. "For our preaching of the good news did not come to you as mere words but with power and the Holy Spirit and full conviction."[37]

Down-to-earth Advice

Granted that what has been said so far in this chapter is true, we can move on to a more prosaic examination of the technical equipment all ministers need for proclaiming the word of God with power. A great deal of the minister's time is spent in learning how to write and deliver a sermon, and some never quite master it. The minister's seminary training is often surprisingly ineffective in the pulpit. There seems to be something lacking. The sermon is either too scholarly or too superficial, with too few illustrations or too many; it is either too sketchy or too meandering, with no clear evidence of what the preacher is trying to get across. The language may be beautiful but the logic shaky, while the voice may repel or barely be heard. There is no escape from the hard discipline of profound thought and diligent research, careful drafting and clear language, illustrations that fit, and the best use of God's instrument, the human voice, in pronunciation, enunciation, and diction—all audible and distinct, with correct pace and emphasis—to say nothing of the importance of gesture and posture.

All of these are pointed toward the one end of reaching the target of all preaching—the listener. There are so many angles to one's preaching, such as using notes or not using notes; making only one point or more than one; the length, whether too long or too short[38] (a sermon is just as long as it seems to the listener); and the content, which must be words for life and death. All sermons should face facts, but also lift up and leave one's spirit high in hope, eager for whatever lies ahead.

I'm sure all ministers who preach have had nightmares similar to the dream I had following a performance of the play *J.B.* on Broadway several years ago. If you saw the play or read it, you may remember the setting. There was a crow's nest, high up toward the fly loft, where God was placed for His dialogue with Job. In my dream this became the pulpit from which I was preaching, and God was not there. The pulpit was so high up that the people spread out below seemed like Lilliputians. I could hear, as from some distant tower or minaret, a call to the people, "Look up and live," and they were all looking up at me as if I were God. I found myself speechless, staring back at them, trying to discern their faces and to read the true meaning back of their expressions of hunger, thirst, fear, and despair. I tried earnestly to find what they were looking for, what they were expecting, in order to have life. My eyes became like a telephoto lens, and I zoomed down for a closer look. All the faces were upturned, but all were not listening. Their eyes appeared to be a bit glazed. What could I say to awaken all those people who filled the pews below, and how could I hold their attention until they found whatever would feed their need and enable them to go forth as "new" men? How could I open up the secrets of their hearts? What I sought for desperately was not just some passing word to toss them which would then be forgotten by both of us, but an awakening, enduring word of life, which would lift them up to where God is—not to where I was in that dream. I wanted to give them a high and uplifting experience like that of Isaiah's in the Temple. I still want to, as we all do, but in reality, not in some dream sequence. So we must awaken from our dreams, or nightmares, and gird ourselves for speaking God's Word with power.

The minister in his preaching must seek to bring alive the root meaning of the word "existence" from *existere,* which means to rise above any moment of existence, even while being a part of it. He is in this sense a prophet, and whatever he speaks or writes will strike this note of standing on tip-toe and seeing a bit farther ahead than the man in the pew. His words are not limited to carefully prepared utterances on a Sunday morning from a pulpit. His daily contacts furnish unlimited opportunities and pitfalls, and he is often afflicted by the all too prevalent "foot-in-mouth disease" of saying the wrong thing at the wrong time because his mind is not on the immediate situation. My wife has struggled with me over this disease which is so hard to cure. But it must be cured no matter how drastic the medicine has to be.

Conclusion

Besides the sermon, there are so many other ways a minister's words, whether written or spoken, reach people, and no one of them is unimportant. For example, I have always spent as much care on my weekly message in the parish bulletin, which was mailed to each individual and family, as I have on my Sunday sermon, for it reached all my people every week, and my sermon did not. But whatever use the minister makes of words, he has but one purpose in mind, namely, "That I might by all means save some."[39] This purpose is not to be forgotten as we move on in the next two chapters to the minister's works and ways.

VI

His Works

All Things to All Men

Professor James Stewart, a magnificent Scottish preacher, in his book *Heralds of God,* gives some blunt advice to those guilty of rationalization. "Beware the professional busyness which is but slackness in disguise. The trouble is that we may even succeed in deceiving ourselves. Our diary is crowded; meetings, discussions, interviews, committees, throng the hectic page. We are driven here, there, everywhere by the whirling machinery of good works. We become all things to all men. Laziness? The word, we protest, is not in our vocabulary. Are we not engrossed from morning till night? Do we not conspicuously spend our days under the high pressure of an exacting life?"[1]

Ever since the Protestant Reformation in Germany, faith and works have been indissolubly linked in the minds of all Protestant Evangelical Christians, and a great deal of the minister's time is given to good works as a result of his faith, in the belief that every assault upon human integrity, dignity, and honor is an attack on our Lord who is a sharer of all human life. The test of every Christian is his treatment of the lowliest and least among us, for Christ is there in each one, revealed only through the eyes of our loving concern and empathy. "Inasmuch as ye have done it unto one of the least of these my brethren, ye have done it unto me."[2]

One of the joys of the minister's life is that there are so many ways of being His servant in the world, in addition to preaching the Word and administering the sacraments. The only possible drawback is that he must remain a counterpart of the medical G.P.; rarely can he hope to become a specialist. Yet his people expect him to be an expert in all phases of his ministry. Review for a moment the kaleidoscopic range of the parish minister's life, which is both his delight and his frustration, as he presses toward greater dimensions of service among God's people who are his people. He is so many things to so many people he often gets lost in the maze of his own roles, and no wonder.

He is a teacher. He is called on to plan a curriculum of study for the children and young people as well as the adults of his parish; to conduct Sunday School classes; to prepare members for confirmation or church membership through lecture series, classes, and private conversations; to give an occasional talk, or series of talks, based on careful research and preparation, presented with imagination and a sense of humor, like Frederick W. Robertson's series, *Corinthians;* to lead preaching missions and schools of prayer, worship, and religion; to make the laws of learning* the watchwords of his ministry; and to manifest his discipleship not only as a willing learner but as a zealous sharer of what he has learned.

This schedule alone is enough to occupy all his waking hours. This means he does not have time to do a thorough job of planning and executing a full-scale parish educational program and, therefore, has to skimp and improvise, which fools no one and lessens the outreach and depth of all attempts at education in the parish; or he has assistance, paid or volunteer, to help carry the burden, seize the opportunities, and make education an exciting experience for the developing Christian life. The local situation differs widely, but as a teacher the minister finds one of his greatest outlets for communicating the gospel to both young and mature members of his parish, and to neglect it is both wasteful and tragic. His zeal as teacher must never flag, nor his passion to teach in order to "make His name glorious" ever diminish.

The minister is forever chasing the will-o'-the-wisp of the ideal Sunday School curriculum. There is none. He must scratch and search without ceasing among what is available, taking a good look at each bit of new material and every method that may offer a better and more interesting approach to the Christian faith as it relates to the lives of his people, from the cradle to the grave. Whatever method he chooses must, of course, be reevaluated continuously as to content and effectiveness.

He is a counselor. The minister is a pastor, counselor, confessor, and spiritual diagnostician. In him is a true trinity of ministering. Early in my ministry I found, first of all, that I must know what Christianity is, and, second, I must know how to apply it in specific instances of need. In searching for answers to people's questions I found the need

* The five laws of learning are: repetition, exposure, understanding, conviction, and application.

for diagnosing my own problems. Henry Drummond helped immeasurably in setting me straight. His essay on "Spiritual Diagnosis," already referred to, with its emphasis on personal religion as it affects each one individually, has helped me grasp and deal effectively with doubts and fleshly ills in myself, and has helped me in learning how to approach others on the subject of their deepest feelings and problems.

There are differences of opinion about counseling today; the so-called "nondirective" counseling is currently much in vogue. I was trained in the school of "directive" counseling, that is, to listen to a person's need, with an occasional question to ferret out as many of the unknown factors as possible, then to prescribe specifically what to do in one-two-three order, based on a thorough knowledge of human nature, moral theology, and the essential ingredients of the Christian faith. My basic orientation in moral theology was based on the complete Kenneth E. Kirk, whose *Some Principles of Moral Theology*[3] still covers the dimensions of all pastoral counseling, and portrays the role of the spiritual director accurately.

The minister's chief function as counselor is to set the lost on the right path and to bring them to reconciliation with God, by the most direct means possible. The art of listening, and letting the "client" or "patient" or "parishioner" pour out his inmost troubles and perplexities—working out his problems by talking them out,[4] with the minister nodding wisely in encouragement occasionally—may have merit, but I have found a balanced combination of the two methods has worked best for me in my ministry. Often, just sitting and listening—which I did once for three hours straight because I did not know what to say—leaves the one who comes for help drained, and perhaps cleansed, but not filled again with a better attitude, a more Christian response, a sense of forgiveness, and a secure feeling of acceptance, all of which the counselor must help provide. The old story of the devils cast out but nothing brought in to take their place is forever true. Most seminarians are weak on moral theology, and too few non-Roman Catholic books have been written on the most effective techniques. Again, every minister is on his own and simply must find by what means he can become a better counselor.

All are in need of a confessor, the clergy no less than the laity, and each word from the pulpit speaks to some need heard in "the confessional." There is a major difference between the Catholic emphasis on auricular confession to a priest and the Protestant emphasis on confessing by word or in silence to God direct, which is the great point in an evangelical faith. This formal confession in a box, so often repetitious, without getting to the deepest need and sin, often fails; while the more informal, conversational, nondirective counseling, which enables the penitent by insight given to see the sin and how to deal with it with God's help, more often succeeds.

The wide range of one's counseling ministry can also totally absorb one's time. Therefore certain priorities must be set up as to the urgency and gravity of the need and his ability to handle the person's problem, with the primary responsibility for members of the minister's own parish. Often those who come for help need more expert care than the minister can give, and, therefore, he must have an adequate list of doctors, psychiatrists, psychologists, and others to whom those in need can be referred.

The minister must understand, and help others to understand, the role of the Christian religion in mental health, and how to prevent perversions of religious belief from leading to mental breakdown. He must be very careful not to assume the full responsibility for therapy when there are signs of a full-blown mental illness in the making, realizing the peril of superficiality, both on the part of the psychiatrist and the minister, and the need for the redemptive and transforming grace of God. All therapists are seeking the truth about the patient's condition and whatever will best remedy the condition, and the psychiatrist, in his dual role as philosopher and scientist, has an obligation to examine the healing power of Christianity.

The counselor must probe relentlessly if he is to find the truth so often buried deep within. I well remember a lovely girl in my parish in Atlanta, Georgia, making a date to borrow a book from my library on a Saturday morning. After a long "song and dance" about books and reading, she almost left with nothing said about her real reason for coming—the festering guilt she had come to share. As she turned to leave with book in hand, she stopped suddenly and blurted out the truth. "I have been living with a married man for the past five years. What am I to do?"

Take one important area of counseling as illustrative. In most churches it is a requirement, or at least a custom, that premarital instruction be given to all couples who are married in that church. This is a responsible task which requires the minister's concentrated attention. All counselors know the tragic results of the wrong kind of home life and the long-term unhappiness it can cause, and they must prepare the young couple for their life in relationship, giving advice on dealing with the inevitable anger to be controlled, selfishness to be combated, inner wars to be ended, tensions to be resolved, and making them aware of human imperfection and perversity. But Christian counselors know also that happiness and peace can be found and that all couples can learn how to live together according to the rules of common courtesy, good manners, decent behavior, and with an attitude of consideration—all marks of Christian love. Each minister must work out his own approach based on experience and the many excellent manuals readily available. He must be ready to refer the couple, or either one of them, to someone else for dealing more deeply with any special need, physical, mental, or spiritual.

The wise old theologian, Pelagius, gave this succinct advice to the bride and groom: "Avoid avarice, ambition, adultery, convenience; have charity, have faith, have children."[5] This is neat, simple, and all-inclusive, but no aphorism is sufficient for preparing a young couple for the "great gamble," the "great adventure." I discovered, after several years in the ministry, that there was never time enough to say all that needed to be said to a young couple, separately or together, therefore I prepared a rather lengthy mimeographed "Manual" as required reading before meeting with the couple for premarital counseling, saving until the personal conversation my presentation of the meaning of Christian married love and the sacramental aspects of holy matrimony. In smaller parishes and communities, premarital counseling can be done more personally and in greater detail, with as many sessions as needed. This phase of the minister's life should *never* be neglected.

Another area of constant concern to the minister is helping willing learners find an adequate devotional life, whether in making their daily prayer life more meaningful or in aiding them to find the fullest possible meaning in the sacrament of Holy Communion and showing them the relevance of the service to their own modern life. I wrote a little handbook, *The Most Comfortable Sacrament*,[6] in an attempt to answer one man's innumerable questions on the subject. We are forever interpreting the words and phrases of the Prayer Book service, from "miserable sinners" to "washed through his most precious blood." There must always be time for this kind of counseling.

But the minister is never too busy to see anyone in need who comes to him, no matter what the problem or how inconvenient it may be for him. He never knows when it may be a matter of life and death to the individual who seeks out a counselor. Therefore, the faithful minister, as pastor and counselor, never loses touch with his people and their several conditions. He always has time, a ready ear, patience, and an empathy that comes from really caring and sharing what his people are going through in this complex century.

He is a financier—of sorts. At least he is expected to be one. Indeed, he is often called upon to be a financial wizard. One of the first parishes to which I was called had incurred a large debt for building the first

unit in a combination church and parish-house plant, just before the
1929 financial crash. The Bishop, in his letter to me, painted an honest
picture in black and red. The insurance company that held the mortgage
was threatening to foreclose. The people were discouraged. The "new"
building had been neglected and was run-down. All the Bishop wanted
me to do was to stop the foreclosure, renovate the building, pep up the
congregation, and raise a lot of money!

Among the many good things for me which came out of this experience was a greatly expanded knowledge of money matters, which are
most often the trial and burden of a minister's life, for rarely is he
gifted with skills in the complex and swiftly changing world of finance.
But he must, regardless of his modest qualifications, do his best with
budgets, stewardship campaigns, investments, annual money-raising
efforts, mortgages, if any, and the best techniques for "selling" the
parish on all the items in the current budget, especially "missions," now
become more often just "mission." He must do his best to make his
people conscious of their full responsibility, as stewards, to make gifts
to special needs in parish, community, diocese, general church, and the
ecumenical movement. He inculcates a sense of mutual responsibility and
interdependence within the Christian fellowship. In other words, he is
to make money an instrument for spiritual things and translate dollars
and cents into life-giving terms and potential. He will be called upon to
walk the delicate line of not catering to the rich because of their potential giving, and not blaming the poor for their perpetual neediness and
demands.[7]

One of the best introductions to a church financial drive I've ever seen
is the following statement, which stunned me when I first read it. When
I checked it further, I found it was an accurate appraisal of one church's
sense of stewardship, and of what potentially could happen when the
"sleeping giant" of financial resources was awakened by the shock of
such an elemental presentation. "Suppose all Episcopalians were suddenly deprived of all their income and all their assets, and every Episcopal family placed on old age assistance or 'on relief.' Then imagine all
these Episcopalians giving a tithe of their income to their Church. If
they did it, the income of the Episcopal Church would increase by over
50%."[8]

The minister must be a responsible citizen in the realm of finance,
conducting his own affairs with efficiency and honesty, not forever in
debt or stupid about his personal income and outgo. He must be especially meticulous, too, about any funds he administers, such as his discretionary fund. My discretionary fund has been the only one I've ever been
able to balance month by month, and how I have sweated over this! I've

always dreaded any discrepancy with this money entrusted to me for the benefit of others.

In the early years of my ministry financial going was rough for me personally; almost everything had to be purchased on credit or on the installment plan. I became a bit of a juggler when I decided each month how much to pay "on account" in order to keep my credit rating. The banks have always been fairly lenient and understanding with ministers because they are often so financially inept—but don't count on it.

The question of income tax, and a correct accounting of "gifts" and "fees," places a burden on the minister's conscience and bookkeeping, but once a system has been devised, and the right columns for deductions and extra income have been worked out, it is really a question of noting down everything day by day. It was helpful to me to consult with an expert accountant for a few years to set up the easiest method for keeping track of my own income tax items. Even so, I still find it hard to settle down on the eve of April 15 each year and put down the final figures taken from my rough notations made in January. When the sealed envelope, with the check enclosed, is dropped into the nearest mailbox, I heave a heavy sigh of relief.

We are all aware that the growth of our national economy accounts for appreciation in stocks when there is no comparable increase in savings (although now as much as $4\frac{1}{4}$ per cent interest can be earned, and even more in savings and loan corporations on the Pacific Coast). To have an increase in returns from securities requires careful investments in common stock, if the minister has anything to invest, preferably with the advice of a layman in the investment counseling business.

From the beginning of our married life I've always given my wife the gift received from the groom at each wedding, which has formed the basis of her savings account ever since; this is listed as part of income, of course, in our joint return. I have always put money received from baptisms and funerals into my discretionary fund, but this each minister must decide for himself. However, my people, knowing this custom, often gave me more on such occasions than if it were simply added to my personal income. When the gifts are personally received, the minister must be constantly on guard to list them as added income, unless they are clearly receivable as nontaxable items. Some of the clergy feel strongly that there should be no fees on such occasions, since all are part of the normal service and life of the church, and that fees *per se* smack of professionalism. They argue a good case, but often forget that such great moments in one's life are the sacramental moments of the Church's life, and people want to make a gift in thanksgiving. I have never felt strongly about not accepting such a gift. Needless to add, there must be no "fees," in the strict sense of the word, that is, asked for, but I believe gifts of gratitude should be graciously received.

He is an administrator. This, too, requires a skill so often lacking in those who are called to be ministers and stewards of His grace. So often the standards and practices of the business world are not applied in running a parish, especially in handling a staff, deploying paid and volunteer workers, getting adequate maintenance done—which requires the same efficiency as that provided by a good professional cleaning service—and making full use of the talents of an assistant minister as an extension of one's own ministry.

I have bumped up against endless frustrations as an administrator. I've often felt it would be a wise use of parish funds to hire a skilled lay administrator, which is done in some quite large parishes, but I've never done it, always managing to limp along with the aid of the best sexton I could find. In my New York parish the problem of maintenance was greatly magnified, for in addition to the constant battle against the city's soot, especially in summer, and snow in winter, the church was open night and day. This required extra staff, continuous warmth and lighting, and the upkeep, cleaning, and guarding of the church, the parish house, the parish house annex, and the rectory. I was blessed with a good sexton, but I sought advice and counsel from an expert administrator to help set up the most efficient use of our manpower. The minister's often unpleasant task is not only to set up a workable schedule, but to check up and see how well it is carried out. Unfortunately the church has usually paid small salaries to its employees and as a consequence has had to put up with many inefficient staff members.

A very sensitive area with which the minister must deal is the hiring and firing of staff. In hiring, pressure is often brought to bear on his taking some worthy member of the parish, or good friend of a parishioner, whose qualifications are very sketchy and shaky. Also, this question must be answered: should one choose to hire members of one's own denomination only, or seek the best person for the job, regardless of race or religion?

Another question plagues the minister persistently: how long must be put up with a member of the staff who has outlived his or her usefulness, or who is disloyal, or who is a gossip or a troublemaker? Disloyalty is the worst "disease" any staff members, lay or clerical, can have, and it must be dealt with at once, either by confronting, correcting, and giving another chance, or by relieving the offender of duties without delay. No minister can afford to keep on his staff any one who is poisoning the minds of his parishioners behind his back by deliberate lies or innuendos. When any staff member is let go under the cloud of disloyalty, no fuss should be made, and it should be done as quickly and quietly as possible, with as little hardship and hard feelings as can be managed. This is always a difficult decision for any minister to make, but I believe he must take the action which is of greatest benefit to the total parish situation, even if this means letting a long-term employee go. But there must always be kindness as well as firmness, and adequate care in timing for finding another job or providing some kind of pension.

I am not advocating for parish administration the same procedures followed in the secular world, but the same wisdom and expertness are demanded of those who must do the Church's business in the world as ministers and stewards.

He is an organizer. His ability here is always tested to a lesser or greater degree, depending upon the size of his parish and his community's needs; also, whether his parish is composed of a "normal" cross section of community life or a special segment—racially, socially, or economically—and whether it is urban or suburban, town or country, for communities differ radically and change continuously. He must come forward with a design and plan for the Church's life in an urban or suburban, town or rural, community. I found, for example, a vast difference between Lexington, Kentucky, and New York City as to what works best in the way of organized parish activity.

One must proceed on the basis of trial and error, in addition to previous experience, to work out a parish program which seems most likely to fit the particular parish and community; and if it doesn't work, something else must be tried, until at last the right type of parish program produces the desired results. Success depends largely on the minister's aptitudes and attitudes, and how hard he is willing to work to implement his designs and plans, and to win leaders to help him do the job. One can never count for sure on what was done successfully in a former parish, for not only are parishes different but the times are different, and what will work now in a particular place may or may not work equally well somewhere else. The minister must be adaptable, creative, and undiscourageable. There is always a right way to reach every parish and the many types of people that make it up. It simply takes time, patience, and ingenuity to find that right way, which is never ready-made, but always developed on the job to fit the measurements of each parish.

One such development that proved very successful was a variation on the Sunday afternoon lecture series held each winter in my New York parish: the innovation of a Sunday afternoon conversation around a coffee table in the parish hall, taking some pertinent theme, leading off with a statement from an expert, and then carrying on a dialogue for as long as the conversation remained fruitful.

The planning of a parish program is usually done in the spring—right after Easter, if possible—in consultation with the parish leaders. All phases of the current and coming parish program are discussed, the work of the past year evaluated, dates dovetailed, and themes, series, events, speakers, and leadership decided upon. This is the ideal plan, but usually summer blows in and fall arrives before all items are in place and locked tight. September, however, is the deadline for final planning, making the announcements, and following through with the implementation of the season's program.

He is a responsible member of his community. This role often seems to furnish a threat to his time as minister, and can force him to make many drastic choices, for he is called upon to lead so many community projects. His outside commitments and committee assignments in the community should not take him away from his primary responsibilities, but only he can evaluate and choose what to undertake. He is rightly involved in good community causes, for the Church is an institution of the community and, therefore, must manifest its concern for community problems. The Church is not only visibly present as a building, but the parish and people are an integral part of the community, not in opposition to it as something apart. The Church must be an inseparable part of community life, bearing its witness corporately as well as individually.

There is a temptation to divide sharply the sacred from the secular, the good from the bad, the churchgoers from the non-churchgoers. But God is in the midst of whatever is going on constructively in the community, and the minister must plunge in and do his bit in all worthy community projects—educational, social, and political—as well as in the work of his own denomination's various departments. He must be careful, however, not to be the willing horse who is worked to death or use his membership on committees as an excuse for neglecting parish duties—say, paying parish calls. This is where Professor James Stewart's warning at the beginning of this chapter needs to be heeded.

It is never possible to budget time in percentiles—so much for the parish, so much for the community, so much for one's private life. But there can be a serious consideration of every new task the minister is asked to take on in the light of how much time it will demand, how many other commitments have been made, and whether it threatens to use up precious hours needed for the parish. Choices must be made throughout one's ministry, and it is essential not to take on too much. Remember the parish is God's witnessing base in the community and has first priority on the minister's time.

He is ecumenical. This is more and more an important factor in the minister's life, and throws him into a new context of existence as a Christian minister in cooperation with his equals, the ministers of other churches. This search for and dedication to unity and a worldwide cooperative fellowship, with significant breakthroughs theologically and in the realm of human aid, is the great new Christian fact of our time. The minister must have ecumenical feet, following in the sure and tireless footsteps of St. Paul, who set the pattern for answering calls for help from Christian brothers in different parts of the world. He must learn to walk with these same Christian brothers everywhere in the world, as one of those committed Christians who realize the impossibility of any person, nation, continent, or any part of the Christian Church, remaining in isolation from atomic fallout or the ideological death struggle, who refuse to panic or ignore the unlimited ills abroad in the world, centering their lives in the Person of Christ, whom they believe holds the answer to the world's "night of doubt and sorrow."

The definition of the word "ecumenical" is much broader than its organized manifestations in councils of churches at the local, national, and world levels. It is really "the world in a word"; the bigness or littleness of the world is revealed in miniature as each one involved in it carries out "one little action on one little front," endlessly repeated. Those with "ecumenical feet" are ready for "movement" and "relations" and "reconciliation," joining in the common task of those Christians who would do their bit to hold the rapidly disintegrating world together.

Let there be no confusion about what we mean by "ecumenical relations," namely, the banding together of the separated fragments of the Body of Christ in a cooperative fellowship for the first time since the Reformation, to do together what cannot be done separately, to provide the means and leadership for unified work and action in every area of Christian concern, and to give the churches opportunities for conversing together for a better understanding of each other.

It is this being together constantly in work, worship, and study which increases knowledge of one another, and brings a gradual "growing together" at other points than Christian compassion and philanthropy. Ecumenical relations are made concrete in the World Council of Churches and the National Council of Churches, as well as in state and local councils of churches.

The World Council, for example, is "really not an organization," as

Dr. Ernest A. Payne points out in his article "Some Illusions and Errors," "but rather an enterprise and an adventure." The World Council is no super-Church nor does it sponsor attempts at organic unity as such, but by its very nature enables such unity to be more readily brought about by its member churches.

No one part of Christendom is the whole of God's work, even the Anglican Communion, great as it is and much as we Episcopalians love it! All of our churches lack something and need each other, or we would not be divided, said Bishop Azariah, in the early days of the Church of South India negotiations. Wherever the ecumenical movement has been taken seriously, the results have been an enrichment, a more effective witness, and, in spite of many differences, a strong bond that will ensure lasting cooperation, because we know that we are in some measure doing God's will for His Church.

Ecumenical relations in miniature, where we are, the actual contact between the fragmented units of Christendom operating at the local level, are still highly idealistic, yet unity is the goal we must always keep before us. The first step toward unity is cooperation.

"No matter how wide the divisions among our separated allegiances in this world, there is one baptism and one death. There may be precious little unity between these two horizons, but in the beginning and in the last things, Christians can't help but come together. . . . To deal with the Church as if she really had nothing to do with the one Lord Christ but only with the opinions of men, as if there were no one truth and one Lord and one faith at the heart of our Church, that is unbearable. And if that is so to you as it is to me, then there is no escape for us from the painful, difficult, uncomfortable, costly encounter we call the Ecumenical Movement."[9]

The Anglican Communion, through its bishops at the Lambeth Conference in 1958, declared that "one of the most serious weaknesses of the ecumenical movement is that it fails to draw the divided churches together at the local level, where actual congregations of Christ's flock live and worship side by side." Therefore, Lambeth called "upon all clergy and people to break out of the isolation and introversion of much of their church life, and to seek, by every means at national and local levels, to establish brotherly relationships and contacts, and to share perplexities and burdens that they may be one with their Christian brethren of other traditions in Christ's mission to the world."

All of us realize that "no single person can know what God is saying to the churches in every area about the next steps in their growing together. Only those who are in that situation and seeking to be sensitive to the will of God for them can know that." But those with ecumenical feet "can encourage experiences and suggest methods whereby responses may be made to the leading of the Spirit," through both word and sacrament, in the process of growing together locally.[10]

The minister, in his role as ecumenist, must keep his vision, his head, and his commitment through the hard times of witnessing, as God bids him speak and do for Him. He must remember that each individual can diminish or add to the problems of the world as he confronts his brother who has also been signed with the sign of the cross. The whole inhabited earth is a large place, and while we must get to know and trust our neighbors, we must head for the still alienated places of the world, carrying Christ's light "to people in unbelief, in conflict, and in distress." When we stay together, grow together, and go forward together, in common "commitment to manifesting God in Christ to the world" for all men in all conditions, far away and next door, we are implementing the ecumenical vision.

The local indifference to or reaction against the ecumenical movement reminds me of this story that first appeared in *The New Yorker*. Wolcott Gibbs, just before he died, included in his latest collection of essays an old piece called "The Mantle of Comstock,"[11] in which he took apart the individual members of a select interdenominational ministerial group in New York City for its resolution condemning Dorothy Parker's play, *Trio*. One leading clergyman of the group offered the resolution, and every other member signed it, including several prominent Episcopalians. Gibbs phoned and asked each member why. With one accord they condemned the play, some at great length, every one of them ending with this refrain, "But of course, I haven't seen it." I have a feeling that this is our main difficulty in the ecumenical movement. Most of our thinking and speaking is based on hearsay. We need to get the facts and apply as many of them as we can at the local level.

He is a crusader. He must exercise extremely good judgment in guiding his crusading instinct, so that it will count when used wisely, and not be dismissed as a "fool's errand." He will need to throw his influence behind many good movements, such as the continuing struggle everywhere for civil rights and the breakdown of barriers between races and classes, achieving the correct balance between the far right and the far left. He will need to back such movements as the drive to eliminate pornographic literature from newsstands and bookstores, particular community problems such as corrupt government, poverty, or crime. All this he must do in spite of the insistence on the part of some parishioners that he "stick to religion" and "stay out of politics," as if anything concerned with human welfare was ever foreign to religious concern. Ministers can never be bystanders or fencestraddlers, even though their crusading may be costly, as many ministers who have been involved in the big push for civil rights have discovered. Martin Luther King, Jr., winner of the Nobel Prize for peace, has said, "Some things are so dear, so precious, so eternally true that they're worth dying for. If a man does not discover something worth dying for, he isn't fit to live."[12]

The Church must always concern herself with moral issues in Christian thought and action, and speak with authority and wisdom on matters involving social ethics and sexual ethics. Although the Church is under no illusion that she still sets the norms for society, in no sense does she capitulate to secular movements and forces outside the Church. Through her ministers, she must seek to clarify the meaning of the gospel to men of today; the Church's teaching must not be allowed to remain obscure or distorted, or to muddle along without vitality and applicability.

The minister as crusader is involved in the ever current problem, "God, Man, and Contemporary society."

He is an evangelist. His evangelistic outreach must never be limited. His parish is the world. His responsibility is all mankind. He can never rest as long as one single man still has not heard that Christ is Lord. By all means at hand he must extend and deepen his ministry to the blind, the deaf, and the lost.

The minister must be a pamphleteer, a specialist in tracts for the times, knowing what is available, especially that which speaks to intellectual doubt and the scientific-secular mind; he must always have ready something to hand another for reading and discussion. The minister must overlook no opportunity for reaching others. One of the vital functions of radio and television is its potential for going through closed doors to reach those untouched by other media.

There are many techniques for "by all means" winning some. One example is the sidewalk preaching I did on Fifth Avenue in New York City. This attempt at evangelism is reminiscent of such "outside the Church" efforts as "The Church in the Street" technique of St. Peter's, London, and many variations in other large cities, to bring the Church to the people and the people to the Church. All such approaches are opportunities for witnessing.

The minister is presenting the drama of redemption in miniature continuously. Indeed, each Christian is a peripatetic theater presenting dramatic skits at unscheduled curtain times. The daily extemporaneous drama of each life is composed of many scenes, *lived* out, not *acted* out, involving or influencing other players in a random and unrehearsed cast, playing to a chance audience, making vivid and concrete God's mighty acts as they are incorporated into one man's existence. For the Christian, especially the minister, the stage is always set. The curtain is always up; there are always watchers of the scene in progress on stage; and each Christian is responsible for what men see and hear, and its effect on them. We prove our faith in the dramas we live out each day with God's help.

All Christians are called on to be the Church wherever they are, and to manifest at all times, in their speaking, writing, and conversing, at least these two marks[13] of the Church: its simple and informal fellowship, in which all who are identified with Christ participate and to which all men are manifestly welcome, both those who are saved and sinners who are not yet saved; and its reach—its existence beyond the church building, in streets and homes, in close relation to every aspect of daily life. Thus, we are all part of the "church" that is carried into my house by me and into your house by you, and so finds its way into the life of the world. No matter how far we are from realizing this ideal, it is still the goal of our striving.

He is a social worker. Dietrich Bonhoeffer summed up this phase of the minister's life. "The hungry man needs bread and the homeless man needs a roof; the dispossessed need justice and the lonely need fellowship. The undisciplined need order and the slave needs freedom. To allow the hungry man to remain hungry would be blaspheming against God and one's neighbor, for what is nearest to God is precisely the need of one's neighbor."[14] More on this subject later.

He is a healer. We will deal with this facet of the minister's works under "When He Prays."

He is a pastor. This we have already discussed under his role as counselor, and it will be dealt with still further in a later chapter on "When He Calls."

He is all things to all men. Or at least he is expected to be, and he valiantly attempts to be, using as his example the ministry of the versatile St. Paul.

In other words, *he is an octopus.* This phrase exactly describes the minister's life. He is into everything. This is both the glory and the pain of his calling. He cannot possibly do justice to everything he is called upon to do, so some of his "tentacles" will reach farther than others, and some will hold more tenaciously to one thing than another, and some will atrophy because of no use at all. He will also need a sharp mind for following his far-flung and varied interests, lest one or more of them be neglected, or left dangling with no relationship to what is going on in his life.

Time and Choice

There is always time to do what must be done. As someone reminded me, "There is always time to be nice." Christians believe that time as well as words are precious, since no one knows just how much of it has been allotted to him. Therefore, while we have time, "let us do good unto all men."[15] Waste of time is not only sinful but foolish. Time is important, not only to the big, hard-to-reach executive, with the unlisted telephone number and a battery of protective secretaries, isolated at the top rung of the ladder, but to each one given a portion of life to live.

We must all seek to learn how best to use this priceless commodity, time. But the realization of time's passing must not lead to panic, pressure, or a frenzy of aimless activity. A part of clock time must always be saved for thinking and planning how the essential chores of life may be most efficiently done; how to take advantage of the hours over and above work time, so they will bring the greatest benefit and joy; how leisure time, family time, and rest time may be fitted in as the clock ticks away the hours, minutes, and seconds of each day; how to assess one's existence and the miracle contained in the words *just to be alive*.

After the year spent out of my life recovering from that almost fatal airplane accident to which I have referred, I found myself trying to make up for lost time, using every second to show my gratitude for being spared to do God's work in this world as His minister. But I soon found myself burning the candle at both ends, rising early and working late. This is a bad habit I have never quite managed to shake off. However, I feel it is important to take care of my body by getting sufficient sleep, rest, and exercise, no matter how heavy the burden of work I have taken on.

We need, above all else, to create a sense and appreciation of time's value and its all too swift passing, and to whet everyone's desire to make the most of it. Yes, the minister makes the best possible use of time, God's time. In no other vocation does one man have to play so many parts, wear so many hats, and be so everlastingly on the job. He can never regulate his day's life by the clock, although appointments must be made and kept. In other words, he can never be out of harness "after hours"; there are no after hours. Only in a large parish, where there are one or more assistants and the parish is "covered" at all times, can there be freedom from the "cry in the night." He is the lifeline, and when people grab for it he must always be at the other end, ready to haul them in.

There is no escape for the minister from the dreadful discipline of time and choice. These must be his daily meat and drink. Some manage it well. Others do not. Dr. Theodore O. Wedel gives three measuring rods to hold over the day's life, as guides to parceling out time and saying "no." In his book, *The Gospel in a Strange New World,* he gives three words under which can be listed the major categories of each day's life: presence, service, and communication. In what he does, the Christian minister must mediate God's *presence,* the result of having been with Him recently and continuously. He must always be ready to respond to people's needs in acts of *service* or referral, so that when people "ask" no one will be turned away. The problem in a big city is the poverty-stricken, glib-tongued, after-hours bellringer at the parish house and rectory, and the beggar on the street. The ability to discern the need, and what to do about it, is an essential part of the urban minister's equipment. He must be constantly engaged in mission, in *communication,* seizing opportunities to witness wherever and whenever they come, as well as in dispensing charity with grace.

One thing has always worried me, the so-called "bum" in the street, who accosts the man with the clerical collar or anyone else who will stop and listen, for a money handout. The minister knows that 90 per cent of the time the money will go for cheap wine. What is he to do? In New York we had meal tickets and flop tickets and were always able to meet an immediate need for food and shelter. For any other *service* these men were encouraged to come to the parish house for more permanent help, but few ever did. One thing the minister must always do is to receive these beggars with kindness and not revulsion, and when they offer to shake hands, which they often do, to accept this gesture with understanding.

The only truly satisfactory answer to all the works demanded in a large parish is a team ministry, like that in Christ Church, Greenwich; or in a semirural area, a regional team ministry, like that in the upper part of the Diocese of New York; or in both urban and suburban situations, a lay-clergy combination ministry, such as found in a parish council, with experts in law, finance, and social service who pool their knowledge and their skills to help plan and guide the parish program.

The minister's works are many and varied, but they always reflect in some way the spirit of Christ, and should convey to the person ministered to the feeling of "the touch of His hand on mine."

VII

His Ways

Latitude

It seems that at a certain university the new chaplain for Episcopal students was very "high church." His predecessor had been "low church." At his first celebration of the Holy Communion he wore elaborate vestments and went through all sorts of extra ceremonial, strange to many of the students. At the time of the announcements he explained his way of doing things. "I've been saying my prayers, and all the outward and visible accompaniments are my way of saying them. How do you say yours?" The chaplain was within his rights; nevertheless there are both right and wrong ways of doing everything.

St. Paul's words are exactly right. "Let all things be done decently and in order."[1] Orderliness is demanded of the minister, not only in worship but in all areas of his life. He may exercise great latitude in the use of his gifts as long as order, decency, and reverence are preserved. In other words, he must never be careless or slipshod in anything done or said in God's service.

A minister's ways and his works are closely identified. What I mean to deal with in this chapter is his own particular way, or manner, of doing things, including his diosyncrasies, if any. In seminary we called this "ministrations." We notice it first in a service of worship as the minister conducts, reads, preaches, moves about, and wears vestments; in short, what he does ceremonially as well as how he deals with the rite, what the actual form and words become as he conducts the service, whatever the service of worship may be. No matter how often we remind ourselves that the service itself carries the impact, we know the minister's role is vital in communicating its meaning to the worshiper.

The Power of the Voice

"The word was made flesh, and dwelt among us." In all his ways the minister is constantly involved in the spoken, written, applied Word of God as found in the Bible, the Person of Christ, and the Church. The minister is called upon to read the Word privately in his daily devotions and to meditate and act upon it. He is called upon to plumb the depths of its mystical and obscure passages, and make them clear and relevant. He must be an interpreter of the Word as he speaks, preaches, writes, and conducts services. As an interpreter of God's Word to his people he must read the Word as if it were the burning bush of God's presence— as if God were speaking it direct. The minister is always seeking the best ways to communicate the Word.

In some churches the Bible is read from a brass lectern which is shaped like an eagle with outstretched wings. This is marvelous symbolism, for the reader stands there as if he were on a launching pad, ready to fire a rocket into the midst of the congregation. This reminder is needed, for so often the rocket, instead of taking off for the target, drops feebly between the outspread eagle's wings and the front pews. This rocket-launching analogy must conclude with launching the hearers by the power of God's Word into a new life of renewal and obedience, making relevant the gospel message in their everyday existence, not allowing it to fizzle out; leading them to choose life, not deadness, to see the promises of life and hold to them in faith, even though these promises are unrealized in a lifetime of striving.

Jesus has called us to be fishers of men, literally to lay hold of other men and capture them for Him, so that, as St. Paul says, "I might by all means save some."[2] One of the chief ways of doing this is by means of the human voice, God's instrument held in trust by every Christian minister. Thousands are waiting for the right voice to speak the right word to penetrate their deafness, indifference, hardness, or timidity, and that voice may be yours or mine. One thing that makes a man different from other animals is language, the highest means of communication. "God gave man language just as He gave him reason," wrote Henry Drummond, "and just because He gave him reason; for what is man's *word* but his *reason* coming forth that it may behold itself? They are indeed so essentially one and the same that the Greek language has one word for them both [$o\rho\eta\tau\omega\rho$, orator]. He gave it to him, because he could not be man, that is, a social being, without it."[3]

After a great deal of listening and observing in my ministry, I have reached certain conclusions about the use and misuse of God's instrument, the voice of the minister, which need to be shared and underscored. Unless the worshiping people are caught, held, and moved by the words of the speaker, the winds of inattention will blow their minds beyond reach and the service will be nothing to them but a string of sounds without meaning, and this precious Sunday morning hour will be largely wasted; the people's "hartes, spirite, and minde, [will not] have been edified thereby."4

There are many unfortunate types of clerical voices in daily use throughout the Church, with no chance of ever being changed unless each minister hears his own voice as it really is and works hard to correct his faults. It might be helpful to check your voice against these common types and to get your wife, usually your only honest critic, to help, or some good voice coach; or make a tape recording and criticize yourself. The *cliff jumper* is characterized by a stretch of monotone followed by a swallow-up of words, with the sense lost; the *breather* is identified by an audible intake of breath, like a rushing mighty wind. The *pious one* deals in honeyed words, sickeningly sweet; the *expressionist* reads meaning into words, not out of them; the *monotone* is the lullaby type, with a deadly soporific effect. The *emphasizer* selects certain words for enunciation and literally pounces on them, usually smashing the sense. The *ogler* keeps his eyes moving up and out, down and in, and from side to side in quick succession, to "hold attention," but instead he is thoroughly distracting—this is sometimes called the "drinking-hen" method. The *dramatist,* conscious of self alone, striking a pose in word and manner, seems to ask, "How'm I doing?" The *jitterbug* uses the nervous ejaculatory method, accompanied by gestures to match. The *singer* makes a tremolo elongation of word sounds, sometimes off-key, and his technique is known as "the Welsh huil," pronounced *wheel,* originally *howl.* The *many-syllabled one* overemphasizes articulation, stretching a word out of shape so it is often mistaken for several words, like the popular singer's use of "lu-huv" for love. The *runner-out-of-breath* takes too long a phrase in one breath, runs out, then snatches a life-saving gulp of air. The *mumbler* sounds like one whose upper plate is loose; he is the lazy-tongued or lazy-jawed one, whose immobile lips makes him a good prospect as a ventriloquist. The *hisser* makes a sibilant sound which is a cross between a whistle and escaping steam; the *roller-coaster's* voice travels up and down with dizzy, meaningless rapidity—again for "expression," so he thinks; the *yeller* is the orator type who intends to be heard, and is. There are undoubtedly many other types, from the *an-duh, er-ah* stumblers, to the utterers of other unscripted and unscriptural guttural sounds, like Mortimer Snerd's famous *duh.* But, "Good Lord, deliver us" from them all.

It is interesting to contrast the profession of the actor with that of the minister and to discover how the former labors endlessly to perfect the use of his voice, while the latter does little or nothing toward perfecting his instrument for the spread of the Good News through reading and preaching the Word of God. The actor often spends hours perfecting a single word or phrase, while the minister spends far too little time to make his reading of the Word of God living and dynamic. Recordings of Bible readings and other selections, made by skilled users of God's instrument can be purchased and studied. Such listening and practice are not based on vanity, quite the contrary, for one of the functions of the minister is to impart the mighty acts of God through the use of the voice, and this is the worthy reason for improving the instrument and the vehicle. Never forget this. The actor doesn't forget his profession.

The voice, however, must never get in the way of the meaning, or make the individual stand out, nor should the manner of speaking be more impressive than what is spoken. That is one reason why the minister in many denominations wears vestments, so that what he represents is not spoiled by idiosyncrasies and there will be no pride in individual appearance or cultivation of the voice. Only one thing matters, that God be mediated through His Word, and that something happens to those who hear and respond. Response in worship depends largely on the human voice, under God's control and direction, and its effect upon the worshiper. Making the most of God's gift of speech is every minister's responsibility.

While not all ministers are blessed with naturally good voices, all can work harder to improve what they have; *and all of them can make better use of their voices* if they are willing to keep at it. Once again, the right kind of voice, correctly used, combines these elements: it is clear in enunciation; conveys the right meaning; is rhythmical, with the accent rightly placed; has the right pace; is natural, not affected; is loud enough to be heard (one of my professors told me, "When you don't know the correct pronunciation of a word, say it loud"); and, above all, does not get between the listener and God. It is not a so-called "ministerial voice," by which is usually meant a pious, phony, sentimental, sepulchral tone which conveys nothing but doomsday gloom or twittery false hope. The best compliment a minister can get is "Why, you don't *sound* like a minister." God forbid!

However, a word of encouragement needs to be inserted here. If the minister's voice is ineffective or unpleasant beyond recall, or if he has defects of speech, God can use any sounding board for the propagation of His Word. All I am saying is that no minister can afford to neglect making the best instrument possible of whatever combination God has given him of lips, tongue, larynx, vocal chords, and lungs. He cannot simply rationalize his laziness in voice training by thinking or saying with resignation, "This is what God gave me, therefore I must be content."

A good text to guide ministers who read the Bible in public is this, "So they read in the book of the law of God distinctly, and gave the sense, and caused them to understand the reading."[5] The big thing in Bible reading is to see that the God who speaks *to* us also speaks *through* us from the pages of His Holy Book. Therefore, we must understand what we read, the whole of it, so that its full impact and meaning come through. This means time spent well in advance in preparation, especially in looking up the exegesis. St. Paul's epistles are particularly tricky in the King James Version, and require much practice to bring out their full and correct meaning, or even to make sense of some passages.

Each lesson to be read must be thought through, and practiced aloud until each phrase is given the right emphasis and each word pronounced correctly without hesitation. Only so will the congregation listen. And forget all the tricks of the "elocution school" of public speaking. Gestures are irrelevant in reading the Bible, and likewise the drinking-hen technique already mentioned, that is, raising and lowering the eyes to "hold" the congregation, when all that is accomplished is the minister's losing his place in the Book. The people are *listening* to the word, not watching it. The sound is received through the ears. All the minister-reader needs to do is to concentrate on what is on the printed page and let his voice "hold" the hearer-listener. This is radio, not television.

During my ten years in a New York parish I occasionally invited churchmen who were professional actors to read the lessons at Morning Prayer. Most of them felt honored and accepted gratefully. They took their assignments seriously and dealt with them as they would the script of a play, but with even more care and practice, so that the sense, feeling, and each shade of meaning would get across.

The minister has much to learn from the actor as he seeks to remedy the defects in his reading style. To accept voice coaching humbly and eagerly is a small mark of greatness. If, as we maintain, the human voice is God's chosen instrument to convey His message to the world, then all ministers must labor diligently to make it even more perfect than the actor's, for they are speaking His Word, not man's, at His command, in His service. (As someone has reminded us, we may speak with the tongues of men as if we were angels, but if we have not clarity, we are nothing, and the congregation is bored and turns us off.)

Among all the minister's ways the use of the human voice in worship is paramount. In His Church, as the Word is read or spoken aloud and the music is sung, the voice makes it come alive, communicating the sense of His living presence. There is conveyed a glimpse of humility shaming our arrogance, a demonstration of industry highlighting our sloth, a note of courage piercing our cowardice, or we are awakened to some incident in our narrow-gage living which is racing us toward a collision with a situation we cannot dodge. The voice is one bridge between God and man.

The Brazen Approach

If we live with people we must live with words, and keep a nice balance of communication between the gravity demanded of us in public and the more or less significant noises we make in private. This is especially true of that important part of Sunday morning worship, the sermon. I keep going back to those two words "brazen persuaders" to describe those who preach, in contrast with "hidden persuaders" as descriptive of the "Madison Avenue approach." While the two approaches are similar insofar as the emphasis in both is on communicating an idea or a message, they are also vastly different—thank God!

In the one, subtlety of approach is paramount, easing a potential customer painlessly and unconsciously, yet relentlessly, into accepting an idea which motivates him to buy a special product. Not that this always works. When I think of how many commercials for cigarettes, beer, and razor blades have been pitched at me while I listened to baseball and football games, I find there has been no impact significant enough to lead me to drink beer, smoke cigarettes, or change razor blades. My suggestibility quotient is quite low for beer, cigarettes, and razor blades.

Perhaps this is in part true of those who listen to sermons when nothing happens to them. Perhaps it is because they are just not tuned in on the right wave length, or the magic secret button to open a closed mind or a hard heart has not been found and pressed. It takes a piercing word to penetrate indifference or arrogance or overconfidence or habit.

But the refined art of manipulation on a mass scale is often a kind of gentle but effective hypnosis, which does not wear off until the object is accomplished, that is, until we are hooked and the product is bought. The immediate and frightening result of the Madison Avenue approach is instant success for a product, or sudden death and oblivion if sales do not increase. Hence the prevalence of ulcers among admen. To state that the goal of the advertiser is to sell his product is not quite accurate. The responsible advertiser wants the worth of his product known and proved by use, and sales to continue because of this. Madison Avenue changes its approach as often as necessary to catch and hold men's attention long enough for them to be persuaded to buy. Never for them the phrase "almost persuaded."

In the minister's approach, subtlety is obnoxious and dangerous. For each potential convert, the minister's presentation of Christian truth must be unmistakable and relevant, allowing no chance for misunderstanding or missing the point. The not-so-immediate results from the pulpit approach are evident in a full church on Sunday mornings or poor attendance and a dead congregation—although sheer numbers can never be the sole criterion for the value of a sermon or a ministry— thank God! Although "you can't save souls in an empty church,"[6] and the minister wants to "sell his product," too, as he proclaims the Word of God to modern ears, he wants even more to present his message in such a way as to convince men of its truth, applicability, and contemporary relevance. The preacher in the pulpit must take his ancient truth and speak it effectively to every generation in a different way, fully conscious of what men will respond to in the light of their mental, moral, and physical environment. The minister who ignores the wisdom and techniques of communication does so at the risk of losing contact with his people and the chance by some means to save a few.

If there were no such institution as the Church, where would the preaching be? With many advocating disbanding the Church as an institution, it might well behoove the minister to sharpen his skills in person to person encounter and confrontation, and in carrying the gospel to men wherever and whenever they will listen.

One Sunday morning in London, I heard a sparkling sermon by Leslie D. Weatherhead in a drab church setting. In the afternoon, in the stunning atmosphere of St. Margaret's, Westminster, I heard a distinguished but exceedingly dull Church of England preacher. The one knew his congregation and spoke on their wavelength; in spite of the uninspiring service and music, they tuned him in. The other seemed oblivious to the need for catching and holding attention in order to give his message a chance, depending on the ancient service and beautiful music; few found his wave length.

I make no brief for Norman Vincent Peale's message, but he has made himself heard and understood by millions of people. The preacher can never simply be popular, although this is greatly to be desired. Mass communication and acceptance may not indicate that the greatest truth has been presented. Remember how Adolf Hitler swayed the masses and to what end. However, the use of the most effective skills in persuading to buy or to believe within a given environment and time are essential. More people know of Norman Peale than know of Reinhold Niebuhr, but I believe Niebuhr's theology has shaped the thinking of more men and will have a more permanent influence. However, can those who hear and understand Peale find any meaning in Niebuhr? The two men are on different wavelengths. Perhaps we need them both.

Symbols and Imagery

The minister must be practical in developing his skills and ways of mediating the gospel, and yet in the process he must not forsake imagination as a balance to reality. The Christian religion is not afraid of either, for imagination and reality are integrally related, and both are required to make truth acceptable and sought after. This is why good novels are grist for the minister's "image" mill, along with poetry and drama, which also furnish word pictures ready at hand for making truth vivid and living. It took me a long time to differentiate between too many purple passages for adding "color" to sermons, and the window-opening word or phrase which illuminates. I am still a bit color-blind. A little poetry and imaginative use of language is good, but too much obscures the cutting edge of the thought to be expressed. We might make a slight emendation of Maurice Barrès' phrase, "Why have words, when their brutal precision bruises our complicated souls."[7]

Words create images, and one of the persistent problems besetting the minister's pursuit of ways and means is to correct the wrong images people hold and to give right images of those things related to religion, such as Church, person, minister, morals, salvation, Christian. The image people hold is often unreal or untrue, and needs to be checked constantly, especially the image we have caused to be created of the minister as too busy, stuffy, out-dated, easily shocked, or interested only in "the better people," socially, financially, and racially.

The Christian Church is not afraid of reality, nor is it afraid of poetic license and imagery—see the Book of Common Prayer for examples of magnificent poetic language. Indeed, the Church always faces things as they are, without using rose-colored glasses, and never ducks the hard explanations in morals or in doctrine. In a day when religious themes tend to be relegated to the realm of the imaginary and the fanciful by modern scientific-minded man, the minister is obliged to meet mysteries and problems head on with as much reality as he can muster.

Take, as an example, the doctrine of the Trinity, with the triangle as one of its symbols. This is the hard-core theme of the Christian religion, and the way the minister deals with it in sermons, classes, private conversations, and writing is of the utmost importance. Most people are confused by it, sometimes even the ministers who have studied theology and should know. The real problem is how to convey the single meaning of the substance without going off the deep end in a complexity of theological language. We have all tried, but the presentation can never be quite as simple as in the days of St. Patrick, when he found that a shamrock was sufficient to illustrate the threefold nature of God for the primitive Celts. The historic Christian creeds tried to spell out the true nature and being of God in order to combat the heretical distortions of the truth about Him.

It was all quite simple at first, when the newly converted Chrstian at his baptism declared publicly, "I believe that Jesus is the Christ." We do not need to know the precise historical moment when each Person of the Trinity emerged as distinct in religious thought, but, more important, we can know when the reality of the concept shines through for us and we know that God, as Jesus Christ, and as Holy Spirit, indwells His Church and us. Man can only nibble around the edges of the mystery of God's nature revealed as three Persons in One, but he can do this and relate what he finds to his life.

Language fails to describe the mysteries of God's nature, but we can surely do better than the religious beatniks who referred to the Three Persons of the Trinity—and not irreverently—as "Daddy-O, Laddie-O and Spook," with no exegesis attempted. Even though such terms are sacrilegious they do give a clue to what the minister is up against as he attempts to articulate such doctrines to modern man. This is what Bishop Pike in this country and Bishop Robinson in England have been grappling with, suffering the taunts of traditional Christians with their orthodoxy in straitjackets, in order to reach the minds closed to the traditional doctrinal approach.[8]

Even though intellectuals often view the doctrine of the Trinity as a "theological hodgepodge" or a "pedantic tangle" and sometimes call theology "the art of befuddling oneself logically," it is for them that the theologians have struggled to express such Christian doctrines in intellectually acceptable and meaningful terms, from St. Augustine's famous *De Trinitate* to Leonard Hodgson's *Doctrine of the Trinity*. Harlan Cleveland's eight-year-old son accidentally hit on a happy phrase when he switched the words of the grace at mealtime and prayed, "Make us needful of the minds of others." Even though we can never completely understand the mystery of the Trinity, we must give our minds to the discovery of how best to speak of the three natures, the three faces, the three persons of God—man's manifold experience of the being of God.

Signs and symbols are used in representing the Trinity, all of them attempting to relate the concept of three to one. The triangle is especially familiar, and can be found prominently displayed in most Christian Churches.

If, as Paul Tillich says, "Religion is the dimension of man's ultimate concern," what is the dimension of God whom we call Father, Son, and Holy Ghost? This Trinitarian God is not a refuge of words to confuse, but the formulation of the purpose and meaning of a God-related existence, reminding us we can and must accept meaning in spite of apparent meaninglessness, and go on the assumption that life is purposeful.

We can appreciate the Trinity, too, through music. There has been a richer, fuller sound to music since harmony was discovered; and since melody was found to match melody, the chord was born. The triad of harmony in music gives some semblance of the new dimension that the doctrine of the Trinity added to man's life. Music and words are often complementary in worship. Creedal propositions express beliefs, but, set to music, they seem to express the states of the soul aroused by those beliefs.

Christian art also makes full use of the Trinity in a hundred different ways. Tintoretto furnishes the best example, perhaps, in his painting "The Trinity Adored by the Heavenly Choir." He paints God the Father as an old man with a beard *above* the Cross, with arms outstretched, holding it up. God the Son is stretched *on* the Cross, with the top and crossarms forming another trinity. God the Holy Ghost is represented as a dove *at the foot* of the Cross.

In art, music, and poetry men have tried to say what the Trinitarian formula, which all Christians subscribe to and are signed and received by, means to them. The doctrine of the Trinity is an attempt by the Church to guide us through the storms of doubt, and guard us against heretical and strange doctrines. God is not a square; He is a triangle. He is not three separate circles, but three circles interlocking. Whether we are conservative and orthodox and unwilling to change any expression or phrase of the creed, or liberal and seeking to revise and modernize the phrasing, we find the healing and reconciling powers of religion repealed in the creedal description of God's nature, with the addition of our Lord's words, "him that cometh to me I will in no wise cast out."[9]

One of the exciting features of the old-time revival meetings was the moment when someone heard and responded to God's call to service, like certain famous athletes of Oxford and Cambridge who responded to the Moody-Sankey mission to Britain in the 1870's and offered themselves for service in the foreign mission field, under the auspices of such groups as the China Inland Mission. They used the very words Isaiah uttered in that famous dialogue with God.[10]

"Whom shall I send?" "Here am I; send me." "Go, and tell."

God has always been and is still let loose in the world through men; the marks of God's presence in the world are still discernible in and through persons; God is still calling, "Who will go?" and men are still hearing and responding, "Here am I; send me"—or not responding. "The sawdust trail" has largely faded from our vocabulary and become a figure of speech. Most men would rather be caught dead than stand up and testify to such a call in a public place; still, sometimes the same call brings the same response, and many do still declare their faith publicly and make costly decisions because of it.

What marks distinguish those who say, "Here am I; send me" from those who don't—and those who hear the Word of God only casually in passing, from those to whom that Word contains marching orders to be obeyed? Christians are marked at baptism with the invisible sign of the Cross on their foreheads. But something more visible is needed to indicate those who are Christians—some outward mark, or sign, or symbol. For centuries the Jews had the Star of David as their symbol, but very few ever paid it much attention until in Hitler's Germany the Jew was required to wear it on his sleeve as the symbol of his race. He wore it fiercely, with pride; he wore it with resignation; he wore it trembling with fear, for it labeled him. It was the mark of death.

The Jews wore their brand as a badge of faith with honor and dignity. I wonder what would have happened if the Christians in Germany had been singled out for mass extermination. Would they have been required to wear on their arms the stigma of a triangle? That is the nearest visible symbol of the Christian faith we have, other than the cross. The Trinity is one distinctive mark of the Christian religion. Suppose we had been there then, and had been required to wear a red triangle instead of a yellow star as a symbol of our faith. Could we have worn it with courage and conviction, and would we have known what it meant? Most of us find ourselves day after day in a rather humdrum and uncertain existence, not knowing where we stand or what we stand for. Our faith is tested only under fire.

We cannot alter circumstances, but God can through us. We can, with God's help, alter a man's situation in his circumstances. There has been a great hue and cry over the Pope's silence about the known fact of Hitler's eliminating the Jews by gassing naked men, women, and children to death and burning their bodies in countless ovens burning furiously night and day. We know that some brave Christian leaders did speak out in God's strength and name. When a word needs to be spoken in defense or in protest, it is a sin to remain silent.

Ground to Stand On

Why did the Christians choose a triangle in the early centuries to symbolize the threefold nature of God? It looks more like a mathematical formula or a bit of hocus-pocus. It sounds a little like nonsense when you hear someone trying to explain the Trinity. What do we mean by the triangle?

We certainly do not mean that there are three gods, but that there are three ways of apprehending God, and having said this we have done the best we can with it. But the doctrine of the Trinity is something we can understand in part, because all we are saying is that we believe in one God. We believe in the one God who created the world. We believe that this Creator-God took human form in Jesus Christ, and we believe that He remains with us continually as the Holy Spirit—at least with those who open their hearts and their minds to Him.

Some people will always say, "It is too complicated." Perhaps you have seen the very simple-looking formula that Einstein put together which, as it turned out, contained the secret of atomic fission. I certainly don't understand that equation; not very many people do. But I don't have to be a nuclear physicist to know that this equation is true and works. Everyone knows what has happened because of it. It would be just as silly for me to call a mathematical formula all tommyrot because I don't understand it as it is for nonbelievers to state that the Trinity is all rubbish. The Holy Trinity is not a lot of mythical nonsense, but an attempt to put into a formula the basis of our belief.

A man has to have something to stand on and believe in, or else what is he?

Let me give one illustration. Some of you have read that very wonderful story, *Through the Valley of the Kwai*,[11] about the Japanese prison camps on the River Kwai in World War II. You remember, perhaps, how the prisoners of war were reduced to the lowest common denominator of animal existence. They thought only of themselves and concentrated on only one thing: "How can I die?" They had no spirit or strength left for survival. Although many were Christians, their belief was feeble until two young men who were practicing Christians came into the camp. These two young men began to say, Yes, there is something here that is bigger than the circumstances; there is something more than death. There is something more than hate. There is something to live for, even in the midst of these ashes, this filth and the odor of death. And that something is that we believe in a God who has been let loose in the world, and if He has been let loose in the world then He is here with us, and therefore life which He has given is a life that we must live to the utmost as best we can, thinking in terms of all of us together, not of each man for himself. Over a period of time these young men, just by their very attitude—the spirit in which they ministered to the needs of others and their willingness to do the most menial and disgusting tasks—manifested Christian love and brotherhood. The other prisoners learned from them, and found that as Christians they could do the most difficult things without question, even forgive the terrible atrocities committed by their Japanese guards. From the Christian example, the prisoners gained a reason for living.

It seems to me we are always in between "bloody struggle and supreme ecstasy"—a phrase used by Dr. Jung in one of his *Reflections*.[12] Somehow we have to keep a balance between the two. If we understand that the Trinity is the symbol of the Christian faith, then we have at least these three ways of apprehending the God whom we know and declare, to help us keep this balance.

There are two more things I'd like to say which may help to clarify a little better what we're talking about. When we get in a bind, not knowing where to turn or what is going to happen, we can get very easily discouraged. We feel that somehow the ground has fallen out from under us, and the very ground of our being is shaken. And yet there is one thing we can know for sure: that this God who was "let loose in the world" (a wonderful phrase from a poem by John Masefield)[13] is apprehended by all those who open the door of their hearts and their minds to receive Him; that He is there—whatever the menial task, whatever the disgusting task, whatever the difficult choice, the Spirit of God is let loose in that situation. Wherever we are, He is. Whatever the situation, He is in it. That we can know.

Something that must always come to our mind when we think in terms of this so-called threeness of God is the fact that perhaps He is beyond our knowing. However, when we look at history we can see that men have found God—men have found God in the New Testament, and men have found God in their own experience. Thus we can say that we can truly apprehend God with our whole being, we can be enlarged by the dimension of God's presence within. Not that we can comprehend all of God. The nature of the triune God will always be a mystery. But we can apprehend Him, in part, through our thoughts, our minds, and by going always deeper into the knowledge of His being. The person who dismisses the Holy Trinity by saying that it is nonsense really is guilty of intellectual sloth rather than intellectual acumen.

We can wear on our arm the red triangle if we will, and begin to live with more and more understanding of what it means to be branded and labeled as a Christian in the world. That is what we mean by God in our minds.

We can feel His presence in our hearts. One of the things I like about the Church of the Ascension in New York City is that it is open all the time, and there is a constant atmosphere of the presence of God for those who wish to walk in any hour of the day and night. We can apprehend God in our hearts by our feeling, and we can know that this God who is let loose in the world is a God who cares for us, a God who loves us, a God who is around us to help us stand up strong against the world. That is what we mean by God in our hearts.

Lastly, God is in our hands. Not that we can feel God as a person physically present, but we can be directed of God. We can be used of God. And one of the things we mean by God's Holy Spirit is that God is in action in us, through the Church, and through us as members of the Church. He does His will and works in the world. That is what we mean by God in our hands.

It seems to me that in these ways of knowing God we can say that the God whom we worship is one God—yes—but that He is known to us in many different ways. And no matter what the world thinks or what the world does, the immutable laws of God are there for a man to stand on and live by; and if he doesn't, you know what happens—the moral collapse of his life in the world. There would have been no Star of David and no yellow armband for the Jews if it hadn't been for the perverted moral sense of a Hitler. And wherever there is a perverted moral sense it means there is nothing to stand on. There is no norm.

There must be something to anchor a person in the fundamentals of the Christian life. He must know what it means to be with Someone. This is essential to sustain life. So I remind you there is something firm for us to stand on and hold to and live by, the God whom we know in the Person of Christ through the indwelling Holy Spirit.

Moral Climate

Two other images relevant to the minister's ways tie in with "God let loose in the world," namely, "existence" and "the new morality." The following is only a brief indication of the connection between the two concepts and the ways the minister can make them both clearer to all his people who are willing to think them through.

The word "existential" is a perfectly good word for Christians as well as non-Christians. We are all in the midst of things as they are. A Christian is both a realist and a man of faith. Existence has to do with things as they are, and as we face what is and reflect on it, we do so, "not as men without hope," but as Christians who believe God has made us for Himself, and that our existence is to fulfill His purpose. We cannot and do not want to ignore or check or deny what is, but we are not overwhelmed by it. Let's admit that most things are imperfect and do not fulfill their own essence or existence, and we are aware of it. We understand fully that a gap exists between what we know ourselves to be and what we are potentially and essentially, and that this gap must be closed. As we listen, learn, and make His Word relevant to what and where we are, we at the same time make manifest the gospel for today as no obsolete message of an obsolescent God.

Interpreting the Bible's contents as significant for man's everyday work life, we shall both teach ourselves and witness to others that God is with us. We shall share a mutual concern for each other's growth in common dependence on the gifts of the Holy Spirit, relate them to the world and its needs, and focus attention on some special area of concern or need leading to postworship action. Our basic search will be how to make the gospel manifest in, and acceptable to, a strange new world. Each one must make his own choice about what he does with his life, discovering by God's help the tremendous importance of such things as prayer, neighbor, attitude, procrastination, and a limited idea of God. We exist, that is, we stand out as recognizable persons. We have being, and are fully aware of the gap between the potential self and its present condition of existence. God has chosen us, nevertheless, and we choose *life* and deal with it as it comes, trying not to limit His vision and purpose for the world by our own limited field of vision, because we believe God is ever with us.

There is no question but what we live in an erotic age, when nothing is left to the imagination, when all is spelled out in words and pictures, and yet we wonder why sex crimes are on the increase, delinquency has skyrocketed, and the number of babies born out of wedlock is booming, even among our younger teenage group, while venereal disease flourishes alarmingly. By the visual flaunting of indecency, and word pictures of obscenity, there has been created a climate of degeneracy which is causing havoc in almost every country in the world, and no one seems to understand why or what to do about it. The old controls are largely gone. The moral standards of our age are dragging in the slime.

As we look into the moral mirror of our day, what do we see? We see not only open pornography nooks in every community—all of which were formerly hidden, back-room, behind-the-barn stuff—but the continuous and endless exposure to the new morality, in movies and books especially. Even though the "message" of many plays and films is *"Don't* go and do likewise unless you want to end up in the same kind of mess and misery," it doesn't seem that the young who feed on these dramas have enough perception and balance to see this. Instead, they are pulled by forces they don't understand, to conform to the new non-law of amorality, and havoc and despair follow all too surely. Every minister can testify to this fact, for he tries to pick up the pieces; he can tell of the far-reaching tragedies for all concerned which result from this cutting loose from the moorings of moral standards and controls. But there is wide disagreement over what or who is moral or immoral. Even those who want to live moral lives are no longer certain what is right and what is wrong.

The Church seeks to guide its members in choosing right from wrong and between two evils, and to furnish moral leadership in matters of sex and in all areas of moral choice. We do know that the misuse of sex can never be right, since it is selfish and sinful in its irreverence for the sanctity of both a man's and a woman's life. So many youngsters are being duped into thinking they are emancipated, when they are actually being entrapped. It's not surprising that this twentieth century attitude changes the moment a girl gets pregnant. Then the nineteenth century morality comes back into full play. Sexuality as entertainment, divorced from procreation and from abiding love, without personal commitment, without relation to responsibility—to family and to marriage—*is wrong.*

But society is no longer accepting the Christian morality of sex life. What are to do—capitulate? What has the new morality done to us? What safeguards are left to guide those who believe in the wisdom of God's laws and who cherish decency and morality? Where are our Christian ethics?

We are not completely bereft. We do have some guidance from our Church leaders. The Anglican Bishops, meeting at Lambeth Palace in 1958, in an unprecedented and frank discussion on sex and family, spelled out in plain English the problem and the Church's position on sex, family, and related matters in contemporary society. They made it clear that God's circle of love includes us all and reaches far, that it takes in saints, sinners, trinitarians, unitarians, "anythingarians," nominal Christians, doubters—all mankind. God's love and the Christian ethic go hand in hand. God's love and God's law set the standards, unfurl the banner of our declared style of life or mode of existence.

St. Augustine's phrase, "Love God and do what you please," makes sense, for if a man loves God he will try to do what pleases God. Behind love is the law—the moral law and the law of the universe. Clearly part of the meaning of Christianity is in the moral restraint of animal impulses and of lawlessness. What is right? What is wrong? That's always the confrontation. That's always each man's choice. Courage and moral leadership are needed within the fellowship as we formulate and enunciate guides to conduct based on the New Testament. There is no substitute for old-fashioned "character" that enables one to hang on to what one believes is right, with God's help, no matter what the temptation.

Music

So much for the addenda on preaching. Now, a further word about music. In most churches the music is left up to the minister, who is ultimately responsible for its quality and the caliber of its performance as complementary to the rite and ceremony in a service of worship.* Music is one of the minister's ways, or instruments, for touching his congregation. Of course much depends on the organist and the choirmaster, for the minister must lean heavily on their knowledge, skill, judgment, taste, and experience. Worship needs neither words nor music, but words articulate its meaning, and music enhances and expands the dimensions of the words. The function of music in worship is to take the worshiper out of the plane of everyday communication, and raise him to a level of praise where he can approach Almighty God with inspired zeal and fervor, like Isaiah in the great experience recorded in his prophetic book.[14]

The worshiper is in a receptive mood. The function of music is to feed the mood, give him wings for his aspiration and praise, arouse and involve all his being, and call forth a symphony of his faculties—emotion, will, intellect—all orchestrated as if the congregation were an orchestra pouring out its praise.

The arts, especially music, help stimulate and kindle the sense of God's glory in ordinary worshipers and have done so from earliest

---

* In *Constitution and Canons of the Protestant Episcopal Church*, Canon 23 says, "It shall be the duty of every minister to appoint for use in his congregation hymns or anthems from those authorized by the Rubric, or by the General Convention of this Church, with such assistance as he may see fit to employ from persons skilled in music, to give order concerning the tunes to be sung in his church. It shall be his especial duty to suppress all light and unseemly music, and all irreverence in its performance."

biblical times. The psalms were the hymns of ancient Israel. A random troubador, by just singing a song, revealed to Elisha the will of God, and demonstrated the power of music.[15] It was David playing on his harp and singing his songs, who comforted and calmed the tempestuous Saul. Music has always been used to soothe and heal, to stimulate and inspire, to accompany joy and sadness, to commemorate high moments of festival and deep moments of mourning. Life would be bleak and barren—bereft indeed—were all the instruments of music silenced and all the voices of singing stilled.

Robert Bridges summed up the meaning of sacred music as "music whose peace should still passion, whose dignity should strengthen faith, whose unquestioned beauty should cheer in life and death. Sacred music is worthy of the holy words of the Liturgy, whose expression of the mystery of things unseen never [allows] any trifling motive to ruffle the sanctity of its reserve."[16] In other words, music is sacred whenever it touches us deeply and divinely and makes us aware of God's presence. Music and worship speak as the "collective voice of mankind that unites men on a higher level of spiritual sensitiveness than they could otherwise attain."[17]

The object of the redeemed life is the praise of God, and music is an aid in attaining it, for music "moves and changes as man's whole being moves and changes; it lives parallel with his life, agonizes with his struggle, mourns with his grief, exults with his joy, prays with his adoration"[18]; it feeds his soul with assurance, consoles and inspires him, awakens and sends him forth. Such music should be the best always, and should expand the mood and meaning of worship. God often speaks in sounds of music—in singing, playing, listening—and men are won to praise Him, making melody in their hearts because of hearing a melody in their ears. The power of the Lord is made manifest through music.

As an example of what happens to worshipers through the powerful influence of music, listen to this testimony of Robert Raynolds, the novelist. "I can remember," he says, "in my middle years hearing a sublime performance of Beethoven's *Missa Solemnis* that opened again and harmonized lost and backward deeps in my life, unbinding strength in which I wrote two novels, *The Sinner of St. Ambrose* and *The Quality of Quiros*."[19] All those who have heard Bach's *Christmas Oratorio* realize it is no Christmas confection but that it unfolds the deep and permanent meaning of the Nativity. Intended for separate use on successive days of the holy season, each part makes a unity in itself, but put together in one performance, the whole eloquently and passionately defines the significance of the Incarnation and, therefore, is not for

Christmas only but a series of cantatas singing the creed for six different seasons of the Church year. Such music was created and designed to plant "Seed for a Song" in the hearts and minds of all who listen, and to nourish growth in the praise of almighty God.

As part of his ways in worship the minister tries to make minstrels of the worshipers: to see that the power of the Lord comes upon them as they sing psalms, hymns, and spiritual songs; to use sacred music to strengthen their religious ideas and feelings, release their minds from life's ordinary activities, and help create for them an otherworldly mood and atmosphere; to select music that will bring devotion to the devout, whether musically sensitive or not, and a satisfying, uplifting experience to the musical person, whether devout or not. The minister's approach through music, as a fellow minstrel and worshiper, is to let sounds of praise be heard; and "with a voice of singing," to "let everything that hath breath praise the Lord,"[20] so that the power of the Holy God may rest upon him and them.

Decently and in Order

All this has a place under the minister's ways as part of his methods, resources, and instruments. However, to return once more to our discussion at the start of this chapter, on the means by which the minister makes sure everything is done "decently and in order," a former dean of my seminary, when it was old Western Theological Seminary on Chicago's West Side, wrote a book by that title which I used for many years as a guide to conduct and usage in matters of worship, along with Percy Dearmer's *The Parson's Handbook*.

In the preface to the twelfth edition of *The Parson's Handbook*, Percy Dearmer has this to say: "When her standard [of worship] is everywhere recognizable and understood by the world, . . . the world will see that there is open to Christendom a way, free from the tottering obscurantisms of the past, which is Christian in its light of beauty as in its goal of truth."[21] The two phrases, "the light of beauty" and the "goal of truth," are especially valuable accompaniments to the minister's ways.

Whatever the minister undertakes must be done "decently and in order," never indifferently or *ad libitum*, without preparation. I'd like to write a small guide book on "The Care and Nurture of Services of Worship." The effectiveness of any service is in direct ratio to the time and care spent in preparing for it, from finding and marking the places in the Prayer Book, Hymnal, and lectern Bible and being absolutely sure of the correct order and the smooth moving from one part of the service to another, to making the transitions without awkward pauses and leading firmly in all the unison parts.

I had planned to look closely at those accompaniments of worship which indicate a minister's churchmanship, but more especially his personality and character, not found in the rubric "stage directions" often printed in red ink indicating what the Episcopal minister "shall" or "may" do as he makes his choices in conducting a service. But I'm not sure how valuable this would be, even if I went on at length about the modern liturgical movement and all the outward and visible signs of a sacramental ministry. Perhaps I should comment on clerical vagaries and my reaction to such scenes as a Roman Catholic basketball player making the sign of the cross before shooting a basket—and often missing the shot—and the extemporaneous praying of any particular Protestant minister and the wearing of a red four-in-hand necktie by an Anglican priest. But I won't, even though some of these ways in church and among ministers annoy and offend, while other bad habits merely amuse and make the minister a character. One of the mirrors of the minister's ways is found in that series of very funny cartoons labeled "Lapses in the Apses." The congregation should not notice such things—but they do—and should not be disturbed by them—but they are.

The greatest asset a minister can have is a loving, honest, observing wife who catches the little habits of gesture and speech in time to eradicate them gently and firmly. That is why celibacy can delay the reformation of a minister indefinitely; but woe betide the wife who marries a minister in order to reform him. Bachelors must find a comparable coach. My wife's keen ears and eagle eyes brought me to recognize gestures like pulling my nose, weaving in the pupit, shaking my head while reading from the lectern, using chopping gestures too frequently to emphasize a point while preaching, mixing up my grammar, using slang words and phrases, moving dangerously close to "hamming it up" at announcement time, and many other bad habits.

There is a great deal I have not covered, especially the use of drama in the chancel, one of the ways of closing the gap between the Church and the arts which is being done so successfully in Coventry Cathedral with a succession of porch plays, commissioned plays for the chancel, special music, and whatever else will win a hearing or a viewing by those who have lost contact with the Christian religion. Nor have I dealt with what the Church must be doing in order to reach the laboring man, the technicians, and other special groups who have not yet been won for the Church by the minister and his ways.

I was fascinated by the story of Bible reading in Elizabeth Goudge's novel, *Gentian Hill*. I include a mention of it here as an example of contrast in ways of doing things. Farmer Sprigg, as a nightly duty, read the Bible to his household and doggedly ploughed a straight furrow down the verses of Holy Scripture. They were without meaning for him and all the other members of his household except his foster child, Stella, who followed each furrow as a path for her imagination and became identified with the living reality of the ancient words. The minister should do everything in his power to give wings and flesh to the words of Scripture. That is why his ways of reading it are so important.

If there were space, a few hints might be added on the conduct of other services, like Baptism, and the importance of the minister's ways as he administers the services partaking of the nature of sacraments— such as holding the baby, instructing the god-parents, preparing the parents for the arrival of their first child, and the many pitfalls of wedding rehearsals and how to avoid them. There ought also to be an apologia for the continuation of Morning Prayer, with its climax of the preaching of the Word, even though Holy Communion is the "central service" in many churches now; and a discussion of the place of the sermon in Morning Prayer, which is not covered by a rubric as it is in Holy Communion. In all these things a minister's ways are most important, for they add to, or detract from, the supreme task of communicating the gospel in words and actions, depending in large measure on the winningness, the imaginativeness, the sensitiveness, the appropriateness of the minister's ways.

VIII

When He Prays

Steadfastness

In a remarkable discourse on prayer, found quite unexpectedly in J. D.
Salinger's *Franny and Zooey* (a "skimpy looking book" he calls it in the
dedication), Zooey uses two passages from the New Testament to
encourage Franny's determination to "pray without ceasing."[1] "I will
therefore that men pray every where,"[2] and "men ought always to pray,
and not to faint."[3] We could add many other biblical admonitions on
prayer, such as "And when thou prayest, thou shalt not be as the
hypocrites are: . . . when ye pray, use not vain repetitions."[4]

The insights of such writers are invaluable. Salinger has Zooey tell
Franny, "Go on with your Jesus Prayer if you want to,"[5] and Liz
Burns, in *The Late Liz*,[6] confesses, "Yes, I know that Someone is with
and within me. All I hope is He'll stick around—no, that isn't right,
He's *always* here; *I'm the one who has to stick around.* Oh, this is what
worries me! I've spent my life running from something to something
else; this won't be like that, will it? It's not God I'm suspicious of, it's
me."

On every occasion, in every set of circumstances, men must pray. "I
wonder whether Christian prayer, [which is] prayer in the light of the
Incarnation, is not be be *defined* in terms of penetration through the
world to God rather than withdrawal from the world to God."[7] In
every place, both public and private, unceasing, universal prayer is
demanded of all Christians, "lifting up holy hands, without wrath and
doubting."[8] Persistence in prayer brings results; the parable of the
importunate widow illustrates this point.[9] Keep at it. Never give up.

Communion with God

The minister is looked upon as an expert in the art of prayer and the devotional life. He prays, he speaks on prayer, he teaches others how to pray. He knows how to quaff the cup of silence, formulate his petitions in words, spoken or written, and how to make intercessions for others. He needs to formulate his thinking and his experience on this theme again and again as he grows in grace. He needs to pray for himself and for his people, knowing Him to whom he prays, and revealing Him to others. The minister makes prayer work little miracles.

But he must not hide his qualms and doubts when they come, nor his occasional spells of dryness when nothing seems to happen. He is not a saint in the generally accepted meaning of that word. He must never give evidence of impatience with those shallow brethren who cry "Lord, Lord" in order to gain God's attention just long enough to tell Him what they want Him to do, and then go on their way, forgetting to call on Him again until they have another favor to ask or demand to make. The language of prayer is often silence, being quiet in the presence of God, waiting for Him to speak; but the experience of prayer can only be described in words.

I have already confessed how hard it was for me to learn to pray, and how it was not until after my awakening that I made any progress in keeping in contact with this God to whom I had given my life through Christ. Going back to those first fumblings at prayer, I soon discovered that even with the foundation of my faith securely laid, and in spite of the vast reaches yet unexplored, I had to find an immediate way of knowing Him, keeping in touch with Him, and finding out what He had to teach me day by day.

Since I had gone beyond my old anthropomorphic concept of God as a visible Being to whom I could turn and hold converse, what was prayer to be to me now? It had always meant communion with God and talking with God, according to the Christian teaching. But how could I hold a conversation with the concept of God as Love and Light and Life? Day after day I sought the answer by reading all the passages about Jesus at prayer and trying to apply His method of holding close communion with the Father. That was the beginning, and I am still learning, some thirty years later. The waste places have often witnessed my tracks, but, in the main, the trackless wilderness and the lost road have given way to an abiding consciousness of God's Presence, not as a human being only, which limits God's influence and cramps His nature, but as the Life and Light and Love that are manifestations of His Person and His presence.

Is it so difficult to hold communion with God in these forms? Not at all. In the spring, for example, when the surge of life once again replenishes the earth, we feel the flow of God's presence as we witness the miracle of nature. We commune with God as we see life in its increase and in its beauty. The very love we have for life, the very desire we have to grow, may be a clear sign of communion with God and a consciousness of our part in the plan of His creation. God speaks in the life of the world and, as we pause in the presence of this mystery, God opens ways of still more abundance and keeps us worshiping as humble partakers of a small but wonderful part of it. Or when we witness a sunrise, especially on some high mountain, and see color and beauty restored to the earth and feel the warmth and companionship of it seep into our deepest consciousness, we hold communion with His presence and know that He is opening the world to our sight, and is keeping us in His light. The same sense of His presence is felt as we watch a cloud-streaked sunset across a moor or from some ocean beach.

God's light shines even in the darkness. He often appears in the darkness as a gleam of understanding and a ray of hope, as when we stare with awe into the night sky and open our hearts and minds to the flow of His presence. Many years after my first shy approach to some workable concept of prayer, the World Council of Churches chose as the theme for its Third Assembly "Jesus Christ the Light of the World," emphasizing the fact that Jesus Christ is not the light of a race, a class, a culture, or a period, but "He seeks out the darkness where it is to be found" and sheds the light of His presence there. Many times of darkness and despair came for me because I was interrupting contact with God by doubt and self-projection in my seeing and feeling. This has kept me at work removing the debris, even the smallest fleck of dirt in my eye which could prevent me from seeing and knowing God in His all-encompassing presence as Life and Light.

I have discovered that we are prompted by God to yearn after those who are hungry, cold, lonely, in pain, in sorrow, or who are controlled by hate and fear, and to desire for them that the great gift of God's way, as revealed in Jesus' life and light, open the way to an understanding companionship with God. "When Christians face the distress of the world in the Name of Christ and in His love, then He sends His light and the spell of sin is broken."[10] This is not the usual selfish me, demanding all and giving nothing. This is God speaking to me and through me; I am making contact for Him with others, and the essence of my existence becomes for the moment the outflowing of God's love.

By nature we belong to the human species; by God's grace we also bear His image. In the very act of reaching out to help another human being we are the bearers of His grace. Our acts of love and concern are God in action.

Daily, God becomes real in prayer, which is, insofar as I have experienced it, the delibrate opening of heart and mind to the complete unfolding and harmonizing of His divine indwelling. Prayer is the choice we make of allowing the God in us to possess us and use us. It is the awakening within to the amazing power of His life, the all of me; the growing brightness of His light, the all-glorious-within of me; and the outgoing touch of His love, the creative fellowship side of me. When I pray, which I do many times a day, it is for the will of God to find perfect response in my very sinews, wherein He dwells; it is for the strength of God to see me through; it is to declare complete dependence upon the God in me who has never yet failed me when I trusted in Him. How quickly and easily our hearts toss up a prayer as we respond to some evidence of His nearness, in such phrases as "Thee I adore," "Lord, have mercy," "Thank Thee, Lord," and "Into Thy hands."

Devotional Experiments

In many ways this early formulation of my experience with prayer is theologically off-center, but it is how I started to learn, and it did give me a satisfying way of thinking and talking about prayer to those who were as ignorant and eager as I was. I learned quite definitely, in those first days of devotional experimentation, that prayer is an attitude of heart and mind toward God, sharing the life He gave, opening it for His Word of guidance and blessing, before a day is spoiled by our human blunderings. I discovered that prayer can transform any life— miraculously—and lead us to understand and accept the fact that God is and what He is, provided we also pray for the strength to really desire what we pray for, and to live it out when it comes. I learned to pray for faith to live believing this is so, and to ask for the courage to help God answer our prayers and the prayers of others through us. I learned, too, that we can pray wherever we are, whatever we are doing, if at that moment we become consciously aware that God is near. We can prove prayer only by praying, and anybody can pray, as long as there is, first of all, the soul's sincere desire, and, second, some conception of the God to whom one prays. The moment one turns from self to that which is beyond self, he is praying.

I hesitate to suggest an order for a minister's quiet time, or to spell out a routine of prayer and meditation for him to follow. He knows the ingredients for an order of daily prayer: some act of praise, some Bible

reading, some recall of a statement of faith, some time given to meditation, some prayers for himself and his ministry, some prayers for others,
and for the mission of the Church, using the Lord's Prayer as both
guide and summary. "After this manner therefore pray ye."[11] He must
do the mixing in whatever proportion suits him best. In arriving at and
settling on his own form of daily private prayer he can give wise
guidance to his people toward the same ends.

If he be an Episcopalian, he must not forget the resources found in the
Book of Common Prayer, the services for family and private devotional
use in the back, and the lectionary in the front as a guide to Bible
reading, covering at least a four-year round of reading from the Old
Testament, the Apocrypha, and the New Testament. Each denomination
has its own guides for the devotional life of its members.

A Quiet Place

Sometimes we find that our daily quiet time of prayer and devotion
can be described as "a cup of silence," or as a "rushing mighty wind,"
or as a "torrent of praise," or as an "agonizing over another's need."
Take each variation and make the most of it, for over a year's time
almost every possible variety of prayer comes our way and keeps us on
our toes, constantly stretching us to new dimensions of knowing God's
way for us.

I still remember and cherish one summer day in the country churchyard at Stoke Poges, when I just sat and listened to the silence. There is
no more peaceful place in all the world, save Fountains Abbey, perhaps.
The ancient trees, with the wind soughing gently through them, the
weathered tombstones, the occasional sound of a bird, all flooded me
with an inner warmth usually experienced only inside a church. Here
life and death had moved side by side for centuries, and were unafraid
of each other. Here Gray wrote his famous elegy, "And all the air a
solemn stillness holds, . . . Far from the madding crowd's ignoble
strife."

In a description of a similar experience inside an English village
church, Josephine Tey tells how one of her characters "turned in at the
south porch of the church and found the great oak door still unlocked.
The light of the sunset flooded the grey vault with warmth, and the
whole building held peace as a cup holds water. She sat on a bench by
the door in a companionable silence which she shared with the figures
on the tombs, . . . the names on the walls, . . . and the slow ticking
of a clock."[12]

In a cup of silence inside a church this woman found peace, just as I did in a span of ten minutes of silence outside a church. Many times, when I have visited the ruins of ancient churches and monasteries, I have found, in such a setting of quiet association with the past, the inner meaning and reality of the phrase, "God our contemporary." He is no temporary or ancient deity. He is the God of the ages who is ever present, and is as up-to-date as tomorrow's sunrise. Troubles seem far away at such moments, when I respond within to that quiet by slowly relinquishing the reins of my life and letting God take over and run the show. The quiet always enables me to pull my scattered wits together and slow my hurried thoughts, so that I am able to find in that moment a new aspect of truth which comes without strain or manipulation. It is then I know with greater certainty that "Christ is all, and in all,"[13] in all men, in all things—and in me.

I recall that while in this mood at Stoke Poges, surrounded by the living and the dead, I was able to shed the old self—the selfish anger, wrath, fear, weariness, and all the other things carried around as excess spiritual baggage—and put on the new man, with his renewed faith, his new knowledge of God, as one forgiven and forgiving, as one reconciled and reconciling.

However, most of us must find our quiet in some commonplace environment where we live and work. How and where can we find such quiet and be still and know that God is near? A quiet place is not always available for our contemplation, and so we excuse ourselves from waiting upon God; for, we say, "there is no quiet churchyard like Stoke Poges handy, and who can meditate during the rush hours on the subway?" As a matter of fact, having had a personal experience of both Stoke Poges churchyard and the New York subways, I can bear testimony that creative waiting upon God is possible in both places.

Father John La Farge, son of the famous artist who painted the mural at the Church of the Ascension in New York City, said that subways were for contemplation as well as for sleeping, and that he intended to form a new monastic order to be called the Holy Subterranean. Contemplation is an inner discipline that can be cultivated by practice, by anyone, at any time, in any place. As a matter of record, the noise of the subway closes around one like the quiet of Stoke Poges and keeps out the extraneous petty sounds that disturb and distract. There's no law against reading good books on the subway, or closing one's eyes in meditation. It is well known that the mind can race through a lot of thinking in a few minutes of clock time. So there is always time and a place.

The end result of our time of prayer and contemplation may be taking away some kernel of scripture read and memorized, keeping it in the forefront of the mind, and letting it dissolve slowly to be absorbed throughout the day, like a lozenge on the tongue, which melts imperceptibly and is taken into our bloodstream to nourish us mysteriously.

What do people do who live in a crowded tenement, or who find themselves in a crowded charity ward in some hospital? No situation is ideal or perfect. We start where we are with what we have, for the real peace and quiet are within, and the noises of the world and the household can be shut out, if we work at it with concentration, even if we live on the noisiest city street.

We can't all visit Stoke Poges, but we can all go into a church on Sunday, and during the week if we can find one near—and open, as is the Church of the Ascension in New York City.[14] We go into a church building at odd hours during the week and at set times on Sunday, whether in private or in public worship, to find peace and quiet, to put off the old self and put on the new, to gain a new perspective in which life in the world can be seen whole and examined objectively, because we are heavily involved in every phase of it. Here the ancient past becomes one with the eternal present, and we are able to apply our Christian frame of meaning to the contemporary situation, for God is in the midst of it. Here we are able to get our thoughts straight and prepare for another week of life. Here we find a haven where we can come and get a cup of silence in order to still our fearful hearts and banish for a moment the cacophony of life. It is here, inside a church, during a service of worship or when we are alone, that we can relate the life of the wide world, and our own little personal universe, to the God we know in Jesus Christ, as we examine, confess, give thanks, and offer ourselves for His service. Whenever a threat or torment that appears to be an unbearable burden is caught and turned over to Him in the quiet of some place of worship, He accepts it and makes us able to deal with critical existential situations in His good time, and with His help we are able to bear with them in the interim.

When panic threatens to stampede us into radical and unChristian behavior, we need to seek a place where "a solemn stillness holds," and focus of our attention on Jesus Christ, unto whom all who travail and are heavy laden, confused and fearful, are bidden to come and find peace and rest in Him. "Some churches when they are empty seem deserted and stagnant, as though the world had no real need of them; others are as restfully alive as a summer river continuously flowing."[15] What makes the difference? I'm not sure, but the churches where His presence is felt the moment one enters them are apt to be those where men and women have been at prayer day and night for years, like the Church of the Ascension, "the church of the open door."

One of the greatest devotional books written by an English church-

man since William Law's *A Serious Call to a Devout and Holy Life* is
William Temple's *Readings in St. John's Gospel.* This great scholar,
who had a fantastically busy life, records how he wrote the book. He is
apologizing for his delay in answering a letter: "Life is rather hectic!
And if I get a clear half-hour I write the next bit of St. John instead of
personal letters." And frequently, late at night, he would say, "I must
do half-an-hour of my St. John . . . before I go to bed."[16] Here is a
devotional classic written in large part during those "clear half hours."

For any of us a clear half-hour each day can work miracles in our
devotional life if we set aside at least thirty minutes a day for undivided
attention to God. I am not referring to a clocked time of exactly one-
half hour, but setting apart some time each day of the week for a deeper
and more orderly consideration of the condition of our spiritual life.
There are many ways of doing it. Start by reading a devotional book, or
studying some section of the Bible, and go on from there; conduct or
attend an early service in the church, or spend a period of quiet in the
church some time during the day; work out and follow a pattern of
private devotion, in some convenient and always accessible nook, at an
hour when it is possible to be uninterruptedly alone with God.

Reading the Bible

One of the best descriptions of Bible reading, as an indispensable part
of one's devotional life, I have found anywhere is in a passage from
Elizabeth Goudge's novel, *Gentian Hill.*[17] She often shows remarkable
spiritual insight, as in this instance when she describes an English farm
family at its devotions; Father Sprigg, Mother Sprigg, Madge the
helper, and Stella the young heroine form the family circle. I quote the
scene at length because it has its best effect only when read in its entirety.
The inviolable custom of the Sprigg household was to read one chapter
aloud every evening. The only other book read on the farm was the
English Book of Common Prayer—these two and no other.

Father Sprigg, after the supper dishes were cleared away, "seated
himself, took off his spectacles, polished them on his scarlet handker-
chief, readjusted them on the beak of a nose, wetted his finger, and
slowly turned the pages until he found the pressed carnation that
marked the place. He worked solidly through from Genesis to Revelation, taking the difficult words with the same courage with which he
took a five-barred gate in the hunting field, charging as fast and furious
as his own bull through the more indelicate passages of the Old Testament, happy in the New Testament with the parables of sowing and
reaping and harvesting and with the shepherds in the fields, but work-

ing his way through the last chapters with stumbling tongue, his ears scarlet with distress, humiliated by his inability to read such a story as it should be read, but shirking nothing from the first page of the Book until the last." It is difficult to say what they made of it all. It was mainly a soporific at bedtime, one of those duties which from generation to generation fall to the master of the house and must be performed with constant patience. "But to Stella, this nightly reading was glory, enchantment, and anguish." She identified with the story and characters, and lived out the old tales of adventure, battles, murder and sudden death. "She was one of the trumpeters who blew their trumpets about the walls of Jericho. She stood with the watchman on the tower and saw the cloud of dust which stirred up in the distance and heard him cry aloud the dreadful tidings. . . . She held her breath while that splendid wicked woman, Jezebel, painted her face and tired her head and looked out of the window to greet her murderer. She mourned with David over Absolom. . . . She listened with Elijah to the still small voice. . . . She was with Daniel in the lions' den, and she wept with Ruth in the harvest fields far from home."

It was a mystery to Stella that mere words could make all this happen—all the sudden change in herself, the magical moment when her mind suddenly sparkled with wonder and her spirit leaped up inside her. "Though words could be formed into a casket to hold visions, and could be at the same time the power that liberated them, they seemed of very little use when one tried to explain to another person what it was they had set free. Words were queer things, Stella decided, to be at once so powerful and so weak."

The Bible should come alive, whether it is read in private or in the family circle; the reader should be stirred and do his best to stir the listener, as Stella was stirred. Bible reading is an essential part of one's devotional life, not as a dreaded duty to perform, without meaning or any connection with life in the world today, but as God's Word spoken to each listener—as personally and as vividly as to those ancient people who march with such vigor and certainty through the pages of the Holy Book.

Listening to God

In these clear half-hours of devotion we find time enough and quiet enough to deal with the rough, raw edges of existence, which constantly threaten to upset, slow down, or distort life and throw it off the track. Life's muddle and puzzle often stem from little things undealt with, perhaps an act of wrongdoing troubling our conscience, or the nagging insistence of regret disturbing our hearts, or a hurt or misunderstanding looming ever larger in our minds, all of which leave an inner discord which prevents us from spiritual harmony and peace. The Bible speaks to these conditions.

By holding sacred each day the rule set for a clear half-hour of devotion, we shall maintain a penitential emphasis to our Christian life and answer its call to apartness and spiritual renewal. In this brief spiritual exercise we do our bit toward saving the human race from itself, by allowing our attitudes to be straightened out, by cultivation of and reuniting with the indwelling spirit of Christ, and by seeking for the light which comes to the minds that know Him. In these clear half-hours we shall find the presence of God very near.

Yes, the language of prayer is often silence—silence and waiting—never simply an array of words nor an intermittent crying aloud of "Lord, Lord." The minister must learn to differentiate between "telling God" and "listening to God," between arranging words and phrases directed to God but meant for men's ears, and articulating the "soul's sincere desire." The words of our prayers are often not prayers at all, but "sermonettes." Over the years I have often been critical of so-called "invocations" and prayers before meetings, and "pastoral prayers" that use such homiletic phrases as "Thou knowest, Lord," and the like. Far better on such occasions to repeat some remembered classic prayer of tested form and worth.

Prayer as Dialogue

Someone has said that "man was conceived in the mind of God as the partner in a dialogue." Thank God man was not left to talk just to himself alone. The word "dialogue" does not appear in the Bible, but the word "conversation" and the phrase "talked with" do, and both refer to man's dialogue with God. Is prayer really man and God "reasoning together,"[18] as Isaiah puts it? How can we sum up the whole range of adoration, petition, penitence, intercession, thanksgiving, and meditation under this one concept of prayer? We can't, actually, but we can assume that any and all forms of prayer are variations of a give and take with God, never a monologue or talking to oneself, but always something done or said or felt in the presence of another.

Above all, God is personal. His Word is heard through and is incarnate in a Person, Jesus Christ. It is to Him and through Him we pray. It is He who speaks through His Word, His life, His laws. All prayer is creative and engaged in as a personal relationship between man and God, for God is not a "Cloud of Unknowing," as the title of an old

English devotional manual indicates, but as near as hands to feet, as close as a whisper to an ear. Our human tendency, in order to make God more concrete and real, is to form an anthropomorphic image of Him as one who walks, talks, and listens, as one who is always near, ever ready to respond. This is an attempt to express our belief that God is, and that we can be in touch with Him. We may never really become expert in prayer and the ascetic life, and we may find the daily discipline of it difficult to maintain. But what little we do learn we will be grateful for, even for so partial an understanding and experience of the vast resources of God's grace as we are able to gain.

As the minister takes on the spiritual discipline of prayer in dead earnest, he must remember that prayer is a pilgrimage, a search, a conversation with God which never ends. He must also not forget that no matter how he prays or what words he uses, or whether he uses words at all, the chief requirement is that he wants God to hear him and is willing to wait for His reply. Dialogue consists of questions and answers, an antiphonal litany and response in both directions, crying "Lord, hear our prayer, and let our cry come unto thee," then waiting to know what is next, as God hears and responds.

Our age is afraid of affections, affectations, and sentiment. That is why so much emphasis is placed on the intellect. But it is important to satisfy the soul—that hard-to-define inner being of man often referred to as "heart"—as well as the mind. There must be some logical arrangement of our prayer life, in order to enable the mind and the soul to get into communication with God. All the creative activity of the mind in meditation, for example, is simply to bring the heart-soul into converse with God.

How is the minister to make all this clear and enticing to laymen who really want to know? There are at least three ways: one, he can conduct from time to time a school of prayer, giving special attention to the budding spiritual life of each one attending; two, he can, through personal counseling over a period of time, help develop the most suitable "clear half-hour," or less to begin with, for newly converted or newly awakened individuals; or, three, he can write out spiritual prescriptions with an outline of private devotions to be tried, and can check them later, to see how they worked, revising them if need be.

Prayer is really placing every part of life in the hands of God, a complete surrender of mind, heart, and will to Him. Prayer has been defined as being, in addition to "a dialogue," "the lifting up of the mind to God,"[19] concentrating on His action upon us and others brought before Him; we are both expectant and receptive. So we come into His presence with heart and mind and soul tuned "like a guitar"— a figure used by St. Peter of Alcantara—thankful for being an instrument ready for Him to play upon, whether He wills to strike a chord or not. At least we come humbly and thankfully, renounce self-will, struggling with whatever "demons" possess us within, and doing the best we can to receive His word.

Devotional Discipline

In accepting the discipline of prayer as dialogue, and the need for a clear half-hour daily of colloquy with God, how do we go about filling up the time fruitfully? As I have said, every minister must work out his own discipline of prayer and devotion, but he must work it out without fail. I have found the early morning best for me, with no day off. First of all, I read some passage of Scripture, varying the translations from time to time. As I meditate on it I seek to expand its meaning beyond any I have yet found, pulling together the familiar and known for advance into the unknown—deepening, enriching, and relating each word and thought, more fully apprehending His love. I ask three questions on the meaning and application of what I have read—using the Sulpician method of meditation, in these very simple and sustained exercises:

Jesus before my eyes—adoration—I ask, "Lord, enlighten me, show me Thyself in this passage, and tell me what it means";

Jesus in my heart—communion—I look at myself in His presence, and seek for identification with His Word and to learn what it means for me as He emerges and His Word unfolds;

Jesus in my hands—cooperation—I say, "Just as I am, with what I have, I offer my cooperation with God's will, reorienting my life around Christ as center, and seeking to know what I can and must do for Him."

These three questions—What does it mean? What does it mean to and for me? and What must I, what can I, do about it?—lead me into prayer for direction and strength. As I read and pray familiar words, a new world comes into view, a country of wider views and greater promise; and as I ponder the meaning of His Kingdom, the goal of it all, I move beyond the frontiers of ordinary existence, beyond the range of common day-to-day experiences, and discover a new kind of world, the kingdom of the spirit which lies beyond the kingdom of the senses. It leaves me forever dissatisfied with sensations alone and demands that I move into a larger area of thought, feeling, and action.

St. Francis de Sales suggests an ideal conclusion for every time of prayer: to carry away a "spiritual nosegay," made up of insights and directions, the manifestations of God's love in forgiveness and restoration, the clear knowledge of some next step to take, and whatever else we have found of beauty and fragrance during our morning walk in the garden of devotion. This is the "little nosegay" of remembrance of our colloquy with God.[20]

Intercession

But nowhere is this partnership in a dialogue more apparent than in intercessory prayer, a conversation with God about another's need. Creative intercession is instinctive, an almost compulsory urge, and we all engage in it. How terrible it would be if there were no one to turn to and share our burdens with.

One of the earliest forms of intercession is the summary parents teach their children to use at the end of their goodnight prayers. Often it becomes a long list of all the names a child can remember, unconsciously used as a delaying action. "God bless mummy and daddy and bubby" and so on and on, ending up finally with "God bless everybody. Amen." Then follows the last sweet hug and kiss, and the child is left to sleep, secure in his sense of both God's love and his parents' love. As we grow older, we pray for others with greater understanding, expressing much more deeply our concern and sense of responsibility for them. Intercessory prayer is truly "love on its knees." It is conversation with God about the needs of others in particular situations. We are ready to have our attitudes altered and corrected, and to become personally involved, laying before God our hopes, desires, and apprehensions about those for whom we have care and concern.

In spite of the commonness and naturalness of intercessory prayer, it is still most puzzling for those who never get beyond the idea that it is simply a question of persuading a trillionaire God to do something. They approach Him as though He were some celestial Ford Foundation, using any lever of influence to get Him to act favorably.

God needs no persuading to do good for His creation. His goodness comes, not like that of some weary parent giving in to the cries of a fretful child when patience is exhausted, but in a continuing abundance of grace and mercy outpoured, when men believe and accept and do not cut themselves off by unyielding self-centeredness. We need to understand and believe that God is doing the best that can be done at the moment, that He, too, is thinking with intensity and loving concern about the person for whom we pray, and that our thoughts and desires are additional portions of grace from the will of God toward that person. Then why pray at all? Because God has made us interdependent. This is no lone-eagle universe. Although it is made up of separate parts and persons, all fit together in an interrelated whole, each one dependent in some measure on the other. The intermingling of our love and thoughts through prayer is an essential flux for the life of man. Also, we need to pray because in our aloneness we cannot help but reach out toward some wiser and greater being than ourselves—God. Life's burdens are too much for us to bear alone.

And yet God's will is limited by the laws which are essential to an orderly universe and to the people who live in it. He gave us free will to set fires, to walk over cliffs, to defy His laws; and even prayer cannot help us to escape from suffering the consequences of such foolish disobedience. Prayer cannot alter the laws of God. This is the way of His creation, even though God at times must agonize over the laws which cannot be suspended even for a moment.

Spiritual Healing

A word here about spiritual healing—discussed in more detail in Chapter 10—which is so often misunderstood. Our instinctive cry for help aims at preventing hurt and curing illness for ourselves, for our loved ones, and occasionally others. We cry "O God, don't let him die!" and "O God, make him well!" Our prayers must concentrate, however, on God's will for the person prayed for, and express our faith in Him as accomplishing better things than we can desire or pray for, now and always. When the shock of sudden death comes, or the shattering pain of a long-drawn-out illness must be watched helplessly, our faith is sorely tried, but we believe our "Why?" will have its answer at last for the sufferer and those who suffer with him. Until then we must leave it all in God's hands—believing and trusting in Him.

Miracles of healing often occur beyond our understanding. There is no sound reason why they do or do not occur. Therefore, we pray for and hold onto our loved ones as long as we can; but we always remember that death is not the end, only another beginning, which all of us must face at last. It is the time schedule which bothers most of us, for we are never ready, nor is *now* ever the accepted time from our viewpoint. There is provision for unction and laying on of hands in some churches, and the distinction is made between functional, psychosomatic, and organic disorders. Spiritual healing is more effective in functional and psychosomatic conditions than in organic.

We who persevere in prayer, and believe in Jesus' terse commands to ask, seek, knock, must want to share in the work of healing and redeeming as His instruments and helpers, and be willing to abide by His laws.

We must always pray to be made adequate for whatever we may have to do in response to our praying for others. We don't know what is best for them. We can't see the whole picture. We must not attempt to make a blueprint for God's action or try to tell Him what to do. We must lift up special situations and persons to God, then leave both in His hands, trusting Him absolutely. We cannot know exactly how God must needs answer our prayers against the long perspective of eternity; all we can do is to concentrate on our readiness to respond as He directs, manifesting empathy for the one for whom we are praying, being identified with the person and his need.

If, for example, a child is born with six fingers today, few parents would panic and think it the work of the devil or a just punishment for some sin of the father or mother. Nor would they ask for a miracle. They would consult a good doctor or surgeon, find the condition could be repaired by a rather simple operation, and get on with it. The healing is in the attitude and occurs within, and while the child's hand is made well, too, the greatest spiritual healing is in the banishment of fear, superstition, and shame—still prevalent in many parts of our world, including our own country.[21] Good Christian common sense usually prevails in such cases today, and the minister can play a key role in bringing this to pass.

While in seminary I was troubled over the condition of my spiritual life. Everyone assumed, simply because I was a candidate for the ministry, that I was a Christian and that all was well with my soul. But it wasn't. I found it hard to pray, among other things. One winter I tried to practice the spiritual exercises of St. Ignatius Loyola. I got down on my knees daily in my room at noontime, behind closed curtains, on the hard rubber-tile floor, conjuring up mental images as directed. Although I tried hard, nothing much happened, except to my knees, and after a week or so I gave it up.

It was not until several years after ordination that I discovered the cause of my spiritual poverty—a self-centered and unrepentant heart—a story I have told in considerable detail in Chapter 4. There had been practically no dialogue with anyone before. That was my problem. Only after a thoroughgoing confession to God, and the first serious fumblings at amendment of life, did I really begin to find His mercy and forgiveness and take my first giant step away from my egocentricity toward Him. Only then was I dimly aware of what I had always been reminded, that Jesus Christ came into the world to save stubborn, foolish, erring ones like me; and I soon began to pray for others, too. The road has been long since then, but that first step along it was the hardest, and even though I may never fully arrive in this life at the point where I am a perfect partner in this dialogue with God, I know it is not a question of where I stand at any given moment, but what I am moving toward— more perfect oneness with the will of God.

We cannot deal with all human needs each time we pray, but we must always be conscious of the endless opportunities for intercessions found in the daily headlines: tense places where peace is threatened—we pray for rulers and all others in authority who must make decisions; trage- dies, such as a teen-age boy knifed to death—we pray for his parents and the parents of the killer; homeless children lost and alone in war's aftermath everywhere, especially now in East Asia—we pray for gener- ous hearts and for love so great it will stop these "little wars," and preparations for another worldwide conflict; or we take the glaring needs of family, friends, and neighbors, and hold them in our prayers. Out in the world there are those who carry heavy burdens which we can help lift, inner feelings of guilt which we can help relieve, and oppres- sive sorrow we can help alleviate. And we begin through intercessory prayer to reach out to them all, lifting loved ones and others up to the goodness and love of God, awaiting His will. No day passes but what there is someone or something to pray for. At night my final prayer is to commit each loved one, and each one on my prayer list in desperate need, into God's hands.

Love Thy Neighbor

In her perceptive book *Waiting On God*,[22] Simone Weil says, "The capacity to give one's full attention to another is a very rare and difficult thing; it is almost a miracle; it *is* a miracle. Nearly all those who think they have this capacity do not possess it. Warmth of heart, impulsive- ness, pity, are not enough." It takes a lot of practice for us to reach the point where "the love of one's neighbor in all its fullness" is attained. And yet, to love one's neighbor simply means being able to say to him "What are you going through?" and really wanting to know. God asks of us a miracle of attention when we concentrate on the answer to this question. The Guild of St. Raphael is dedicated to this in many Epis- copal parishes, where its members intercede for others with intense and loving concern for their plight.

Bishop Stephen Neill recommends making a list of those we would pray for as a regular part of our daily quiet time of Bible reading, prayer, and meditation. This quiet time is the place, he said, where 90 per cent of time, energy, and concern for others must be spent. Each one must make a list of those he feels are within the realm of his own responsibility. No matter how frail or how poor or how imperfect we are, we can still break out of the narrow limits of self-concern and pray for others. Thus we express to Him our anxieties, hopes, and fears for those we love, making known our concerns and desires for others; and it is this healthy concentration on others which saves us from attempting to limit God's loving power to ourselves alone. Prayer is always dialogue.

Importance of Prayer

The toughest problem to lick in all kinds of prayer is just doing it. We are far too lazy, or too intent on other things, and this includes us all. But being with others at prayer stimulates and inspires our own praying. For example, every time we gather together for worship we engage in intercessory prayer—reflecting our private devotions, emphasizing the corporate life and action of the household of faith. Within the one Body of Christ's Church the true interests of one are also the interests of all; no one or no thing is too small or too insignificant to be included.

In worship the focus of our praying is on the world's cry, "Pray for us." One of my most vivid memories from a visit to Hungary in the summer of 1956, just before the revolution that fall, was the constant request from church people we met to pray for them. I remember especially an old lady, heavily shawled, who placed a note in my hand after a church service in Budapest; a seminary dean—shortly afterward placed under house arrest—who spoke unguardedly from his heart to a session of the Central Committee of the World Council of Churches; a Lutheran pastor at the final banquet in the Parliament building who whispered to me in broken English, "You do understand what we are going through?" Each one ended with the same request, "Pray for us." That, at least, we can always do for one another: never cease to make mention of each other in our prayers,[23] and never forget that man was conceived in the mind of God as the partner in a dialogue, a dialogue which God has already begun within each one of us.

Prayer is important. No Christian questions that statement. As William Stringfellow puts it, "Prayer is nothing you do; prayer is something you are. Prayer is not doing but being," it is being with Someone. "Prayer is about being alone in God's presence. Prayer is being *so* alone that God is the only witness to your existence. The secret of prayer is God affirming your life."[24] The minister continues to remind his people, "don't stop praying," and when the doubter asks, "What is the use of praying?" he can always reply that at least it keeps the circuits open.

IX

When He Reads

Reading Maketh a Full Man

Many famous men have written on the value of reading. Most of them were addressing, quite naturally, the general reading public. Nevertheless, their words are wise and helpful. I quote a few as illustrative. Michel de Montaigne: "When I am reading a book, whether wise or silly, it seems to me to be alive and talking to me." Edward Gibbon: "The use of reading is to aid us in thinking." Henry David Thoreau: "How many a man has dated a new era in his life from the reading of a book." Anthony Trollope: "Book love . . . is your pass to the greatest, the purest, and the most perfect pleasure that God has prepared for His creatures. It lasts when all other pleasures fade. It will support you when all other recreations are gone. It will last you until your death. It will make your hours pleasant to you as long as you live."[1]

The prophet Habakkuk also has a word on reading: "that he may run that readeth it."[2] In other words, the message must be so clearly stated that it can be read at a glance, on the run. But Habakkuk does not mean for us to eliminate difficult and subtle books from our reading list! Some time must be given to reading which is more than merely journalistic or comfortable, easy, and relaxing.

Earlier, in another context, I quoted from this passage by Henry James: "The house of fiction has the possibility of a million windows, any of which can be fashioned to open on the spreading field of the human scene by the pressure of an individual will and vision. The windows can be of any shape, either broad or balconied or slit-like and low-browed. They represent the literary form the writer chooses. Yet in themselves the windows are as nothing without the posted presence of the watcher, the consciousness of the author."[3] Books are windows, and the aim of this chapter is to look out of some of the windows, describe the view, and suggest what it tells to the posted watcher.

The minister's library is his tool chest, and his reading habits proclaim the man. He is the inheritor of a scholarly tradition, and yet he is hard put to keep up his ancient reputation as a man of superior knowledge. In the time schedule of a modern minister's life, learning often takes second place, and his reading becomes a snatch-as-snatch-can kind of rat race. The next sermon is always immediate and demanding, so there must be wide theological reading to keep his thinking up to the mark of his calling. There must be continuous contact with both secular and religious magazines for information and for keeping in touch with people, ideas, and events. There must be time for an occasional dip into a volume of poetry, classical or modern, or for reading a novel or a play. Not only must the minister be *au courant* with art and literature, but he must have on tap fresh material to keep sermons and conversations from running dry or becoming drab and colorless. It is a constant battle to be won daily, as each minister devises how he can best find the time to read for preaching, living, and keeping in sharp focus "the face" of his parish.

My professor of homiletics in seminary, George Craig Stewart, did his best to teach us good reading habits and to encourage us in finding a way to make readily available the fruits of our reading, especially for sermons. He seemed always to have a book in his hand, ready to open in a moment of leisure. Even at a dinner party or a meeting he could not resist sharing a good passage from his current "find" with his neighbor. His most prolific reading, however, was done in the summertime while vacationing in northern Michigan. He carted with him all the unread magazines accumulated over the winter, and all the books laid by which he had been unable to read. When he discovered good material in magazines, he tore out the pages and marked them for filing under one of the endless subject labels he kept for future reference, ranging from "birth control" to "love" to "zeal." That filing system may be seen today intact, in a special room at the College of Preachers, Washington, D.C.*

Not every man is a George Craig Stewart, as most of his students discovered when they tried to emulate him as a preacher. Each man must find and develop his own system for reading and keeping in mind what he reads—for its memorable content or as material suitable for illustration, analogy, pump priming, or quotation. Alas! Few of us are blessed, as George Craig Stewart was, with a photographic memory.

* 3510 Woodley Road

Reading as Background

I've always been a voracious reader; in most of my boyhood memories there linger names like Tom Swift, the Rover Boys, Horatio Alger, Jr., and countless stories of flying heroes in World War I. I grew up in an ordinary household where our stock of "literature" consisted of a few sets of books, bought from door-to-door salesmen. I remember our set of Edgar Allan Poe's stories, mainly because of the picture of a huge ape with bared fangs clutching a woman by her long hair, illustrating that thrilling story, "Murders in the Rue Morgue," which gave me nightmares. I lack the literary heritage so many ministers have as a result of their rich and privileged background, with the ability to recall bits of Shakespeare and Browning, Thackeray and the Brontës, the Iliad and the Odyssey, to say nothing of great stories and passages from the Bible. But I have an innate love of books and reading, and this urge gave me a good start toward making up for my literary lacks, which I've been doing now for many years. But I have barely touched the surface of the priceless treasures buried in the covers of volumes, new and old, which fill libraries to overflowing. One yearns for the pre-printing-press days when it was almost possible to keep up with learning and master the few manuscripts in existence. Today it is an impossible task to do more than make an earnest attempt to catch up on a few of the classics and snatch an emerging "best" among the deluge from the publishers of the world.

Selective Reading

The minister should keep his mind abreast of what men are thinking. He certainly should not compartmentalize his reading, but he would do well to keep a mental check on how balanced his reading list is. I have found it helpful to keep several kinds of reading going at once—an assortment of the following types: a stiff and demanding theological work which requires concentrated attention, such as *Nature, Man, and God* by Reinhold Niebuhr; a devotional work such as *The Cloud of Unknowing;* a selection or variation of the many "schemes" for daily Bible reading, not overlooking the lectionary in *The Book of Common Prayer.* I include a serious novel or biography, which is often, unfortunately, delayed until the summer, as when I read Sandburg's *Abraham Lincoln* and Freeman's *R. E. Lee.* I have discovered that a really good detective yarn serves for bedtime reading or while traveling—not just any murder or suspense story or mystery, but only the best, selected by author—such as one by Sayers, Tey, Gardiner, Fleming, and many others. To round out the picture, I read a bit of poetry and drama, by such authors as Dylan Thomas, Robert Frost, and Tennessee Williams; a book of history now and then, such as a good solid review of the Reformation or the Early Church; and, of course, the current best on world and national affairs. Add to this the daily paper (I never get *all* the New York *Times* read), a weekly news magazine, a denominational weekly or monthly, some interdenominational journal—*The Christian Century,* perhaps—along with a wide range of general magazines, and anyone can see how impossible it is for the minister to "keep up." We have not even mentioned other journals, house or school organs, which we are expcted to peruse. But keep up we must, and never slacken in our desire to be the prototype of the "learned" minister who "knows all" and "forgets nothing," an image which has not yet lost all of its historic luster!

To be selective in our reading and waste no time on nonessentials is in itself no mean accomplishment—even though the *Readers' Digest* is kept handy for a free moment or two of light entertainment. We are the watchdogs of our own time and the guardians of our precious eyesight. I remember from childhood the often repeated admonition to have the light coming over my left or right shoulder when reading, and to sit so that the light would never be glaring into my eyes. I was taught that lamps should be sufficiently strong and well shaded to make reading easy on the eyes.

I find it possible to read on streetcars, trains, planes, ferries, and subways, but not busses, which vibrate too much, except when they make stops. Incidentally, when reading or writing on a train I use a pillow to absorb the vibration. When a reader is interested in the subject matter of his book, nothing will disturb him—neither noise nor swaying coaches nor people crowding in, even when some of them lean over him to catch a glimpse of what he is reading. There is always a way to find time to read when there is a will to do it.

As we read we must not be like a bomber refueling at high altitude from a fueling plane, just filling our mind with "stuff," not knowing what we read. During the filling-up process we must always be concentrating, always alert, and relate and remember whatever is taken in. As an aid to remembering, passages may be marked for later use. When no pencil is handy, I often mark a passage lightly by using my thumbnail to make an indentation, which is easily found if soon returned to. In time the mark smooths out again and is hard to discover, so no harm is done to the page. But a minister should always have a pencil handy, even in the pocket of his cassock or robe during a service of worship, ready to jot down any idea which awakens in his mind, so that it will not slip away and be lost beyond recall. Some find it helpful to use a pencil for underscoring, marking alongside, or writing in words and symbols in the margin of their own books, whatever comments they desire. George Craig Stewart taught us to index subjects for reference on a blank page in the back of the book as we read along. However, for really keeping in mind a thought or a line of argument or a story, it should be read aloud, or told aloud, to another, as soon as possible after reading. I find this most difficult, but my wife has been working hard to teach me the value of this immediate sharing for remembering. In your own books you can "circle" or "thumbnail" or "dog-ear," but with borrowed books whatever method is used must not mar the pages, and any trace of markings must be removed before returning.

How hard it is to keep up with books borrowed or loaned. If one procrastinates in returning a book, soon it is "lost" among the countless others in stacks and on shelves. No one ever intentionally "loses" a book, even one which is out-of-print and a sore temptation. But we are apt to forget, and libraries dwindle in consequence. The minister consoles himself for books he has loaned which have not been returned, for they may be doing a missionary or pastoral task, and must be credited to the "hazard" of his calling. His most used "tools," however, are kept close at hand and never loaned. One such tool is a reference Bible given to me by my mother-in-law, which she bought from an itinerant book peddler. For a long while I disdained to consult it, until one day I thumbed through it. From that day to this it has been my constant companion and greatest treasure.[4]

Reading in Spare Moments

I try never to be without a book handy (this may be so I won't always have to think or converse), waiting to be picked up and read, and always to have some "work in progress." I try to use to advantage the odd moments of travel. Even while calling in New York City by bus or subway or taxi, I found that I could read at least one book a week, preferably a small, slender volume that fitted into my pocket—this made the paperbacks very useful. Also, when one drives a car, outside the situation peculiar to New York, there are opportunities for snatching a bit of reading time during waits or rest periods, even in homes while waiting for your host or hostess to appear or in business offices. On longer journeys by plane or train, I keep my reading trilogy going: a solid, difficult book on theology or something else; a sound, but not too demanding book of fact or fiction; and some light reading for relaxing a tired mind. I read in round-robin fashion, one chapter or so in each book at a time, with a brief break in between for stretching. I like riding on trains and deplore the drastic changes being made in railroads, for I get so much more reading of all kinds done traveling this way. Magazines I leave at home, unless I happen to get my copy of *Time* to take with me on the journey.

How does a minister select, from the mass of every kind of material pouring from the presses, to give a proper balance to his reading fare? This problem he must solve both for his own sake and in order to give advice to his people on how to fit in recommended reading of devotional, study, and other religious material, as part of a parish or personal program of development. He must find the answer both professionally and personally. A minister must guard against limiting his reading to material for his preaching, speaking, and counseling. All reading inevitably, in some measure, nurtures and forms one's life: helps mental and spiritual growth, shapes attitudes and convictions, expands horizons, and broadens knowledge. And all reading should have this advice as a slogan: "read, mark, learn, and inwardly digest."[5]

Selection

There are many guides to selection from the wide-ranging choice of literature constantly before the minister. Almost every magazine, paper, mailing piece, and the like, which he scans can give him clues to his desires and needs. The book reviews, of course, usually succeed in bringing to the fore the cream of the crop, although they overlook an occasional "sleeper" which becomes a best seller, like Bishop Robinson's explosive *Honest to God*.[6] We often judge the value of a book by our faith in the reviewer, who is "almighty" and can "make" or "break" a new book, as the Broadway critic can determine the future of a play. I shall always believe a reviewer of one of my earliest books killed it as a successful confirmation manual by thoroughly misunderstanding one chapter. He accused me of advocating the dismissal of the creeds as ancient appendages, when all I said was that we should see if we could not revise the language of the creeds to say the same things in words more understandable and relevant today. This is a rationalization, perhaps, as to why my book did not become a best seller.

Another good source for discovering new books is the recommendation of persons whose judgment we respect, who enthusiastically plug a book they have read—"You simply must read so and so." If a good case is made for the book, it should be given a chance to prove itself. However, books, like sermons, strike people differently; what is one man's joy, excitement, and nourishment may be another man's utter boredom and waste of time. But we can afford an occasional gamble in the hope of finding hidden treasure. In this way, and also from browsing, we often discover something new to recommend from the pulpit and in calling.

No matter how hard we try, there is simply not enough time to squeeze in all we want to read during at least nine months of the minister's round-the-clock ministry. Therefore all through the busy months of fall and winter, the minister must be on the lookout for good books with which he plans to fill in the many gaps in his knowledge come summer.[7]

Vacation periods vary, but most ministers get one month, with an occasional summer conference thrown in. It is only the privileged few who can take two months or more. Therefore it is all the more important to squeeze in all the reading possible during the winter and not leave too much for the short, quickly passing summer. In one hammock period under a tree I spent a whole month at Summer Rest, Virginia, reading Tolstoy's *War and Peace*. At least, for most ministers, the pace slows a bit after Easter and makes "leisure" seem more realizable than it does at the "height of the season."

In one period of my ministry I was forced to read widely and generally from the current batch of novels and other books in the news and on the best-seller list, in order to select one book each month and know it thoroughly, for I had agreed to give a monthly book review, sponsored by the business women of the parish, to raise money for the new organ fund. This was exceedingly good for me and, fortunately, came early in my ministry when I had considerably more time to play with than ever again.

All books are grist for the mill of public utterance, but there is demanded from the reviewer some insight as to the worth of the individual book he has read, an evaluation of the human beings involved in it, and how it all relates to the local and world scene. One example is a book I reviewed back in 1938 in Atlanta, at the Church of the Epiphany, which was a smash success and moved the organ fund along famously. I selected and read *Mein Kampf* largely because Dorothy Thompson was urging all leaders to take Adolf Hitler seriously and to look upon the reckless inflammatory book as the Nazi Bible, a blueprint for the future. It caused quite a furor, because members of the local German-American Bund appeared in force, sat in the front row, and took down everything I said. One of my members, a professor at

Georgia Tech, took me aside afterward, much disturbed, for, as he had recently resigned from the Bund because of its pro-Hitler tendencies, he knew what was going on. He said all my remarks would be reported to Berlin, and I would undoubtedly be marked for arrest or liquidation on "Der Tag." Few of my reviews attracted so many avid listeners, stirred up so much excitement, or made so much money.

Through this reviewing commitment I did get a lot of valuable reading done, and trained myself to do more than I ever thought possible before. It is in reading and recognizing the value of such books as *Mein Kampf*, that the minister can render a great service to his people and his community. Reading is for relating to living, as well as for deepening and illuminating the minister's sermons.

A minister whose wife is an avid and discriminating reader is doubly blessed, for his range of reading, especially in the field of general books and magazines, is enormously increased. Many a gem has been turned up for me by my wife in some magazine which could never have been unearthed in my normal round of reading. I am deeply indebted to her, for she reads with discernment, discrimination, and understanding, and remembers what she reads and where she read it. She has found many "just-right" quotations and illustrations, and has sharpened my own insight by articles she has literally forced me to read under the guise of "so we can discuss them together," and the dimensions of a sermon have often been stretched because of some comment she has made on the subject or the text. I never seem to catch up on the marked stacks of newspaper clippings, magazines, and books she carefully hoards for me, but I can usually depend on her to remember and pinpoint vague references and illustrations which come to mind, especially in novels and plays.

Scholarly Pursuits

One of the major problems for the twentieth-century minister is how to carry on any kind of serious study or scholarly work, which used to be so large a part of the minister's life. We can't all pretend to be scholars, or even scholarly, nevertheless there must be some time given to serious study. I find this easiest to arrange when a deadline is set, at least mentally, for, say, a series of lectures in the parish on "St. Paul's Letters to the Corinthians," or a series of sermons on "The Prophets and Twentieth Century Man," planned, scheduled, and advertised well in advance. I remember reading, during one summer vacation, Frederick W. Robertson's lectures on Corinthians—given before his Brighton

parish—as the beginning of preparation for a winter study series in my
own parish on the same subject. He gave two series of lectures on
Corinthians while at Brighton. He spent hours in preparation, consulted
current commentaries, and read both epistles in the Greek for whatever
fresh insight the original language could give. He also spent long
devotional periods in meditation on the several parts, seeking for a
relevant word to speak to his people and his day. Just as he slanted his
lectures toward the issues of his day, so I did mine.

In our day there is a spate of materials at hand on the various aspects
of critical issues such as nuclear war, labor, the political far right and
civil rights. This last is to the fore in every section of the country; the
innumerable facets of the controversy flash from all parts of the nation,
north and south. The minister who tackles it—and he cannot ignore it
for long—will know his own denomination's position, will dig deep in
an attempt to understand all sides of the question. He will read James
Baldwin's novels and plays, perhaps, and such perceptive books as Sarah
Patton Boyle's *The Desegregated Heart*.[8]

Many of these issues were raised in my lectures on Corinthians, for St.
Paul really "covers the waterfront" in these two epistles. I pursued my
studies by consulting all the commentaries in my library, including *The
Interpreter's Bible,* which is used by thousands of ministers today as the
source of their inspiration in lectures and sermons—I find it should be
balanced by other commentaries with perhaps a bit more depth. My
Greek was never very fluent, but I turn to it from time to time and find
an occasional new vista opening in a word or a phrase not quite clear in
any of the English translations.

I have several favorite modern translations, in the following order of
preference: Goodspeed and Smith, the Revised Standard Version, and
the New English Bible. But a number of others are also good, especially
of the New Testament. The Apocrypha in a modern translation is
available in the RSV, made possible by profits from the huge sale of the
RSV of the Old and New Testaments, which has sold in the millions.
With such excellent translations at hand, I find it less and less necessary
to consult my Greek New Testament. This may seem a pity to many, for
the minister has always been fluent—at least so people have imagined—
in Greek, Hebrew, and Latin, and at home in the classics.

A most important point must be made about the lecture series: do not
attempt a program of study which is too ambitious and for which there
is too little time. And by all means start preparing far enough in
advance to have the subject well in hand by the time the lectures are
scheduled to be given. A detailed outline should be drawn up before the
decision is made to advertise the proposed series, and the minister must
be absolutely sure of the material to be covered and the number of

lectures to be given, and schedule enough time to get them in shape. The lectures, when formal, should be given in a place large enough, but not too large, to accommodate the estimated attendance. Far better to overflow a small room than to fill but sparsely a large one. To maintain some semblance of the scholarly image the minister should wear his academic regalia, his gown and hood, if he is sure the content comes up to the outward show.

I recall my first lecture series in my first parish, a general survey course on the Bible, which I called "The Modern Approach to the Bible." It was a job well and thoroughly done, based on my seminary courses, but the small town was not ready for it. I was labeled as a "destroyer of the faith." Each week's lecture was covered in the local paper and caused quite a stir, but my own congregation was with me, save one who couldn't get over his cherished belief that the whale really swallowed Jonah. This course proved to be a backlog for future use, which I consulted many times and used in two other parishes with minor changes. The careful preparation of lectures is also a valuable discipline for material that is potentially publishable. While not many lecture series get into book form, the polish and effort expended is never wasted. Every minister has to get as much "mileage" out of his labors as he can, and repetition can be a useful law of learning when the same material is used in different forms even in the same parish—as lecture series, as quarry material for sermons and addresses, as kernels for essays, papers, and articles, and, maybe, a book.

One of the greatest disappointments the people of a parish can have in their minister is to be led to expect so much of his lecture series and get so little, because what he says does not live up to their expectations. They often expect too much, but if the result is something superficial and largely unsuccessful for a thinking audience, any lecture series will leave a bad memory, small attendance records, and very little hope of any future series succeeding. No minister can really excuse himself by using the old crutch "too busy." Lectures should never be undertaken at all unless they are carefully prepared and open up new territory for all who hear them. Far better to invite in someone who is prepared to do the job.

Finding the Answers

It is almost trite to remind the minister that out of his dealing with his own needs arises the capacity to help others. And we find the current personal need of the moment the one we are best equipped to handle. Much of the minister's time is given to reading for answers he must find for those in need, and for comments on the vast questions of his day. Every minister must have at his command reading references for almost every kind of pastoral need, from sorrow to alcoholism. He must become expert in the many possible uses of the tract or pamphlet or paperback ministry, provided in such variety today, such as the Forward Movement Publications, various paperback series, books like *The Late Liz,* and many more. There is nothing more disillusioning than a minister who does not know the answer to a question or who does not know where to find the answer.

One of the saddest scenes I can remember in a recent motion picture was in *Whistle Down the Wind.* The scene is a conversation that Kathy, played by Hayley Mills, has with the vicar in a local tearoom. The children, Kathy and Charles, her younger brother, thought a murderer hiding in their barn was Jesus. They had fed him and not told anyone he was there. It was a secret. Charles had given him his sick kitten, named Spider, to keep and make well. But the kitten had died. This troubled the youngsters, and Kathy wanted to know from the vicar why Jesus let people and animals die. The vicar fumbled when he sought to come up with the answer, as we all might at the suddenness and depth of the question. The little boy watched Kathy and the vicar from another table, wide-eyed, and listened intently as he sucked his soda through a straw. But the vicar was preoccupied with his own pet project of catching the young vandals who had been destroying church property, and held forth with great emotion on this theme as he skirted the more difficult question posed by Kathy, and left it unanswered. The poignant ending of the scene is what Charles says to Kathy as they leave the tearoom. "He doesn't know, does he!" There are always questions of great moment to those who ask them or who do not put them in words, and the minister must be alert and prepared to find and articulate the answers, not only in preaching and teaching, but in casual opportunities like the one the vicar missed in the tearoom with the puzzled children.

Such questions as "Why do innocent men suffer?" are never finally answered, for we cannot know the complete answer. We can only make guesses and surmises based on our knowledge of a good God, and try to give as much hope and comfort as possible by using the insights and glimpses God has given to those who have pondered this question deeply and trusted Him beyond knowing. Both novels and plays give us aid, as we look to men of stature who have suffered and have delineated their near answers as best they could, leaving the ultimate and final answer up to God Himself in some future time.

One of the most moving examples of this unanswered question was experienced one evening several years ago when my wife and I saw

Archibald MacLeish's play, *J.B.* As the play unfolded there was a growing concern over how the author would come out in wrestling with the
ancient theme of the Book of Job. I heard, and grasped at, each clear,
poetic word as it came from the actors' lips, searching for every crumb
of hope, every glimmer of light, every shadow of an answer. I was so
thoroughly involved in the mood of the play that at intermission I hated
to look at those nearest me; I did not want to see the questioning of
their hearts and minds reflected in their eyes, for they expected to find in
the play some sort of an answer to the ancient question of innocent
suffering. All I wanted at the moment was to marshal from the play any
answer possible to ease the aching hearts of those around me, there and
everywhere. The play resumed after the intermission, and the tragedy
deepened. It was only in the final scene, after sharing all evening the
agony of the characters, that there was something—not much, but
something. Sarah, the wife, after walking out on J.B., comes back after
the world is destroyed, because of her love for him. She had thought
"there was a way away," but she returns with a forsythia twig she has
found "growing in the ashes" of the world's destruction. All is in ruins.
It's cold; it's dark; even God seems far away. But Sarah is able to say to
her husband, "Blow on the coal of your heart, and we'll know, . . .
we'll know."⁹

The play overwhelmed me with pity, terror, and reverence for the
human race, and set me thinking once again on this ancient theme of
innocent suffering, so full of meaning for us. That is why the minister
must forever follow the admonition and promise, "search and you will
find," for "the one who is searching will always find," not everything
he searches for, but sufficient truth, light, faith, and understanding to
live by. We cannot know everything, but we must find what can be
found and know what can be known, and take the rest on faith.

In my search I was compelled to read the play when it came out in
book form, and I was also forced to reread the Book of Job and ponder
once again this great "lyrical meditation." The Book of Job is closet
drama of the highest order, that is, not written for acting but for
reading; even more than this, it is a poem of faith. The poet who wrote
the main body of the Book of Job, a giant in his day, took an ancient
folktale of a suffering servant of God, which captured his imagination,
and expanded it. As he retold the story he was inspired to ask such
questions as these: Who is God? What is man? What does God require
of man? What is the meaning of human life? Why do the righteous
suffer? The mighty Book of Job is a collection of poems dealing with
the meaning of life, and the unknown author uses the problem of
undeserved suffering for the pursuit of a broader and higher purpose. A

much more fundamental issue was at stake for Judeans of the sixth century B.C., whose world had crumbled under their feet, that is, What is the meaning of faith? There are no abstractions in the Book of Job. It contains the very stuff of life, delineated sharply and compellingly, and demands concentrated reading and pondering to sift out its message for us today.

The story is familiar to every minister, that is, the saga of a man who is not guilty of any offense and who, when swept by the most extraordinary kind of adversity, demonstrates the most uncommon integrity. Through all his travail Job refuses to "curse God, and die,"[10] but clings to his belief in a just and omnipotent deity. Job's physical pain is not as important as his mental anguish over what he does not know, what does not fit into his frame of meaning for his life. Man's ignorance about God and the great unanswered whys of life are spiritual torture much harder to endure than physical and moral grappling with undeserved evil.

We could go on and on about Job and J.B., but the point I am making is that a play or a novel can create a climate in which such subjects as innocent suffering will be discussed widely by everyone, and the minister is forced to come to grips with answers. Archibald MacLeish chose the Book of Job as the ancient structure on which to build his play, because it was the only one on which our modern history would fit, so he tells us, in dealing with a question which was too large for him, but which would not leave him alone. Job's search, like ours, was to find some meaning in his afflictions. Job wanted justice from God and His universe. Our age is haunted and driven by the need to know. But Job is brought, not to know, but to see that "man can embody truth but he cannot know it." He can live his deepest truth but cannot speak it. Both J.B. and Job affirm the worth of life, its wonder and beauty, when they accept life back in order to live in love. In the end they get no justice, only love, but on this basis life begins again. The touch of the forsythia twig in the finale of *J.B.* is the note of resurrection and continuing life. Every minister has seen this happen over and over with people who think there is nothing left to live for, but in spite of all, life goes on. The Christian view is almost like these two notices which appeared side by side in a London newspaper in wartime—"Blackout 6:37"—"Moon rises 6:38."

Many of life's questions will go unanswered, but the sharp hard lines of them will be less hard and less sharp as men move on in faith, aware of and believing in their God-given capacity to suffer, and in some measure to understand. Men need to live at their highest and best, where suffering and pain have a real part to play. Life must be lived as it comes, with courage, strength, and patience, all God-given. Paul Tillich's words, "The Courage to Be," mean for us the courage to accept what comes, in faith, remembering that innocence has nothing to do with suffering, and that Christianity has never guaranteed freedom from suffering.

Time Out for Contemplation

This is only one example of the reading demanded of the minister as he copes with life and its problems *in extenso* and *ad infinitum*. *J.B.* makes easy reading, for as poetry it is as clear as journalism, moving swiftly, yet with a pace slow enough for its meaning to sink in and linger for contemplation. "He who runs may read," but he who is able to settle quietly with a good book in the undisturbed sanctity of his study will profit far more from his reading, which can both consciously and unconsciously sharpen his own thoughts and modes of expression, and lead him to ever larger dimensions of thought and feeling.

I am reminded again of the child Stella in *Gentian Hill,* who identified completely with the young hero of the story, Zachary, as he appeared at the Sprigg farm looking like a tramp. Elizabeth Goudge says there was such empathy that "she *was* Zachary, hungry and thin, his feet wrapped in bloodstained rags. She was both of them coming from unknown darkness, going back to darkness again."[11] She also identified with Old Sol who ploughed the fields and sang, and who, at times when he needed self-expression, got out his "bull-roarer," made of a bit of string and a piece of wood, which gave out an awful roar when he whirled it rapidly above his head. "It was the medium through which he expressed deep feeling. When another man would have played a fiddle or written a poem, Sol swung his bull-roarer."[12]

In whatever the minister reads, he will be on the alert for insights leading to answers, especially to such painful questions as those posed by the play *J.B.* When "the wit won't burn and the wet soul smoulders,"[13] men find it very disturbing to face such dilemmas as God's goodness, mercy, and all-powerfulness as opposed to the frightful things which happen to men on earth. Christians face such questions quietly and confidently, for they believe "God is there, too, in the desperation,"[14] and concentrate on the positive side, making both wit and soul burn with a flame of understanding.

It is from his reading, pondering, and discussing that the minister keeps hold of his basic assumptions of the Christain faith, sharpens their expression, and enriches them. After every such experience as seeing *J.B.* or reading *Job,* he runs over his assumptions once more and checks them against the insight and mood of the experience of such

moments, to see if they hold up. After seeing and reading *J.B.*, I jotted
down the following summary: God is good, for He cannot be less than
the best insights of His highest creatures, and does not deliberately will
or send suffering and evil; God is all-powerful, but limited by the laws
of His own creation; God made man to live obedient to the laws of life
in harmony with the universe; God also gave man the power of choice,
that is, free will, to obey or disobey His laws; God wills goodness, but
allows the opposite, for men are not automatons; God does not inter-
vene or alter His laws or control men's actions; God created man to
work together with Him and ever seeks to win men's hearts and minds;
God's will is to replace such human failures as ignorance with knowledge, willfulness with wisdom, folly with integrity, sinfulness with
holiness, rebellion with obedience, discouragement with faith. It is such
basic assumptions that form the sword of belief we use in the battle of
life, and which are the hope we hold to when the clouds form and
storms approach in fury. They are our hitching posts in the universe.

Life's journey takes us often through a belt of fog or a dark tunnel,
but we are not anxious, for we stand with Paul in his mighty declara-
tion: "[Nothing] shall be able to separate us from the love of God,
which is in Christ Jesus our Lord."[15]

What really matters is what happens *in* us, not *to* us; that is, our
reaction to life's circumstances, and how we face the conditions of
existence; whether we can hold onto our faith in a good God or not,
and keep on saying "yes" to Him. God would protect us against much
suffering, but He cannot store us safely away any more than we can our
children. He can only label the dangers and point out the best way for
us to follow or not as *we* choose. We are everlastingly exposed to errant
ideas. We must learn many things, most of them through suffering.
Both suffering and pain are essential for life, but the most effective
weapon against the wrong attitude toward innocent suffering is faith,
which is a glorious guess based on all that is already known. Even the
unknown quantity of death becomes fulfillment, not calamity, when
each one has hope of eventual oneness with God, and can declare with
Job, "I know that my Redeemer liveth, . . . whom I shall see for
myself."[16]

Discoveries Shared

A minister must always be alert to find books that speak to human
need, as well as books to help him preach sermons, and be able to
recommend them or, better still, to have copies on hand ready to give or

lend to the needy; later, the contents and application may be discussed. Reading for pastoral use is most important, and a wide knowledge of available books and pamphlets is an essential part of the pastor-minister's everyday task. Making such discoveries known through notices and reviews in the parish bulletin, or displaying them in the parish book mart or library, or mentioning them from the chancel steps on a Sunday morning, can be very helpful. For example, in the spring I have always tried to make available the best books on premarital instruction for the current crop of brides and grooms, and to stress particularly anything new or old which would underscore the Christian approach to marriage.[17]

This chapter draws to a close, with the solemn emphasis reiterated of the minister's need for reading widely and continuously for preaching, helping, and living.

X

When He Calls

The Doorbell Ministry

In his book, *Return to Christianity,* Nels Ferré said "We may have to have live cells of Christian community springing up like oases within our parched Churches."[1] He was simply reaffirming our Lord's words, "For where two or three are gathered together in my name, there am I in the midst of them."[2] In this statement is found the core of the minister's calling ministry as proclaimed by Isaiah. "The Spirit of the Lord God is upon me; . . . he hath sent me to heal the brokenhearted, to preach the . . . recovering of sight to the blind, to set at liberty them that are bruised."[3] Here is a statement of Isaiah's consciousness of his mission to the world: to spread the word of God that sets men's minds and spirits free, redeems their suffering, and makes the blind see. The prophet is appointed to proclaim God's coming to all men, in every age, and in every area of life; and so is the minister.

People are the minister's business, and "pastor" is his other name. Therefore, he must look after the flock in the sheepfold, in the grazing fields, and in the wild lost places. More "sheep" are in the fields and the lost places than in the fold, and every good pastor-minister must go where the people are to be found. This means seeking them out, not content with seeing only those who come by appointment to his study. Often, the big-city minister thinks "routine" calling is superfluous and not worth his precious time. I heartily disagree. One of the most important facets of the minister's "business" with people is the doorbell ringing ministry—everlasting calling—and the minister can never afford to forget it. No minister called to a parish ministry is exempt from it, although he'll find there are a thousand excuses ready at hand every day for *not* calling. But usually, deep inside him there is the conviction that something vital is lacking in his ministry when he yields to such temptation. Unless the pastor knows his flock and their everyday concerns, and he is known by them, how can he minister to them or speak God's word relevantly to them? He can't. There are no ivory towers left for the minister to escape to. He is in the mainstream of the world's life—and life means people.

One of the gravest blindspots in a minister's life is the danger of allowing some people to remain outside his immediate sphere of concern. No pastor can really lead his sheep unless he stands side by side with them and actually knows and feels what they are going through. This kind of identification has been lacking, thus far, between white and Negro Americans. Reading *The Desegregated Heart*[4] gives the reason why, and opens the way for the minister to find his bewildered way to understanding at last. The pastor is sensitive to only one thing, the needs, feelings, attitudes, and problems of the human heart.

Some may wonder why just plain calling could be considered important enough to include in this book about the minister. The answer is: simply because of what can happen during, or as the result of, his visit—what he writes on a card and leaves behind when no one is at home; what he learns and records in his file about a person or a family; what he writes back in his letters about some point arising during his visit; or what he produces as welcome literature for newcomers in his parish and neighborhood to win them to his flock. These are all evidences that he cares and has a concern for people, the "little" people, the "important" people, the "saved" as well as the "lost."

It takes some ministers a long time to forsake their dignity and strike out in all directions—not playing hop, skip, and jump geographically, racially, or socially, but ending up ministering equally to all. It was not until my wife read a James Baldwin novel, and called my attention to the kind of people he saw and knew within my own parish bounds, that I realized how blind and neglectful I had been. It takes a few ministers like Mal Boyd, who are at home with those who frequent saloons and Greenwich Village *avant garde* coffee houses, to make us all realize we need to recapture the gospel approach to saints and sinners alike.

Calling will always present a problem and be a challenge to the city minister who finds it difficult to visit the haunts and dives of the lower strata of the city's life, but he must wrestle with the problem and find a way within the geographical confines of his parish at least, to reach out and touch those whom he is privileged to serve. The solution is not to move the parish to where the "better" people are, but to adapt the ministry of the parish to the people who are there under the shadow of its wings—the down-and-out and the up-and-coming, and those in-between.

Ringing doorbells is an important part of the daily life of every minister-pastor. I was inspired early in my ministry by George A. Buttrick, then minister at the Madison Avenue Presbyterian Church in New York City, who declared he must make at least a thousand calls a year in order to keep in contact with his people. I've proved to myself the truth of this in every parish where I've served. There is no way to rationalize successfully the non-calling minister's life.

But another form of keeping in contact, a twin to doorbell ringing, is telephone-bell ringing; no matter how limited the income, almost everyone has a telephone. I've discovered, much too late in my ministry, that a telephone call is a worthy accompaniment to ringing doorbells, and takes much less time. I began some years ago, largely because of frustration over finding so few people at home, to call my parishioners by telephone, beginning late on a Saturday morning. I could average about twenty-five calls an hour. The conversation was often no more than a few words of greeting, to let people know I was thinking about them and really wanted to know how they were. This often led to making a definite date to get together, for lunch or at their home or in my study at some convenient hour. People in large cities need to know there are those who care about them, and even a telephone call can do the job, or serve as an opening wedge.

Every minister must take seriously his responsibility for pastoral calling, and be grateful for any hints or aids that can help him change doorbell-pushing from a routine chore into the open door of opportunity. The suggestions in this chapter have been tested many times over the years but of course each minister has to find his own technique for the particular *milieu* of his parish.

The Importance of Calling

No less a person than one of the Presiding Bishops of the Protestant Episcopal Church placed pastoral calling high on the minister's priority list. This is what he wrote about his own experience in ringing doorbells. He said, "I am told that times have changed and what with the modern tempo of life and the new housing conditions, this home visiting is impractical. I do not believe this for a moment. It is a rationalization of the unwillingness of many to undertake an apparently pedestrian task. I realize that there is great pressure upon the clergyman of today to have the institution of the parish move forward in all of its organizations and activities. However, in the past twenty years I have travelled throughout the breadth of our church and everywhere I have heard the same complaint from the laity that they do not see their clergymen in their homes. It apparently makes no difference whether the parish is large or small.* If I were to suggest a means of spiritual revival in the Church, it would not be the creation of new organizations or slogans, but having every minister call every day, resolutely and persistently. I belong to an older generation, but it strikes me that many ministers are too concerned with themselves. Perhaps there is excessive introspection encouraged in our seminaries. To find his life, the best thing any minister can do is to lose it in the lives of his people. This is not done by uttering broad generalities about sheep, but by knowing well each of his own flock."[5]

Bishop Sherrill's penetrating observation on excessive introspection applies to a great many ministers today. Many of us are too concerned with ourselves; we peer too intently, too often, and too lengthily at the inner condition of our own lives. The minister's primary task is out in the parish and the world where other people are. Certainly, I would never discourage frequent times of devotion and regular intervals of self-examination, but most of the time the minister is so busy with people that he is lost in their troubles rather than his own.

There are too many weary and frustrated ministers with that "poor me" feeling. There's simply no room for feeling sorry for oneself in the ministry. All I can say to discouraged ministers, who have given up too easily and feel put upon for no reason at all, is that God has called us to do a job for Him, and has given us the courage to be His witnesses in the world. There is no time for moaning, complaining, and getting into trouble, if the minister is about God's business. He is under orders and under discipline and, to recall Churchill's words, he must like what he has to do. The minister, as are all Christians, is called on to lose his life in a cause in order to find it has value and meaning; and his freedom is measured by the goals to which he surrenders himself—one of which is the spread of His kingdom.

There are many variations on this calling theme. Each minister must set up his own priorities and find his own way of handling pastoral calls, based on his experience in the local situation, which can vary vastly from parish to parish and from city to city, to say nothing of the incredible differences between regions—Chicago versus Jackson, Missi-

---

* In my little country parish of Holy Trinity, Dickinson, Texas, I called on every family once a month; in drastic contrast was my large city parish of the Church of the Ascension in New York City, where I found it a mad scramble to see my parishioners in their homes more than once every few years, except the sick, the newcomers, those in some kind of trouble or sorrow, and random social contacts.

ssippi, for example. In one sense every situation is a "peculiar" one, and calling techniques must be flexible. Let us look first at some of the varieties of calling which confront the minister in the parish. He will need to consider the best ways of handling the following categories of calls.

He must see newcomers without delay—to get acquainted, to make them welcome, and to get facts for his "dossier" on them. He can get all the necessary data in about fifteen minutes, including full names, addresses, telephone numbers for home and business, church affiliations, what they do for a living, family conditions, hobbies, ailments, fears, and whatever will give insight into what the minister can do for each individual or family.

He must find ways of knowing and keeping in touch with each name on the parish list, an almost impossible but truly essential task, for a minister knows and cares for everyone related in any way to his parish. There are many ways of locating those who move without leaving a forwarding address; any good parish secretary can supply suggestions.

He must see absentees from church services and Sunday School, to show concern and find out the reason for their absence. Telphone calls may do the trick here, but tact must be exercised by the one who does the telephoning or the calling, whether teacher, assistant, or the rector himself.

He must see shut-ins to cheer and bless them in their loneliness. This involves the knowledge of how to use one's assistant's and other callers' time. However, the lonely older person needs attention from the rector himself, as well as other callers, and an occasional remembrance, such as a potted plant or a letter, or a card while on vacation, when the rector cannot call in person.

He must see those in physical distress requiring attention under the category of "social service." Funds for this are always needed, and he must know when to "ante up," how much and for how long, which is always a difficult problem, for the minister's discretionary fund is not unlimited, and many such demands made on it may be unjustified by the actual circumstances. Usually church funds are for emergency interim relief only, until something permanent can be worked out. In a few instances granting a small monthly subsidy helps make ends meet and preserves dignity.

He sees those who are sick, both in hospitals and in nursing homes, with "healing" always to the fore. He must give priority to this calling on the ill, with special reference to their attitudes, giving them the impression that he has endless time at their disposal. He must know each one's condition medically and spiritually; he must know, or sense, when and when not to pray aloud, when to apply the healing touch of his hands, what to do with his coat, the correct timing of his visit in the hospital routine. When death is near, he must know how to deal with the relatives and with the patient. He must be intent on learning these and a host of other things.

The minister must find time to visit the sick and those in need. He must know their real condition promptly and keep up with them from crisis to cure; here much cooperative staff work is needed. He will find it valuable to keep individual case records and to make case studies for long-range involvement and treatment.

This has always been a fascinating part of my ministry. Many systems were tried and discarded, until at last all information was put on the individual's calling-record card, revised and expanded as needed, and always, of course, kept strictly confidential. I gave what I call spiritual prescriptions with as many specifics as possible. Early in my ministry I developed a blank, like a doctor's prescription blank, and used it to review my suggestions, conclusions, and actions, adding, in cases of pastoral counseling especially, any concrete directives concerning reading, action, devotions, or disciplines to the one in need.

The best time and place for counseling must be ascertained, but preferably some quiet place where privacy is assured; the minister must always be a good listener. The minister can be, and often is, called upon by doctors or psychiatrists to see one of their patients whose problem is more spiritual than mental or physical, but he must accept only those cases he can squeeze in and do justice to; he can suggest some other minister to help the patient whenever he can't manage it.

He must interpret the clues on the intercession box requests and, whenever possible, incorporate the suggestions into his parish ministry. My experience at the Church of the Ascension, open day and night to the flow of needy persons in and out of the church, gives me some basis for comment. An examination of the hundreds of intercession requests which came in over a period of a year reveals a cross section of the concerns of men and women who live in a city, and brings an acute awareness of the often critical needs of the human spirit which demand the ever-present ministry of Christ's Church. Both the intercession cards and private conversations have indicated that the two great illnesses of our age are, first, loneliness, and, second, fear, and more specifically, the fear of possible loss of income or job, of old age, and of death, in that order.

The calling ministry involves much more than just seeing someone for

a few minutes and then dismissing them from one's presence and one's
mind. Every visit, every contact, is an opportunity to share something,
and leave the place and the person spiritually blessed and enriched.

Pastoral Counseling

There are many aspects of "evangelism" which claim attention under
this subject of "calling," as well as pastoral counseling. The former can
be anything from correcting beliefs to persuading someone to believe.
The latter can be of two kinds: one, formal and by appointment in the
minister's study; and, two, informal, by chance, when calling. Almost
everyone has a problem or concern which needs attention; whenever the
minster presents himself there is an opportunity, and he must be, or
seem to be, leisurely enough for the person visited to seize it.

The pop-in-and-out-again call is not good. Neither is the overlong
call which invokes a question never asked, "Will he never leave?" The
happy medium must often be sensed rather than timed by a clock. There
is great value in a wristwatch on such occasions or a clock visible in the
room; never take out your watch, for even a quick glance will be
noticed. The problem with calls by appointment at a definite time is that
it may be necessary to leave for the next scheduled call too abruptly or
before the business in hand is finished. Far better, I've discovered, is to
call from a near-by phone booth just before arriving, to see if it is
convenient to call since you are in the neighborhood. I try to arrange my
calls so as to spend the afternoon in one locality, grouped according to
urgency. However, no set procedure will work in every situation. You
are on your own when calling. Be sure to have plenty of dimes—and be
nonchalant if the phone call must be made from a nearby bar.

Points of Contact

How can a minister prepare for making the most out of every pastoral
call? It is so easy to fall into the trap of trivial conversation without
getting very deep into things that matter. This is the value of having
some point of contact. When I was in Richmond, Virginia, I had a daily
radio program called "Haven." This always gave me an opening,
whether the person visited listened to "Haven" or not. I could always
refer to something I had said that morning to get the conversation into
more serious channels. The same is true for the reading from the daily
devotional guide, *Forward Day by Day*.[6] Here is an opening gambit

which can be used when the opportunity presents itself. Last Sunday's sermon can also be referred to, or the contents of some book read (the one you have with you might well do), or a play seen. It is always possible to channel the conversation in the direction it should continue, as clues are given and openings made. The minister must carry the ball and be skilled in leading the conversation. Among the many possible conversational leads, there are at least three surefire subjects which the minister can have at the tip of his tongue, as the expert; one of them will surely fit almost any calling situation. They are "Christian healing," "changed attitudes," and "new resources for the Christian life."

Take first, the whole subject of Christian healing and how it may be applied, in a vast number of pastoral calls, to make manifest the real concern and power of the Holy Spirit, without arousing false hopes or avoiding the real issues of life and death. I've been able to use parts of the following presentation on healing in almost every week of my ministry. I preached it first as a sermon, but kept it fresh in my mind as a pastoral tool. Since all of one's preaching, writing, and speaking should be used as often and as long as possible, the better one knows his sermons the more useful they can be. It is a waste of good source material to spend so many hours in preparing a sermon simply to file it away and forget it the moment after it has been preached. I have gotten a lot of mileage out of my sermon, "Christian Healing," especially when I called on the sick. Here is the substance of that sermon.

Christian Healing

Once upon a time there was a cripple, who, along with a great multitude of other helpless folk, waited daily by the pool of water near the sheep-market gate in Jerusalem.[7] According to legend, at a certain time each day an angel of the Lord went down into the pool and stirred the water, and whosoever stepped first into the pool after the "troubling of the water" was cured of whatever disease he had. So the blind, the lame, and the paralyzed flocked to the pool of Bethesda and sought to be the first into it. This crippled man had never been first into the pool for he had no one to help him. By the time Jesus saw him, his hopes had worn thin and "his bleak and wintry life" seemed doomed. When the poor soul realized Jesus had paused and was looking at him, he once again grabbed at a straw and begged for help in getting into the healing waters.

Jesus asked this miserable and lonely man, "Do you want to be healed?" The man was stunned by the question and fumbled with his reply, for "how often had he prayed in fierce agony that God might touch his tortured soul back to wholeness once more."[8] But he could not articulate his intense longing for help. Jesus knew the man wanted to be healed and spoke without waiting for an answer. "Rise, take up thy bed, and walk." Looking at Christ, a complete stranger up to that moment, the man found not only that he *wanted* to get up and walk, but that he *could*. Christ had reached in and inspired him, that is, had aroused in him supernatural energy, and he found powers within, dormant and invisible before, which he could now grip and hold and use. The lifelong cripple had not lost the power to respond, which brought his desire and hope to full flower, stimulating and marshaling all the latent spiritual power within, and the story is quickly brought to its climax. "And immediately the man was made whole, and took up his bed and walked."

This cripple's lifelong plight was connected in some way with sin, and Jesus warns him, "Behold, thou art made whole; sin no more." No one had ever probed into this deep-seated trouble before, nor brushed aside his self-pity, his discouragement, his blame of others for his condition, nor had anyone been so concerned about his helplessness and misery.

God's attitude to sin, and to the persistent, unrepentant sinner, is one of condemnation, and we know, too, that sin has its inevitable consequences—pain and suffering. We also know that God, while judging the sin, forgives the penitent sinner; and we know that man remains in his sinful condition of impotence, or gets up and walks away, as he himself chooses. This man chose to obey. Never before had he felt enough strength and courage and will to do anything. Jesus aroused in him a strong desire, which enabled him to act, and he made a complete and immediate break with the habits of the past; thirty-eight years of not-doing and not-believing were erased in one moment of believing and doing.

Such miracles of healing made up a large part of our Lord's earthly ministry. The blind saw, the deaf heard, and the lame walked. All this happened in the days of the Magi, long before the era of medical science as we know it, with its miracle drugs, surgical operations, X-ray therapy, and psychiatric techniques. It was assumed then that if a man had enough faith he could be cleansed from leprosy, healed of lameness, or restored to sanity. And yet the Church is not quite sure where the healing ministry of our Lord, as found in the gospels, fits into our miracle-scoffing age. If Jesus was so successful in handling human affliction, then why all the ages of suffering and dying since that time, when by a word, a prayer, a look, or a touch in His Name men could be healed? If this was once so, the Church's neglect since then is criminal. What is the proper role of the Christian Church today in bringing wholeness to the lives of men, and, more important, in bringing her ministry of healing to individuals under affliction? Everyone is interested in spiritual healing, and this interest is growing beyond the private pressures of the tent evangelists and sideshows of fundamentalist sects, and such shrines as Lourdes, which is the refuge of the supersititious.

But *all are appointed to die.* This is where the Christian approach to healing often breaks down. There can be no promised miracles of cure for blindness or lameness or deafness or for one riddled with cancer. Remember, we are talking about *spiritual* healing. How can we at any given moment determine if this is the instant when this particular person is appointed to die? We can't. Only God can. Our business is with "holy dying" and "holy living," in the spirit of Jeremy Taylor, who worked out a plan for both by bringing the fact of death into life. Do you remember that the article about the airplane accident which almost cost me my life was first entitled "Not Appointed to Die," but in its final form it came out as "The Day I Learned to Live"? All who are concerned with life and death—doctors, nurses, ministers—if they are Christians, learn sooner or later that "only when we face the inevitability of death can we find meaning in life."[9]

The big and all-important question which dominates our thinking on this subject is, "Do you want to be healed?" If the answer is "Yes," the then the next question is, "What can Christ through His Church and His ministers do about it?" (See the section in Chapter 8 on prayers for healing in connection with this question.)

Through the centuries, the Church has had its say on the subject of man's need of God's healing power and how he can best get at it or have access to it. The Church's teaching on healing has fallen under several headings. First, the Church has nearly always embraced joyfully all valid means of healing which God has provided through man— medicine, psychiatry, psychology, hospitals, drugs, surgery, prayer, and sacraments. Second, the Church has always proclaimed that God does the healing, and that man only provides the best setting and removes the obstacles, so that the healing powers of God can operate more effectively; all healing, whatever the process, comes from God. Third, the Church has maintained the wholeness and interrelatedness of man, that man is an inseparable entity of body, mind, soul, and emotions, and that whatever affects one part cannot be isolated from the rest. The Church has insisted that holiness means wholeness. Healing and health are of God, but we must do all we can to know and live by the laws of good health in all areas—physical, mental, spiritual, moral, emotional—and leave the rest up to the "Good God." Fourth, our creation is still unfinished, and what we call miracles, that is, anything that is medically and scientifically incomprehensible, means simply that there are laws of God operating in the universe which man has not yet discovered, and indeed may never discover, for he is not God, after all, and he must accept this fact. A miracle is not something which couldn't happen but did; rather, it is something that God only knows how it happened and why. Fifth, the existence of sickness, pain, and death are realities which must be faced, since they, too, are of God. Man's spiritual growth is dependent on how he handles these realities.

Even though healing and survival are things to cling to, Christians are committed to His will in the larger realm of His universe and eternity, believing that they, in God through Christ, will be triumphant at last over pain and death, that this life is not the end, but only the beginning, and give themselves willingly and unquestioningly into His hands. No man can be the judge of his own or any other's longevity, nor answer the questions of innocent suffering, old age, the existence of evil, and the flaws in creation. Only God can, and we must therefore trust Him with the answers.

We know, however, that there are miraculous spiritual forces at work, and that they do effect marvelous changes which no one can adequately explain. We know that the sick are suggestible, and that faith and hope help immeasurably in any recovery. We know that so-called functional disorders, where nothing organically wrong can be found, exist, and that they respond more readily to healing techniques than do organic ailments. We know that "the cause of almost every illness is the wear and tear of the soul upon the body."[10] We know that "a neglected or disaffected spirit can poison the body no less fatally than a lethal dose of a corroding acid. And until we face the fact that man's spirit needs at least as much nourishment and attention as his body and brain do, we shall go [on] needlessly, like fools, crippling and killing ourselves."[11] There are miracles of healing which no doctor will deny, for who can tell the exact moment when a word or touch or chemical compound at the point of crisis starts the patient on the road to recovery? Words and attitudes both can be turning points.

A man's inner spiritual condition is an important factor in healing, and, therefore, the minister's job is to do all he can to see that the outward sickness is not caused or prolonged by an inner disharmony. We know that through confession and forgiveness the burden of sin is relieved and we feel better, for the bodily powers are released to concentrate on physical restoration, and this is the beginning of the healing process and of being made whole. That is why the minister seeks to assure a troubled conscience of God's forgiveness, to remove hatred and resentment before they have a crippling effect upon the body, and before the body is weakened and made susceptible to the virulent disease germs always lurking within. That is why the minister tries to produce, through prayer, in those who are sick, a different orientation, no longer with self as center, but self in orbit around God, whose love surrounds us, through Jesus Christ.

God's intent for His creation is that it be whole. The Christian religion presents man with the "promise" of wholeness and loveliness. Sickness is the loss of wholeness and loveliness. How can both be restored and thus produce healing in one's soul? At the moment of forgiveness, of the longing for another chance fulfilled, the promise of life and the Kingdom have become more than a doctrinal formulation; they have become a bracing, clear-cut hope; the sick one has arrived at the point where and when life and/ or death becomes meaningful.[12]

The Fact of Pain and Death

We all possess the healing or demonic touch, and affect others by just being with them, but God's healing gifts are greater through some than through others. Visitors in hospitals, even ministers, sometimes upset the patient, when to calm him is their only excuse for being there. The reason the Church does not shout from the housetops, "God can heal you now," is that there are so many dangers "with charlatans, devotees of the lunatic fringe, and ruthless publicists playing craftily upon desperate hopes and fears of thirsting souls in the hour of trouble,"[13] often leading to worse tragedy. However, we must keep the door open and recognize that there are many ways of overcoming the troubles of the world and producing effects, not just the one which happens to occur to us at the moment. We are not omniscient. God is!

We recognize also that pain is an essential part of life, even though we dread it. Thornton Wilder takes the story of the helpless cripple to make tersely and beautifully the point of the therapeutic value of suffering.[14] We deal with what we can, knowing that love drives out fear, trust drives out suspicion, forgiveness drives out sin, hope drives out panic, and that being determined to live, with God's help, gives us a better chance of overcoming illness; but the last things we must leave to God.

The miracle of Brian Hession's life, after he was condemned to die, according to the doctor's diagnosis, in a matter of days, is unfolded in his last few most creative years in *Determined to Live*.[15] I can bear personal testimony to the miracle of this man's will to live, since he was my friend; and how nobly and quietly he died, after five extra years of grace. God asks us to hold onto life as long as possible, then to "let go," and leave the rest in His hands.

From the time of birth each man knows that he must die, that life is a long or short preparation for death, and, therefore, that he must live each day as if it were his last on earth. At some point, before it is too late, a man must make his peace with God by confession and forgiveness, clearing out all the clutter of regrets and preparing to face the universal ultimate fact of death. We must all be ready for a holy death, still trusting in a good God who cares endlessly for us. We certainly do not want to die sick at heart. Spiritual healing can help make a strong soul in a weak body, and make a triumph of the moment of death.

If pain and abnormal cell growth, and the victory of a virus and any physical malady, are all darkness and He is light, why can't we banish darkness forever by accepting Him into our lives? I can't answer that question, although I make intercessions daily, holding people and their needs in God's presence, committing them into His hands, asking Him to lighten their darkness. But in so praying I must travel in the darkness beyond what I know is best or right, and leave it all with Him.

I once went through pain and physical handicap, and it was a long miracle. I often pondered my airplane accident while lying helpless in a hospital bed and wondered if prayer could have righted the plane, softened the landing, spared my bones, and stopped the flow of blood. If so, I realized the whole of creation could be upset by the prayers of a single person, and chaos would result. Each time these thoughts came I remembered I was alive and getting well slowly, and, in the process, coming much closer to God with ever deepening faith.

I found time in the hospital for the practice of devotion, for surrender and composure, and found peace in the new knowledge that my life was being transformed, that one's life is in God's hands. I missed the religious side of my life, the rites and ceremonies which helped me express my faith in concrete acts of devotion, but what was more important was the inner assurance that all was well.

My old rector came by often and laid his hands on me, asking God to make me whole, not again, but for the first time. I clung to life tenaciously, but what was more important, I learned to cling to Him more firmly. Once adjusted to the long miracle, and my share in it, all was well within. One's attitude while in a prone position on a bed of sickness makes all the difference, and Isaiah's words came to me as a revelation, "In the year that King Uzziah died I saw . . . the Lord."[16]

I have no answer as to why I was spared and another, in a similar accident, was killed.

I have witnessed miracles of healing in both mental and general hospitals. I have also witnessed what men called failures. I have felt the healing power of God flow through my hands to a patient, and I have known the immediate healing power of sin forgiven. I know, too, that penance, the laying on of hands, and the sacrament of Holy Communion, are all parts of the Church's healing ministry, which is to be used to the utmost for help in realizing God's intent for His creation, which is, "To heal sometimes, to relieve often, to comfort always."[17]

How does all this apply to man's impotence today, whether it be mental, physical, moral, emotional, or spiritual? We have all, without doubt, procrastinated, compromised, and excused ourselves much too long. All who are impotent in body and sick in heart, who really want to be made whole and who are willing to do something about their condition, must stir the will and not wait for someone to stir the water. No one of us can have all the answers. The mystery of God's ways will never be completely fathomed. But we can do our part by clearing away the obstacles, living in hope, facing the facts, and by obeying all the known laws of health. As we respond to His command, "Rise, take up thy bed, and walk,"[18] we will discover it is He who inspires and stirs up within us a supernatural energy we have never known before, which enables us to get up and get going, leaving the rest in faith in God's hand. But there are also those who are appointed to die.

Attitudes

I have mentioned several times in this chapter the importance of attitudes. I'd like to pursue this theme a bit, but all I can do is to state categorically that attitudes can be changed, but it is very hard to do, that attitudes are *not* inherited but are definitely passed on, and that it is a man's attitude of mind and heart which determines his reactions, his conduct, and his point of view. A Christian is always concerned with the right attitude of mind, and many a pastoral call furnishes the minister with a chance to bear down on some needed change of attitude. Our attitudes motivate us; therefore we must beware of how and what we think. God gave man a mind and it is a grievous mistake not to use it for good ends—not to keep it open for creative interaction with God and other men. Since it is of God it should be used for God, helping to shape the ends He has in store for mankind.

Often we are guilty of wrong habits of thinking, of unhealthy attitudes, but we are unwilling to lose face by admitting they are wrong, even to ourselves. The minister is always alert to the need for renewing the mind and correcting wrong attitudes. Whatever is the answer to the world's dilemma, we can be sure the major problem is that of our own attitudes—what they lead us to do and to stand up for, and whether they are right or wrong in God's sight. We can do our bit toward saving the human race from itself by allowing our attitudes to be straightened out by the cultivated, invited, indwelling spirit of Christ, and by seeking for the light which comes to the minds which know Him, rather than remain in the dark holes of their old ways of thinking.

We deal with attitudes and every kind of healing in our calling, and, in addition, we offer new resources for the Christian life to those whose resources are depleted or gone. One good example is Pastor Dietrich Bonhoeffer, who, during his two years in a Nazi prison, discovered spiritual resources adequate to carry him through all the tests of loneliness, uncertainty, and threat of death. In his letters we find his resources referred to: not only Bible study and prayer, but books, past and present, family and friends, memories, and the certainty that Christ was with him. All who saw him or heard from him in those days knew he was receiving the food and drink which nourished his soul. Bonhoeffer discovered deep within his heart and mind that the sources which had begun to run dry for lack of use were now starting to trickle and flow again. In his reading, praying, and writing, vast new dimensions of insight sustained him in his confinement, and he found a frame of meaning for assessing the madness of his world during those two years covered in *Prisoner for God*.[19] The least any minister can do is to share what he has discovered of these resources that enable him to carry on.

The Spirit of God

People *are* the minister's business; their care and nurture are in his hands, and calling is one means of reaching them, an important part of that business. Each visit springs up like an unexpected oasis in someone's parched life, bringing to it "the Spirit of the Lord God."

XI

When He Plays

Diversion

I've always dreamed of a hideaway near at hand, a kind of holy island of retreat where I could go each week and get a bit of quiet and perspective. My wife and I have worked on this project for years, but have never quite solved it. There is always too much to do. I've never been able to take Mondays off, either, a day often considered sacred as the minister's "let-him-alone" day; I am too anxious to plow into the things left undone and get started on what will, I hope, be a better sermon next Sunday. While in Richmond, Virginia, during the war years, I did manage a golf foursome with my brother clergy each Monday afternoon—that is where I was when our daughter was born.

I've found Saturday is my best time each week for a spot of relaxation with the family, especially Saturday afternoon, if no wedding or funeral or baptism is scheduled. This has varied considerably over the years, with golf and lawn-cutting in Lexington, Kentucky, matinees and gallery-hopping in New York. My winter sports are ping-pong, piano duets, and walking. In summer it's tennis, golf, bicycling, reading, and swimming. Over the years one steady diversion, which waxes and wanes, is the piano duets I play with my wife. We used to dream of having two pianos, but that never materialized, and while the children were growing up the piano was usually preempted for their practice or for playing their favorite songs. Both children are musical, inheriting their mother's near-genius talent, and play and sing well. I need to sit down and play more often to release tension and soak my soul in harmony. All too seldom I listen to our fine record library—more often in the summer over our hi-fi than at any other time. My wife and I love concerts, the opera, the ballet, the theatre, and enjoyed our stay in New York immensely because of this. Sports, too, have been at times of passionate interest. For example, in Lexington we were rabid basketball fans. In New York I watched the Yankees as often as possible. But my wife fails to share my enthusiasm for baseball, except to "keep me company" when I go to the games.

Since our children are now grown up, it is hard to recall all the ways we spent our family times together, but we managed a great deal of this, with many family councils and family devotions during their growing-up period. I'll never cease to be grateful for the intense years of participation in Dr. Ernest M. Ligon's Character Research Project, and how conscious of our parental responsibilities and opportunities it made us feel. We worked hard to make Christian education effective.

As I look back, I realize we often took it too much for granted that our children, being immersed in the life of a Christian parish, would by some kind of spiritual osmosis absorb what they ought to know and how they ought to act as Christians. We've tried to fill in the gaps as we've discovered them, especially during their college careers. I've tried never to be so busy that there was too little time for the family. If we allow thirty minutes a day for God, we cannot be as stingy with our time for wife and children as Douglas Southall Freeman was reported to have been, allotting each one exactly ten minutes a day, no more. Perhaps there ought to be a separate chapter in this book entitled "His Family." There isn't, but I would like to emphasize the joy of family life and the wonder of life unfolding, no matter how often we as parents botch the job. Bachelors miss a great deal in not living through the cycles of growing in the normal environment of family life; and as for me, I believe the minister's life is more blessed and more useful when he has a wife and family.

Vacation

The minister must praise the Lord in everything he does. This is just as true of his off-time extracurricular activities as it is of his professional on-the-job duties. He must always be prepared to praise the Lord at all times in all situations. "Let everything that hath breath praise the Lord."[1]

But is there no letup in the demands of the minister's calling? He most certainly has to have a regular vacaion and, in addition, an occasional spot of recreation; Jack in the ministry also gets dull from all work and no play. I've often advocated some variation on the educator's sabbatical leave for the minister, who both needs it and deserves it if he stays in one place as long as seven years.

However, the question is, can he ever vacate his vocation? That is, can he cease being a minister when he has a day off, or is he like a policeman who when he is off duty carries his gun and is often in the news acting as a policeman even when out of uniform? When the minister takes off his collar, if he wears one, and his "holy" look, if he has one, and lapses into his nonclerical voice, if he has a choice, can he really be out of character or cease to be ready to respond to that "call" when it sounds? This does not mean that, like a fireman waiting by the slide pole, the minister is forever poised for the jump at the ringing of the bell, with his mind unable to relax and think of other things than those connected with his ministry. But, seriously, he must have some variation of his routine or he will go stale and be less than his best when a call does come. He must have both regular times of recreation all through the winter and a longer time apart for a vacation in the summer.

"Vacation" for me has always meant a month away from the parish, "having fun" somewhere, usually out in the open, coming back with a good suntan. For years it was back to good old hot Texas, the home State for both of us, to visit the grandparents. Later it was an occasional longer jaunt; our first visit to Europe was in 1948, when I was one of the preachers on the British American Preachers Exchange Program— we left the children in Texas. This was a marvelous vacation of some three months, climaxed by going as an accredited visitor to the First Assembly of the World Council of Churches in Amsterdam, which launched me into the mainstream of the ecumenical movement.

When a longer summer vacation was possible in a New York parish we settled on Nantucket as our "holy island," and it has become for us a true sanctuary, where the summer months are spent in true re-creation— under the warm sun, in the cool breeze; on the beautiful beaches, lying prone listening to the surf and the drone of planes overhead; soaking up healing from just being there. Barefoot strolls, with the dry sand filtering through one's toes, breathing the fresh clean air, catching glimpses of the water or Sankety lighthouse from across the moors, staring at the star-filled sky at night, being wrapped in the gray mystery of the fog, hugging a driftwood fire as a roaring nor'easter rattles the windows of our cozy 1763 cottage, all add up to a little bit of heaven on earth.

Summer on Nantucket restores me mentally, physically, and spiritually. I can sleep snug each night without the expectation of the telephone's sharp jangle or the shocking alarm of a clock set to awaken me in the early morning hours. The day's routine of morning work, afternoon at the beach or on the golf course or on the tennis court, with loads of reading and bicycling in-between, and games in the evening, or a play, or some other satisfying entertainment in public or private, all adds up to an ideal vacation. But inevitably a crisis or two breaks in, or a meeting must be attended somewhere in the world, and, of course, letters must be written and the parish program for the fall thought about, and one can never completely get away from those in need; but all this is manageable, and I look forward, from September on, to the next visit to the little gray lady, our island home.

Socializing with a Purpose

All this is well and good, and should be mentioned here, even in such summary form, but there is another form of recreation—usually during the winter, but also in the summer—which comes under "fun" and "play" while at the same time it must be listed as "business," that is, socializing with a purpose.

The ability to enjoy himself under all conditions is the mark of a well adjusted minister. Without this he is very often miserable as he attempts to hold up his end socially. How he lives and acts in the world is also important, for he is a marked man in every community. Therefore, where, how, and with whom he spends his time is known by all. The word "circumspect" applies at all times in all relationships, and he will see to it, whether in mixed company or in gatherings for men only, that his conduct is always befitting his position. No, the minister is never out of character or off-duty, and even when vacationing or socializing outside the parish circle, he is on the spot and always alert to another's need. He is available wherever he is for an appropriate word which may help to ease a given situation or to be of positive assistance in some person's time of need. Lest this chapter sound a bit grim, as if the minister's playtime was a grind, a busman's holiday, and his life chained to the treadmill of duty, let me assure you it is not meant to be, for there is no greater joy than to combine his business with his pleasure. Here are a few examples from my own life and ministry.

Business with Pleasure

One of the hardest things a minister has to do is to keep his mind on his ministry while "socializing." He is torn between the desire to seize each opportunity as it comes for bearing witness to the Christian faith as it relates to that person at that moment, and the fear of being a "wet blanket" at the party. If he could only be a split personality with a clear conscience, how easily he could resolve his dilemma, but he can't. Whether "in uniform" or out, wearing a clerical collar or a red tie, he is always on the job and can never really be out of character or incognito. Every contact can be turned into at least some small witness, leaving behind a question that plagues someone's conscience, perhaps, or a word that awakens understanding, or a strengthening thought that stirs hope and helps someone to bear up.

Whenever there is a social occasion, there are people; and wherever there are people, there are hurts, fears, and problems covered up, waiting and ready to be shared. This means for the minister, who is never off the hook of Christian responsibility, that whatever he, or anyone for that matter, can do to cheer or bless others must be done, and that it is his bounden duty to give undivided attention to the unexpected which comes, or may come, with each new contact. The casual encounter often turns into a vital one, as deep questions of life and death emerge, and the opportunities once given often never come again. The old Boy Scout motto, "be prepared," is never out of place for the Christian, especially the committed, deeply caring Christian minister.

In the last century, in the world of the university, the descendents of the Schoolmen—men like Newman, Pusey, Froude, Keble, and Ward— were eloquent in the exposition of Scripture. They discussed theology in the course of long country walks. But these same men were resentful of any change in the established order of things, and contemptuous of the "march of the mind" which was revolutionizing the world outside. Today, the minister can never live in a cloister or with a cloistered mind, shutting out the world's life. That is why socializing with a purpose is part and parcel of a minister's calling.

Each century has its own changes, for time and men's minds are ever on the march; the tempo of change is immeasurably faster now in the jet stream of time. The gospel must always be communicated in the milieu of time and place, by those who dwell in that time and that place, "according to the various exigency of times and occasions."[2] The twentieth century seldom offers to the minister country walks for extended leisurely conversations about things that matter. Instead, he is faced constantly with the coffee hours, receptions and other gatherings which demand long periods of standing still and talking. To some ministers this is a bore and a waste of time. But wherever and whenever people come together can furnish an opportunity for socializing with a purpose. The minister must train himself to attend all such social occasions and accept them as pleasurable opportunities to be with people in the world. He can never afford to become a semi-recluse or anti-social or allergic to parties large or small, even though many of them take place on a Saturday afternoon or evening, a time when he would prefer to be free for last-minute checking for the next day's sermon and services. If early in his ministry he learns to put on his best clothes, his most cheerful countenance, and approach the mingling with people, especially those outside the fellowship of the church, as an opportunity to do God's work by witnessing in bearing and attitude, if not directly by bits of dialogue now and then, he can bear even the long upright stance in one place by developing a special surreptitious horselike shift, standing on first one leg and then the other.

I was helped by this description of John Henry Newman at the height of his powers in the year 1839. He was always ready for any "providential nudge as guide, an unlooked for event, a word casually spoken, a printed phrase, a sudden encounter or a separation."[3] This quotation convinced me of the wrongness of my attitude and, further, gave me the "providential nudge" I needed to make me more alert to every avenue of approach which might be opened to me by those who walk in any kind of darkness.

I have been, ever since this widening of my outlook, more ready and willing to engage in impromptu dialogue at any time, in any place, with any person. It took me a long time to recognize that conversation—which is really dialogue, a give and take between two or more persons—is an important part of the pastoral ministry. There is no prepared script, nor can there be successful ad-libbing. The minister's frame of meaning must be clear, and whatever is dealt with at any given moment must come within that frame, without inconsistencies, procrastinations, or subterfuges. He must be ready to deal with the topics and the temper of the day head on; if he runs out of ammunition he must hasten to the arsenal for more and, if possible, return to the fray. Thus equipped, the minister often finds that civic affairs, receptions, and dinner parties can be God-given opportunities for "speaking a good word for the Lord Jesus," to recall a phrase from one of Ian MacLaren's poignant stories in *Beside the Bonnie Briar Bush.*

No minister can have notes on his cuff at a dinner party, or glance at a foolscap outline during a cocktail party, or have handy a set of guidelines to follow in an impromptu conversation. These things he must have in mind as his frame of meaning. He needs to think out concretely the answers to the questions people ask most frequently, work out his own belief, and be "ready always," as St. Peter put it so accurately, "to give an answer to every man that asketh you a reason for the hope that is in you."[4] The angry young men, the superintellectuals, the ultraconservatives, and those with a mission, are always ready for an argument, and the minister must have a backlog of information and conviction, as well as a carefully thought-out opinion on the news of the day on tap, ready to engage them in dialogue, with an infinite supply of patience, an endless supply of love, and, if possible, a good story to make his point.

While no one can know in advance what the subjects of conversation will be a given party, some idea can be formed as one considers the host and hostess, the people they might invite, and the reason for the particular occasion. No matter what kind of a party one goes to I have discovered that when drinks are served, even though there is a tall glass of ginger ale in my hand, and someone discovers I am a clergyman, one sure-fire question comes up, namely, what is the Church's view on social drinking? There is always the lurking suspicion that the minister is easily shocked by such a question. I have a backlog of information on which to draw when this subject comes up and there is a chance to make a few points stick. Robert Penn Warren describes the order of subject matter at such a gathering: "the conversation moved from the discovery of [me] to politics, adultery, or money."[5] At least with the minister the conversation gets to "me"—not the minister first and last, I hope—and politics (especially around election time), as well as making forays into various aspects of morality, but seldom touches adultery; he must nip obvious gossip in the bud. But back to the party discussion of alcohol and alcoholism, pushing the ministerial "I" forward to make a point.

Christian Views on Drinking

I grew up in the roaring twenties, during prohibition, when most of the so-called "good cheer" at the holiday season was procured illegally and of very inferior quality. Getting "blind drunk" was more than a phrase. As a soda jerker I served "near beer," but there were speakeasies where the real stuff could be procured even by youngsters like myself. I saw my generation drink a lot. The gangster era, inaugurated by war's end and the Eighteenth Amendment, produced in some of my high school classmates its inevitable overtones of drunkenness, theft, and other crimes. We were not a "beat" generation, we were just a beat-up generation; we took our cues from adult behavior in a time which was pretty well out of hand. I recall my first New Year's Eve dance, when I discovered the strange custom, begun in Saxon times as a family toast, of welcoming the New Year with our particular brand of wassail then—bathtub gin. But the young people overdid it. Almost everyone at this particular dance was beyond the point of enjoyment by midnight. It just didn't figure, somehow, or jibe with the "*Happy* New Year" we all desired, for there was no happiness in it for anybody, only hurts and hangovers left behind to remind us of our fancied "happiness."

The consumption of alcoholic beverages has become an accepted part of the social pattern of our time, and drinking is legal, except for minors in public places. The finest liquor, domestic and imported, is available in every block of practically every city, and at road stops at frequent intervals along the highways just in case of an urgent thirst to be assuaged. Drinking is here to stay and the minister must come to terms or come to grips with it, whether as a pleasure or a problem. I realize some churches take a more rigid stand than others on this subject and that all Christians, as well as all Christian ministers, do not agree about alcohol as evil or not evil when taken in moderation as part of a social custom.

The Episcopal Church, which I serve, has never been in the forefront of the temperance movement, but its position is often misrepresented or misunderstood, and it has been severely criticized by Christians of other communions. I was raised in a Southern Baptist home in Texas, however, where liquor was considered the tool of the Devil and I, along with my four brothers and our sister, was never exposed to alcohol of any kind. Whatever my father did in the way of social drinking was certainly not done at home. There may be some connection here between my upbringing and my present abstemiousness—involving some deep-rooted moral sense.

The Episcopal Church, not officially but through a special commission, has this to say in "Alcohol, Alcoholism, and Social Drinking," the report of their study released in the fall of 1958. The pamphlet begins with some facts and figures on the alcohol problem today. The consumption of alcohol per capita in this country is well below that of our pre-Prohibition era, mainly because more people drink weaker spirits such as wine and beer, and there is less total consumption of distilled spirits. Even so, seventy million persons drink today, averaging $150 per year per drinker, and all of them are likely to manifest, on at least a few occasions, what the report calls "deviant behavior" attributable to alcohol. What a person becomes under the influence of too much alcohol is not pleasant. This annual ten-billion-dollar business has been more of a curse than a blessing, and as a direct result of drinking alcoholic beverages, there has been an increase of crime, insanity, poverty, alcoholism, taxes, and fatal motor accidents—economic and social waste.

The drinker himself is always liable to consequences he never intended or desired; remember, too, that some people are allergic to alcohol and more easily affected than others. The gradual buildup of social drinking may lead to loss of control; then there is no longer free choice of behavior, and the lost weekends begin. The other people who are involved, and who are often injured, are the employer, the family, and the victim of the holiday motor accident—but the widening circle of disaster is almost endless.

I read the following about the opening of Britain's first superhighway: their motorway code warns drivers not to take even small quantities of alcohol or drugs before driving on such highways—as a matter of fact, so does our code. At the party given after the opening ceremonies of this new superhighway, only soft drinks were served. The press release said it was possible that alcoholic drinks would be banned from motorway restaurants—in a land where drinking has always been, to the casual observer at least, well under control.

Since the tempo and tensions of American life often demand some release from the pressures all around us, alcohol has offered to many a temporary relaxation. But the potential danger of using it as an escape to anesthetize existence is ever present and should be recognized. Most people, in what is thought of as "civilized society," engage regularly in social drinking with no harmful effects, and few today are total abstainers. The pleasure of one another's company is enjoyed by all, and this is what we mean by social drinking, when a few or many people get together for a relaxing time of wholesome good fellowship, aided and abetted by "wassail" in some form, in the good old Anglo-Saxon tradition. However, such drinking together must be rewarding; the happy fellowship must be the primary function and purpose, and the drinking purely secondary. When the drinking becomes primary, it is a danger sign. When the cocktail party begins to deteriorate, as it sometimes does at last, into pointless and unhealthy confusion, it has destroyed its reason for being, which is recreation and fellowship. What I am saying is that we must be aware of the possible dangers in social drinking and let our moderation be known to all men, for usually present are also alcoholics and potential alcoholics, those who cannot drink moderately, and who must say "No thank you," to the first drink or go off the deep end—these last should never be present at all, but there they are, finding it difficult or impossible to refuse that first drink, and the second, and the third.

The widely divergent points of view among Christians on social drinking must be recognized—ranging from absolute abstention, which is anybody's privilege and should be respected with no questions asked or eyebrows raised, to approval of moderate drinking. Certainly the prevailing view among Episcopalians, clergy and laity alike, is against all abuses of alcoholic drinks but does not insist that the only remedy is total abstinence for all Christian people at all times. To them "a little wine for thy stomach's sake"[6] is quite all right. Ultimately each Christian must make the decision for himself as to whether he will drink and how much he will drink, in the light of all the facts about alcohol. Whether a man drinks or does not drink, he should do it or not do it for the right reasons. The nondrinker can never afford to be self-righteous in the presence of the drinker; nor can the drinker allow himself to think of the nondrinker as a goody-goody.

The minister will be expected to know the biblical evidence, which is both pro and con. Basically, everything was created by God and "is good," but man can and does misuse this good creation. The Bible makes it clear that food and drink are part of God's creation, and, therefore, are to be reverenced and received as His blessing, moderately and responsibly used. We can never forget that our Lord Himself took "the fruit of the vine" and gave us our greatest sacrament, although some Christians prefer the unfermented fruit of the vine, which is quite all right. There has been far too much bickering over this point in unity discussions. The Bible cautions us against doing anything that makes our brother stumble, and tells us that all immoderate use of food and drink are sinful. The Christian view is: everything in moderation.

The minister is always on the hot spot, the degree of heat depending on the time, the place, and the company. To some persons a minister taking a drink, especially in a public place, is shocking. By others it is accepted as a matter of course, both natural and right. It is interesting to note that the alcoholic priest has fascinated many writers, from Daudet to Graham Greene, and there have always been actual examples of this phenomenon, for ministers, too, are human, and subject to the same temptations that all men are. A clerical collar offers no magic protection. The minister must make his own individual conscientious decisions—unless his ordination vows take care of it for him—regarding the claims of total abstinence, or moderate, careful, and responsible drinking, before God and his fellowmen, just as any Christian layman is called upon to do.

It has been almost too easy for me to decide against drinking. I don't drink for two perfectly good and legitimate reasons: one, I don't like it, or feel any need for it to pep me up, cheer me up, or hold me up; and, two, I have worked with too many tragic cases of alcoholics ever to be unaware that there may be present, in any group, some ex-alcoholic (which is a contradiction in terms, for potentially he still is one), who might be helped to say, "None for me, thanks," by hearing someone else ask for a nonalcoholic drink. I don't think I'm ever a wet blanket—or rather, a dry one—in such gatherings, because I enjoy being with people, even though my drink is nothing stronger than ginger ale or Coca-Cola.

Wholesome Freedom

The minister must help parents and young people to discuss the subject of drinking responsibly and maturely, and help them to understand the problems involved and to make prayerful, sensible choices regarding each one's own position. Parents must be helped to be sensitive to these problems and to the needs of others. The minister must help the host or hostess see that their responsibility is to keep alcoholic consumption in their home secondary to sociability: by not delaying dinner overlong, by serving food with drinks and always having a choice of nonalcoholic drinks on hand (as in England), by not insisting on guests drinking more than they really desire (the good-host fallacy of thinking the more drinks the more fun), and in general creating an atmosphere of wholesome freedom. The minister, who represents the Church, can never forget his responsibility toward the real alcoholic and his family and his problem, and must be ready to use every available means to help.

All Christians, I believe, would agree in condemning the excessive use of alcohol at any time, as the pamphlet I mentioned points out. Irresponsible drinking is a serious kind of immorality, and the driver who has had even a few drinks is a dangerous driver. Too much drinking at parties is not an exercise of Christian freedom, but of unchristian license, and those who believe that moderate, seasonable, and reasonable use of alcoholic beverages is proper, must prove by their own actions that moderation is a feasible rule, and disprove Henry Ward Beecher's maxim, "To speak about a moderate use of alcohol is like speaking of a moderate use of the plague."[7] Social drinking in moderation, for genuine pleasure and as an aid to one's health, can be kept within the bounds of healthy good fellowship, and the old "Wass hael" can really be the kind of toast it was in Saxon times, "To your health" and "Be thou well."

The Moral Issue of Gambling

Another favorite subject in any gathering is crime, which is always current, front-page stuff. David Alexander, author of first-rate suspense novels, recommends murder as the crime a novice could most easily succeed in committing, for, he said, you can get away with murder a larger percentage of the time than any other crime. Mr. Alexander knows his murderers and always brings them to justice; but this happens, he says, only in fiction. In real life the murderer is not always discovered, and if caught, is too seldom convicted and punished by the law. That is why Murder Incorporated flourished for so many years.

But, of course, Mr. Alexander was in a facetious mood. He knows that most of the time the murderer *is* punished, if not by law and hanging, then by his conscience and living in a hell of his own making, as Dostoevski makes clear in *Crime and Punishment* when he has young Roskolinkov break under the strain of holding within himself his dreadful secret and finally betray himself. You *may* get away with the crime of murder, as far as discovery and prosecution are concerned, as David Alexander says, but never with the crime of gambling.

In Gambling Incorporated, the odds are stacked against you; the American public loses forty-seven billion dollars a year in *illegal* gambling alone. Only the professional gambler is sure to get a lot for a little, while the poor-sucker victim is certain to get nothing for something and end up cleaned out and broke. And yet, even though this fact is common knowledge, gambling, with its attendant evils of bribery and confusion, continues to be the treasure chest of the underworld. Every minister knows that personal tragedy, scandal, and corruption always attend widespread gambling. No one who bets regularly on horses or other sports with bookies, or bucks the house percentage in craps, roulette, or slot machines, has the slightest chance of winning in the long run. Rather grim, isn't it? What can we ministers do about it? We can obey the law. We can raise the moral issue of right or wrong and keep it to the fore, with emphasis on moral integrity and honor among public servants, and in our lives. We can stand up and be counted and "cease to pervert the right way of the Lord."[8]

We are all gamblers, whether we play the slot machines, haunt the race tracks, and frequent the "bookies" or not. In one way or another we take chances, live dangerously, and engage in risk, sometimes for high stakes. Something in us responds to a dare, the promise of adventure, the mysterious unknown. Some forms of gambling are instinctive, and not necessarily evil in themselves. The gambling instinct can, of course, be put to constructive use. It is a terrific gamble, for example, to get married, to have a child, to develop atomic energy, or to bet one's life there is a God. Using our instinct for taking a chance according to God's will is good, for the motive is a projection beyond self to the service of mankind. But when we pervert our divine instinct by using it for selfish ends only, then we deny its God-given potential.

The problem of gambling is complex, and it is hard to lay down a blueprint to cover all the angles. The literal meaning of the word "gambling" is "to amuse oneself, a game." When such petty forms of "gambling" as penny-ante poker, "quarter on the corner" bridge, friendly bets between husband and wife, secretary and boss, or friends, even a two-dollar pari-mutuel bet on a horse at a race track, are made just for fun—for recreation or amusement—with no expectation of getting something for nothing, there is no moral issue. But when "betting to amuse oneself" moves over the boundary of the definition and turns into a compulsive habit and a disease, with no other motivation than gain and the bright-eyed expectation of hitting the jackpot, then watch out, for this can lead many an otherwise good man down the wide and easy path to destruction. Each man must choose for himself what he will do, and what he will be and become, but a Christian will always be mindful of the moral question, the motivation, the end results of his choices on character.

Gambling is not mentioned in the Bible, but the attendant evils are, and covetousness heads the list. All gambling based on the motivation of something for nothing is a moral and social evil, and leads to corruption. George Washington called gambling "the child of avarice, the brother of iniquity, and the father of mischief."[9] It is true, you may get away with murder—although I would strongly advise against it— but I'm positive you'll never get away with gambling, that is, the passionate hope of getting something for nothing, which pays off only in misery of one kind or another.

Conversational Gambits

If, after a thorough-going discussion of wine, women, song, and gambling, you want to get onto "Devils, Drugs, and Doctors," use the material found in Chapter 10 to open up avenues of dialogue on "there is no health in us," or the well-rounded man, or physical fitness, or, last of all, "physician, heal thyself."[10]

A catalogue of all the subjects for possible discussion at cocktail and dinner parties, to say nothing of coffee breaks and teas, would be too long. What I have said about alcohol gives the kind of approach needed to straighten out the misconceptions and prejudices so often met with on such occasions. I recall lengthy and serious discussions on everything from gambling, the John Birch Society, and "the new morality," to existentialism, modern art, *War and Peace,* suburban sexual mores, and ailments. It is quite easy to get on the subject of ailments and troubles in a casual conversation at any party with almost any person one happens to meet, for whatever happens to "me" looms disproportionately large.

Yes, indeed, a minister plays, and enjoys all wholesome and healthy recreation, both indoors and outdoors, both in summer and winter, and he learns early how to combine the business of his ministry with the pleasure of other people's company, and on all occasions to "praise the Lord."

Don't Sweat It!

Lest I leave a wrong impression that the minister is a drag and a bore, and never ceases to be the shadow of men's conscience even in his moments of innocent pleasure, let me add this note. He can and must relax from the duties of his calling while he plays, even though he can never be completely free from being what he is wherever he goes. He takes in his stride whatever comes his way, and takes to heart what my teenage son and daughter used to remind me, "Don't sweat it, Dad."

XII

His Future

In God's Hands

Ambition is often a curse to the minister's life, straining the present through the sieve of the future, conducting a horoscope ministry, doing and saying today what will lead to the desired tomorrow. But that little matter is in God's hands, the work of the Holy Spirit, and few can shape their own destinies smoothly toward a predestined end. All our destinies are likely to be roughhewn and beyond our sight. But I covet the same ending to my story as that of the hero of *The Sinner of St. Ambrose* as he looks back on his life and muses. "At the heart of any story I could tell would always be tragic wonder of the human spirit and the greatness of its search for God. I have found out that a man's life is a religious experience. Now in my old age I begin to tell my religious story, of passionate action in the world, more for the fellowship of the bewildered than for the delight of the orthodox. God is my perpetual guest. I still am busy at learning how to be His joyous host."[1]

"Therefore seeing we have this ministry, . . . we faint not."[2] Horatius Bonar picks up these words and uses them in a hymn. "Toil on, faint not, keep watch, and pray; Be wise the erring soul to win; Go forth into the world's highway, Compel the wanderer to come in."[3] The minister keeps fit, keeps his integrity, never loses heart or falters or despairs, for God's grace is sufficient; and he leaves the future in God's hands.

Faint Not

This brief word about the minister's future is my conclusion to this rambling excursion through one minister's life, words, works, and ways. Wherever we are on our life's journey, we can pause for a wordless prayer of gratitude to God for what we are and where we are, asking that we "faint not" nor grow weary, and that we always remember Archbishop Leighton's prayer, "Deliver me, O Lord, from the errors of wise men, yea, and of good men."[4]

There are always a few times of supreme discouragement when the minister doubts his calling, wants to chuck it all and leave a parish or the ministry, especially when he is on a critical hot spot. There will always be trials and tribulations, like St. Paul's thorn in the flesh, in the form, perhaps, of difficult individuals whom one cannot shake off; or it may be some battleground of parish policy which seems to be lost; or the threat of a rapidly changing neighborhood to be coped with; or a spiritual, mental, or physical fatigue, when a sigh comes frequently unbidden to one's lips. At such moments the minister longs for some avenue of escape to open up—a call, a miracle, or even a death. But rarely is an escape offered, and he must take his stand and see things through.

I remember vividly my toughest and lowest moment, when all seemed black and the future looked like a stone wall I could never breach. It involved a matter of principle, upon which I had to stand firm against tremendous opposition, for although what I upheld was in the canon law of the diocese, it had never been enforced in my parish, and to do so meant a drastic change in mores. I knew it must be done and did it. I tried to "chicken out," but God simply would not let me. The crisis was weathered only with God's help.

Again, when the Oxford Group definitely began to compete with the Church, to be a substitute for the Church, I had to withdraw from what had been for me a brief rich spiritual experience. My hope of its sparking a revival within the Church was ended when its meetings were called regularly on Sunday mornings at 11:00 A.M. Of course, I could not continue. It was hard to go against "group guidance," but the right choice seemed clear to me then, and still does, in spite of all the disturbing words spoken, then and now, about the Church and the Christian religion.

Things will never be easy. God never promised they would be. But the minister is called and committed to do God's will, and He promises to see him through—"Lo, I am with you alway."[5] I recall so many foolish mistakes in judgment—from an early political blooper, to fears which locked my lips and let things pass by default. Many a minister has sold his soul to the devil because of fear, like those who keep silent in the face of scandal, wrongdoing, and ghastly inhumanity. And any fear sets up a chain reaction. As St. Francis de Sales said, all fears shake each other's hands.[6] Bystanders are never innocent. Struggles there will always be, and the minister must choose his side and help fight the battle without faltering, with God's help.

Priorities

We are "called" to be ministers. God has laid this task upon us. All through the ages God's chosen ministers have rebelled, have been frightened, have wanted to quit or never begin, like Aaron, Moses, Isaiah, and Jeremiah. God's promises are sure and direct. It is "no strange God" we worship. Therefore, what better words for the minister to hold to than these from Deuteronomy? "Be strong and of a good courage, fear not, nor be afraid . . . : for the Lord thy God, he it is that doth go with thee; he will not fail thee, nor forsake thee."[7] Ever since that hospital experience following my airplane crash, this passage has been for me the theme song of my life and ministry, and has been passed along again and again to those at low tide spiritually. These are ancient words for modern times, never out of date or out of mind.

In this modern world, so changed from George Herbert's eighteenth-century parson's world, the pace and demands make for a killing burden, and confront today's minister with daily choices of how best to use the hours of the day and how to keep from spreading a meager talent to the breaking point. He must often, for example, engage in a period of trial and error before he finds a daily quiet time that fits and works. It sometimes takes years, and in a few cases a heart attack, to teach the minister how to say "no" gracefully. My accident made me want to say "yes" too quickly and too often. But choices must be made and priorities set or the minister's task is hopeless.

The modern maelstrom of urban, also suburban, pressures on time, make it imperative to live a disciplined and orderly day, every day. This means that the minister must find the best time and place for his daily devotions, creative work, and all the rest of his activities. Some find early morning best for concentration and work. I do. I am ten times more alert and creative in the early hours of the morning than at any other time. But others find late evening or night best. My wife fits in this latter category, and it took many years for us to adjust to this tug-of-war within the hours of each day's life. However, it is not always possible to hold to a rigid, unyielding schedule, for the unexpected is liable to break at any moment and knock any day's plans out of kilter.

Flexibility, adaptability, and the power to adjust quickly, are essential in the life of the minister. It is usually the minister's involvement in multitudinous outside activities, which yank him out of his parish orbit, that makes his preparation for speaking so limited and so inadequate. He often plunges into the affairs of the world so precipitously that he must give short shrift to writing carefully and pondering deeply. I have often wondered how a man like Martin Luther King, Jr., does it. The answer, of course, is that he stays close to the heart of his faith. In other words, the minister is on the anxious bench largely because he has not disciplined himself to make the choices necessary for giving the correct priorities to time and talent; he has strayed too far from his Lord and Master, Jesus Christ.

The purpose of this book has been, not to overwhelm the minister with the endless demands of his task, but to encourage him to make the most of what God has given him of word power, written and spoken, so he can give his utmost to implement the gospel of hope in an age of despair, where response and responsibility go hand in hand. This is his chosen task, which he must pursue to his life's end, using to the full every scrap of his powers, thanking God that "each of us has been given his gift [of grace], his due portion of Christ's bounty,"[8] as apostle, prophet, evangelist, pastor, and teacher, and that God's grace never runs out, nor His love, nor His forgiveness.

"Now unto him that is able to do exceeding abundantly above all that we ask or think, according to the power that worketh in us, unto him be glory in the church by Christ Jesus throughout all ages, world without end. Amen."[9]

PRAYERS FOR TODAY

The following prayers were written for the syndicated series appearing in daily newspapers across the country over many years, under the sponsorship of the Division of Christian Education of the National Council of Churches. Each one appeared as a "Prayer for Today," a general or special prayer written in the language of the marketplace, geared to the tempo of today's living.

In the Sermon on the Mount our Lord attempted to do something like this when He said, "After this manner therefore pray ye,"[1] and then gave us the familiar words of the Lord's Prayer, a prayer which is not only a summary of the content of all prayer, but a guide to its order, and is useful in both public and private worship and devotions. Indeed this whole section of the Sermon on the Mount dealing with prayer is most suggestive and should be given frequent and deep scrutiny.

KEEP ME FREE this day, O Lord, from fancied slights and hurts; let me by concentrating on my immediate task, push aside every "poor-me" feeling which threatens to possess me, by remembering I am a member of Christ's family on earth and a prospect for God's family in the life which is yet to come. And keep me free, O Lord, from finding anything relative to life overwhelmingly irksome, ever seeking Thy way in every contact, every task; for I am Thine this day and always. Amen.

CRASH DOWN the barriers I may erect, dear Father, and let me block off no one from my life this day by preconceptions, undue self-regard, preoccupation, biting words, or failure to give attention to another. Give me this day such a continuing sense of Thy presence that others are included in my knowing and feeling, speaking and doing. May my sense of being with Thee continue with me as I go about my business, and may it carry over into every relationship, every need, through Christ. Amen.

DEAR FATHER of us all, break our stubborn wills, wherever they hold fast to bigotry and bitterness; open our eyes to behold and accept all men as related parts of creation, with malice toward none. By Thy love transform us so that we may feel toward all others as toward Thee, and reach out toward them in good will; in Christ's name. Amen.

O LORD, take from me the spirit of idleness and of empty talking. When I would do nothing, spur me on to do something constructive. When I would speak without thinking, hold my tongue and stimulate my thoughts. In both my work and my leisure may I glorify Thee. In both my words and my silence may I bear witness to Thee; through Christ. Amen.

O LORD, we need Thee daily more and more. Grant that we may increase in Thy Holy Spirit until we come to know Thee and Thy will, until we trust Thee and find in Thee strength for carrying out Thy will. O Lord, we do not ask for a magical crash approach to our inner change, but help us to grow just a little each and every day; through Jesus Christ. Amen.

A PRAYER FOR THE LENTEN SEASON

O GOD, hold me to the disciplines of my Christian life as I review my commitments and seek to make up for the lacks, the misses, and the feeble enthusiasm as a disciple of Thy Son, Jesus Christ. Help me to honestly and thoroughly look at myself and my inner spiritual condition as I plunge into this day's life, leaning heavily on Thy strength to see me through the special disciplines I have undertaken, for Christ's sake. Amen.

O GOD, help me never to judge another until I have walked in his shoes for two weeks and endeavored to see him with open eyes and mind. Close my mouth and clamp my teeth to prevent the rush of unkind words, which hurt and bring regret. Lord, guide my steps alongside my brother this day and let nothing separate us as we walk together; in Jesus' name. Amen.

A PRAYER FOR EASTERTIDE

I THANK THEE, dear Lord, for springtime, which ever comes again and leaves no corner of the world untouched with life returning from its retreat into the earth, with beauty touching up the drabness of the long winter, and with the warmth of the sun thawing our bodies and our spirits. I thank Thee, dear Lord, for making it so that all through the winter's cold and dark, spring is ever on the way. Now that it has come again, we lift up our hearts in thankfulness; in Christ's name. Amen.

DEAR LORD, we're not what we want to be, and we're not what we ought to be, and we're not what we're going to be; but, O Lord, we're thankful we're not what we were. By Thy grace keep us moving in directions that will bring us closer to Thy way for us. Defend us against our worst and keep us growing day by day, until we become in fullest measure Thy sons; through Christ. Amen.

I THANK THEE, O God, for night and day, for wind and weather, for earth and sea, and for the visible evidences of Thy creation. As the earth grows green and the sun warms it to life again, so may I grow in grace and manifest more fully Thy love where I am. In each place where I stand, help me to bear witness to my belief in Thee as the only God and my devotion to Thee through Thy Son Jesus Christ, who is the Lord of my days and my nights. Amen.

DEAR LORD, may the mysteries of our tomorrows not deter us from the realities of our todays; may the realities of our yesterdays not be stumbling blocks to the glories of our tomorrows. Help us this day to live fully each and every moment with thankful hearts, grateful for everything, especially for those near and dear, even though they sometimes cause us anxieties. Let us be glad and rejoice in Thy gift of another precious day; in Jesus' name. Amen.

DEAR GOD, keep close to me this day, for the sea of the world is so wide, and the frail boat of my life is so small. Help me chart my course aright and keep my bearings. If the winds and waves are against me, let me head into them and keep full steam ahead; and, O God, keep Thy hand on mine as I stand watch and hold the wheel, unafraid, steady as I go, in Christ's name. Amen.

A PRAYER FOR THE EARLY FALL

O GOD, the lazy days linger in my memory and the lethargy in my spirit persists. Keep me aware of the work to be done, the plans to be made, the rush of time I cannot stay without feeling harrassed. Help me to get down to the work immediately before me. Wipe out my lazy lethargy but keep my re-creation from the summer intact; in Christ's name. Amen.

O LORD GOD, we thank Thee for time and clocks, for days and hours, minutes and seconds, to measure life and alert us to its passing. While there is yet time, help us to do what we can to make life more complete for ourselves and others. Let us not be slaves of time but disciples of relaxed orderliness, counting the gift of time a precious commodity to be used worthily. At every ticking of the clock and every sound of bell or chime, let us say "Thank Thee, Lord, for the gift of life." Amen.

GOOD LORD, deliver me this day from ignorance and procrastination— from ignorance by keeping open to new truth from all sound sources; from procrastination by not putting off until some tomorrow that which can be done now. Help me so to live this day that by the time I sleep, my work will be done, and my mind stirred to new insight and endeavor by Thy help; in Jesus' name. Amen.

O GOD, this day guide first my wishes and mold them as may please Thee so that my whole self will follow. And, as I wind my way through the day's journey, help me to distinguish little things from great things, and good things from evil things, wishing for and choosing the magnanimous and the good, as Thou dost direct. And, good Lord, deliver me from wanting the moon and crying when I don't get it; in Christ's name. Amen.

O GOD, I do not ask for a smooth path to walk in this day, but for a steady faith to hold me upright wherever I walk. I do not ask to have things made easy this day but to be made ready to face all things as they come, no matter how hard, and to know that Thou art near. I ask only for Thy guidance and strength to live this day to the full, for Thee; in the name of Christ. Amen.

O LORD, lead us this day and help us to follow fearless and unafraid. Hold us fast so that we shall not stray. Move us steadily along when we would lag, and make the day's journey long enough to get done what must be done before the night falls. In trust we would begin the day and live through it, following step by step where Thou dost lead us; in Christ's name. Amen.

O LORD, help me to walk unafraid this day, because I know that I do not walk alone, but that with every step I take Thou art alongside me. By Thy grace help me to face what must be faced without hesitation, except to ask for Thy guidance as to what and how to do and say what must be done and said, in the spirit of love and good will through Christ. Amen.

GIVE US courage this day, O Lord, to struggle for what is right. Help us, as we roam about, to stay our thoughts on Thy way and will for us. Prevent our tongues from keeping silent when a word needs to be spoken, and from ever speaking out to bear false witness, slander, lie, or brag. This is the day Thou hast given us. Help us to be glad and to rejoice in it; through Christ. Amen.

DEAR LORD, be Master of my tongue this day and keep it gentle and considerate. May it speak softly and never in taunt or sarcasm. Let the words it utters be of encouragement and appreciation, never to tear down or to start false rumors. Before a spoken word escapes my lips, hold it until haste and anger and impatience are past; then make it well considered and loving. Amen.

O GOD, help us to pray a little, seek a little, think a little, love a little, and do a little this day in response to Thy love for us expressed in a thousand ways of insight and revelation, especially in Thy Son Jesus Christ, in Whom we find what Thou art like. Teach us how we fit into Thy plan for Thy creation. And help us each day to grow a little more toward Thy likeness. Amen.

DEAR FATHER, help me to keep this day a bright penny exposed in my hand for all to see, hiding no part of it in a dark pocket of sulking, complaint, or envy. Let joy and peace radiate from an inner commitment of the day into Thy hands, and help me to brighten my own small corner by Thy grace; in the name of Jesus Christ. Amen.

GOOD LORD, deliver me from uttering meaningless words and from making vows I do not intend to keep. May no good resolution made by me be forgotten. Only by Thy help can I be a generous, loving, kindly person this day; but by Thy help I can be. Lord, help me to be the best I can be this day; in Jesus' name. Amen.

NOTES

Preface

1. II Cor. 3:6; 4:1.
2. Eph. 4:7.
3. Samuel Miller, "To Minister to This Age," *Harvard Alumni Bulletin,* February 15, 1964.

I. His World

1. St. John 16:33.
2. Jack Fishman, *My Darling Clementine* (New York: David McKay Company, Inc., 1963), p. 146.
3. See Arnold Toynbee, *An Historian's Approach to Religion* (New York: Oxford University Press, 1956).
4. Fishman, *op. cit.,* p. 292.
5. From the Headmaster's matriculation sermon, October 8, 1964.
6. St. John 14:6.
7. Elizabeth Drew, *The Novel* (New York: W. W. Norton & Company, Inc., 1963), p. 282.
8. G. Stephen Spinks, *Religion in Britain Since 1900* (London: Andrew Dakers, Ltd., 1952), pp. 147 and 196.
9. D. R. Davies, *In Search of Myself* (New York: The Macmillan Company, 1961), p. 215.
10. D. E. Roberts, *The Grandeur and Misery of Man* (New York: Oxford University Press, 1955), pp. 55–56.
11. John Baillie, *The Sense of the Presence of God* (New York: Charles Scribner's Sons, 1962), p. 150.
12. C. S. Lewis, *The Case for Christianity* (New York: The Macmillan Company, 1945), p. 25.
13. Edmund Fuller, *Man in Modern Fiction* (New York: Random House, 1958).
14. *Ibid.*
15. *Ibid.*
16. Jer. 31:33.
17. Rom. 7:24.
18. Martin Esslin, *The Theatre of the Absurd* (Garden City, N.Y.: Anchor Books, 1961), p. 290.
19. W. C. Heinz, *The Surgeon* (New York: Doubleday & Company, Inc., 1963), p. 69.

II. His Church

1. George Casalis, *Portrait of Karl Barth* (New York: Doubleday & Company, 1963).
2. St. John 1:12.
3. Phil. 2:15.
4. *Mission of Studies Bulletin,* World Council of Churches, April, 1964, p. 8.
5. See Frederick C. Grant, *Basic Christian Beliefs* (London: Oliver & Boyd, 1960).
6. *The Book of Common Prayer,* pp. 284-285.
7. William Stringfellow, *A Private and a Public Faith* (Grand Rapids, Mich.: Wm. B. Erdmans, 1962), p. 56.
8. James W. Kennedy, *Venture of Faith* (New York: Morehouse-Gorham Co., 1948), p. 58.
9. *Ibid.*
10. I Cor. 11:23.
11. John Baillie, *A Diary of Private Prayer* (New York: Charles Scribner's Sons, 1936), p. 71.
12. Acts 2:42.
13. James W. Kennedy, *Henry Drummond: An Anthology* (New York: Harper & Brothers, 1954), p. 224.
14. Phil. 2:15-16a.
15. Deane William Ferm, "The Time Has Come," *The Christian Century,* July 15, 1964.
16. James W. Kennedy, *He That Gathereth* (New York: World Council of Churches, 1952), pp. 76-78.
17. *Ibid.*
18. *The Hymnal 1940,* Hymn 551, verse 2.
19. Hos. 8:9.
20. Heb. 12:1.
21. Eph. 4:15-16.
22. Heb. 13:8.
23. Heb. 13:9.
24. Pope John XXIII, in calling the Second Vatican Council, used the word *aggiornamento,* meaning "bringing the Church into tune with the modern world," which accurately describes our Christian task.

III. His Parish

1. Georges Bernanos, *The Diary of a Country Priest* (New York: Macmillan Paperbacks, 1937), p. 30.
2. I Pet. 5:2.
3. St. Matt. 28:20.
4. Gal. 6:10.
5. Colin Williams, *Where in the World* (New York: National Council of Churches), pp. xx and 96.
6. *Ibid.,* pp. 43 and 56.
7. Quoted in Stringfellow, *op. cit.,* p. 33, from *The Presence of the Kingdom.*
8. Source unknown.
9. Williams, *op. cit.,* p. 83.

10. Acts 20:28.
11. Quoted in Williams, *op. cit.*, p. 10, from P. Kraemer, "The Urban Church," *Concept III.*
12. I Cor. 3:13.
13. Quoted in James W. Kennedy, *The Unknown Worshipper* (New York: Morehouse-Barlow Co., 1964), p. 75.
14. Roger Lloyd, *The Ferment in the Church* (London: SCM Press, 1964), p. 105.
15. Acts 17:28.
16. Stringfellow, *op. cit.*, p. 34.
17. For further information, write the Rev. Eric James, Director of "Parish and People," 177 Half Moon Lane, London, S.E. 24, England.
18. Quoted in Tom Allan, *The Face of My Parish* (New York: Harper & Brothers, 1957), pp. 56–57.
19. Forward Movement Publications, 412 Sycamore Street, Cincinnati, Ohio.
20. Kennedy, *Henry Drummond, op. cit.*
21. George Casalis, *Portrait of Karl Barth* (New York: Doubleday & Company, 1963), p. 53.
22. *The Book of Common Prayer,* p. 67.
23. Elizabeth Burns, *The Late Liz* (New York: Popular Library Inc., 1961), p. 183.
24. Kennedy, *Henry Drummond, op. cit.*, p. 227.
25. Presiding Bishop's Sermon, General Convention, St. Louis, Mo., Oct., 1964.
26. J. D. Salinger, *Franny and Zooey* (Boston: Little, Brown and Company, 1961).
27. Quoted in Tom Allan, *op. cit.*, p. 13.
28. Jer. 31:33.
29. Ps. 95:7.
30. Quoted in Roger Lloyd, *The Ferment in the Church* (New York: Morehouse-Barlow Co., 1964), from R. C. Hutchinson's novel, *Interim,* p. 87.

IV. His Life

1. "The Private Ethic and Self-fulfillment," *The Christian Century,* August 19, 1964.
2. From Wykeham Rise brochure, 1964.
3. Presiding Bishop's Sermon, *op. cit.*
4. Quoted in Laurence Stallings, *The Doughboys* (New York: Harper & Row, Publishers, Inc., 1963), Prologue, p. 4.
5. Fishman, *op. cit.*, p. 274.
6. Williams, *op. cit.*, p. 98.
7. *Ibid.*
8. Source unknown.
9. New York: Harper & Brothers, 1953.
10. Davies, *op. cit.*, p. 214.
11. Kennedy, *Henry Drummond, op. cit.*, p. 28.
12. Werner and Lotte Pelz, *God Is No More* (Philadelphia: J. B. Lippincott Company, 1964), p. 31.
13. *Ibid.*
14. Eph. 4:7, *The New English Bible.*
15. St. John 1:4.

V.   His Words

1. William Strunk, Jr., *The Elements of Style* (New York: The Macmillan Company, 1959), p. 17.
2. Colin Williams, *What in the World* (New York: National Council of Churches), pp. 43, 44.
3. Gibson Winter, *The New Creation as Metropolis* (New York: The Macmillan Company, 1963).
4. *Ibid.,* p. 129.
5. Col. 4:6.
6. Stephen Neill, *The Christian Faith and Other Faiths* (New York: Oxford University Press, 1961), pp. 127–128.
7. From the leaflet, "The Pulpit, One of the Most Important Places in the World" (Washington, D.C.: College of Preachers).
8. Martin Luther King, Jr., Episcopal Society for Cultural and Racial Unity, General Convention, St. Louis, Mo., Oct. 12, 1964.
9. New York: Pocket Books, Inc., p. 184.
10. Source unknown.
11. Source unknown.
12. King, *op. cit.*
13. Pelz, *op. cit.,* p. 56.
14. St. John 1:14.
15. I Cor. 14:9.
16. I Cor. 14:19.
17. Source unknown.
18. I John 1:1–2.
19. Rom. 1:20.
20. *The New York Times,* Theater Section.
21. Phil. 4:13.
22. The St. Andrews Statement of the World Council of Churches, 1960.
23. Isa. 33:17.
24. A. R. Vidler, Ed. (London: Cambridge University Press, 1962).
25. John A. T. Robinson (London: SCM Press, 1963).
26. Ezek. 37:1–14.
27. Casalis, *op. cit.,* p. 7.
28. Elizabeth Goudge, *Gentian Hill* (New York: Coward-McCann, Inc., 1959), p. 160.
29. Casalis, *op. cit.,* p. 18.
30. *The Book of Common Prayer,* p. 44.
31. Ps. 31:8.
32. Paraphrased from *Forward Day by Day,* Late Trinity, 1964.
33. Source unknown.
34. New York: The Macmillan Company, p. 155.
35. *The Works of George Herbert,* F. E. Hutchinson, Ed. (Oxford: Clarendon Press, 1941), p. 231.
36. St. John 4:23.
37. I Thess. 1:5, Goodspeed.
38. I have found a stop watch, with a sweeping second hand, invaluable in keeping me within the bounds of time and in pacing my points; ministers are sometimes poor time estimators.
39. I Cor. 9:22.

VI. His Works

1. Quoted in Tom Allan, *op. cit.*, p. 103.
2. St. Matt. 25:40.
3. London: Longman's Green & Co., Inc., 1921.
4. See Salinger, *op. cit.*
5. Robert Raynolds, *The Sinner of St. Ambrose* (Indianapolis: The Bobbs-Merrill Company, Inc., 1952), p. 68.
6. New York: Seabury Press, 1961.
7. *The Living Church,* August 30, 1964, p. 8.
8. *Ibid.*
9. From Bishop Bayne's address at the Ecumenical Mass Meeting, General Convention, Nov., 1955.
10. See pamphlet, *Growing Together Locally* (British Council of Churches), p. 33.
11. *More in Sorrow* (New York: Henry Holt and Company, Inc., 1958), p. 297 ff.
12. King, *op. cit.*
13. The classic marks of the Church are that it is one, holy, catholic, and apostolic, *The Book of Common Prayer,* p. 291.
14. Dietrich Bonhoeffer, *Prisoner for God,* Letters and Papers from Prison (New York: The Macmillan Company, 1959).
15. Gal. 6:10.

VII. His Ways

1. I Cor. 14:40; the entire fourteenth chapter is pertinent here.
2. I Cor. 8:22.
3. Kennedy, *Henry Drummond, op. cit.*
4. From the Preface to the first Prayer Book, 1549.
5. Neh. 8:8.
6. David Ogilvy, *Confessions of an Advertising Man* (New York: Atheneum Publishers, 1963), p. 97.
7. Simone de Beauvoir, *Memoirs of a Dutiful Daughter* (New York: World Book Company, 1959), p. 203.
8. See the letters received by Bishop Robinson in response to his far-reaching little paperback, *Honest to God,* published in *The Honest to God Debate* (Philadelphia: The Westminster Press, 1963). See also James A. Pike, *A Time for Christian Candor* (New York: Harper & Row, Publishers, 1964).
9. St. John 6:37.
10. Isa. 6:8–9.
11. Ernest Gordon, *Through the Valley of the Kwai* (New York: Harper & Brothers, 1962).
12. Source unknown.
13. John Masefield, *op. cit.*
14. Isa. 6:1.
15. II Kings 3:15.
16. Source unknown.
17. *Ibid.*
18. *Ibid.*

19. *See* Robert Raynolds, *The Choice to Love* (New York: Harper & Brothers, Publishers, 1959).
20. Psalm 150:6.
21. Percy Dearmer, *The Parson's Handbook* (London: Humphrey Milford, 1931), p. vii.

VIII. When He Prays

1. Salinger, *op. cit.*, p. 110.
2. I Tim. 2:8.
3. St. Luke 18:1.
4. St. Matt. 6:5,7.
5. Salinger, *op. cit.*, pp. 193, 199 ff.
6. Elizabeth Burns, *op. cit.*, p. 159.
7. Roger Lloyd, *op. cit.*, p. 51.
8. I Tim. 2:8.
9. St. Luke 18:2–8.
10. Source unknown.
11. St. Matt. 6:9.
12. Josephine Tey, *op. cit.*, p. 64.
13. Col. 3:11.
14. James W. Kennedy, *The Unknown Worshipper* (New York: Morehouse-Barlow Co., 1964).
15. Source unknown.
16. F. A. Iremonger, *William Temple, Archbishop of Canterbury* (New York: Oxford University Press, 1949).
17. New York: Coward-McCann, Inc., 1959, p. 41 ff.
18. Isa. 1:18.
19. Source unknown.
20. *Ibid.*
21. Morton Wishingrad, *The Rope Dancers*. There was a Broadway play on this theme a few years ago.
22. Simone Weil, *Waiting on God* (London: Routledge & Kegan Paul, Ltd., 1951).
23. Col. 1:9.
24. *The Christian Century*, Oct. 10, 1962.
25. Ross Macdonald, *The Wycherly Woman* (New York: Alfred A. Knopf, 1961), p. 210.

IX. When He Reads

1. Found on the dust jacket of Robert Penn Warren's novel, *Flood* (New York: Random House, Inc., 1964).
2. Hab. 2:2.
3. Drew, *op. cit.*, p. 9.
4. *The New Chain Reference Bible*, 3rd ed. (Indianapolis: B. B. Kirkbride Bible Co., 1934).
5. Collect for Second Sunday in Advent, *The Book of Common Prayer*, p. 92.
6. Back in 1940 John Hadham wrote *Good God* which caused no stir at all.
7. My engagement book blanks for the coming summer are filled with names of such books jotted down as they come to my attention.

8. New York: William Morrow and Company, Inc., 1962.
9. Archibald MacLeish, *J.B.* (Boston: Houghton Mifflin, 1957), last line.
10. Job 2:9.
11. Goudge, *op. cit.* p. 71.
12. *Ibid.*, p. 72.
13. MacLeish, *op. cit.*, p. 153.
14. *Ibid.*, p. 39.
15. Rom. 9:35, 37–39.
16. Job. 19:25, 27.
17. Many pamphlets on the subject are available, for example, from Forward Movement Publications, 412 Sycamore Street, Cincinnati, Ohio.

X. When He Calls

1. Quoted by Tom Allan, *op. cit.*, p. 63.
2. St. Matt. 18:20.
3. Isa. 61:1; St. Luke 4:18.
4. Sarah Patton Boyle, *The Desegregated Heart* (New York: William Morrow and Company, 1962).
5. Henry Knox Sherrill, *Among Friends: An Autobiography* (Boston: Little Brown and Company, 1962).
6. Forward Movement Publications, 412 Sycamore St., Cincinnati, Ohio, 45202, $1.50 for two-year subscription.
7. St. John 5:2–15.
8. *The Interpreter's Bible.*
9. Cicely Saunders, "Death," *The Living Church*, July 26, 1964, p. 8.
10. John Ellis Large, *The Ministry of Healing* (New York: Morehouse-Gorham Co., 1959), p. 17.
11. *Ibid.*
12. Paraphrased from Werner and Lotte Pelz, *God Is No More*, *op. cit.*, p. 65.
13. Large, *op. cit.*, p. 84.
14. Thornton Wilder, *The Angel that Troubled the Waters, and Other Plays* (New York: Coward McCann, 1956).
15. Geoffrey Bles, London.
16. Isa. 6:1.
17. Large, *op. cit.*, Preface.
18. St. John 5:8.
19. Bonhoeffer, *op. cit.*

XI. When He Plays

1. Ps. 150:6.
2. From the Preface to *The Book of Common Prayer*.
3. Eleanor Ruggles, *Journey Into Faith* (New York: W. W. Norton & Co., 1948), p. 247.
4. I Pet. 3:15.
5. Robert Penn Warren, *Flood* (New York: Random House, 1964), p. 61.
6. I Tim. 5:23.
7. Source unknown.
8. Acts 13:10.

9. Source unknown.
10. St. Luke 4:23.

XII.   His Future

1. Raynolds, *op. cit.*, p. 13.
2. II Cor. 4:1.
3. *The Hymnal 1940*, Hymn 573:4.
4. David Ogilvy, *op. cit.*, p. 15.
5. St. Matt. 28:20.
6. Quoted by Pierre van Paassen, *To Number Our Days* (New York: Charles Scribner's, 1964), p. 13.
7. Deut. 31:6.
8. Eph. 4:7, *New English Bible*.
9. Eph. 3:20–21.

Prayers for Today

1. St. Matt. 6:9.

INDEX

DATE DUE